American Warriors

Five Presidents in the Pacific Theater of World War II

Duane T. Hove

BURD STREET PRESS
SHIPPENSBURG, PENNSYLVANIA

Unless otherwise noted, the maps were prepared by James Murray.

Photographs of the presidents on the chapter pages are credited as follows: Johnson: Naval Historical Center Web Site www.history.navy.mil/faqs/faq60-6.htm; Kennedy: Naval Historical Center Web Site www.history.navy.mil/faqs/faq60-2.htm; Nixon: Naval Historical Center Web Site www.history.navy.mil/faqs/faq60-8.htm; Ford: Gerald R. Ford Library; George H. W. Bush: George Bush Library.

This Burd Street Press publication
was printed by
Beidel Printing House, Inc.
63 West Burd Street
Shippensburg, PA 17257-0708 USA

The acid-free paper used in this book meets the guidelines for permanence and durability of the Committee on Production Guidelines for Book Longevity of the Council on Library Resources.

For a complete list of available publications
please write
Burd Street Press
Division of White Mane Publishing Company, Inc.
P.O. Box 708
Shippensburg, PA 17257-0708 USA

Library of Congress Cataloging-in-Publication Data

Hove, Duane T., 1945-
    American warriors : five presidents in the Pacific theater of World War II / Duane T. Hove.
        p. cm.
    Includes bibliographical references and index.
    ISBN 1-57249-307-0 (alk. paper)
    1. Presidents--United States--Biography. 2. World War, 1939-1945--Biography. 3. World War, 1939-1945--Campaigns--Pacific Area. I. Title.

D736.H7 2003
940.54'1273'0922-dc21

                                                        2003041750

This book is gratefully dedicated to
Lieutenant Commander Forest Wilson—survivor
of the sinking of the USS *Princeton* and recipient of
two Distinguished Flying Crosses

and to all the men and women who fought
in the Pacific Theater of War.

Contents

Illustrations

Maps

Preface

Five United States presidents served their country as Naval Reserve officers in the Pacific Theater of World War II. Very few people can name all five, and almost no one knows the details of their service. Presidential biographies gloss over this important period of their lives and are often inaccurate. This book attempts to set the record straight with a systematic and dispassionate look at the five presidents' service. The presidents' military roles are reconstructed using primary sources, including Reports on the Fitness of Officers where available, ships' logs, and interviews with more than one hundred Pacific War veterans. Each president's service in the United States Navy is discussed in a separate chapter, arranged by the order in which each entered the Pacific Theater. Maps of each region are included enabling readers to orient themselves with geographic details.

The Japanese attack on the American Pacific Fleet at Pearl Harbor, and the subsequent United States' declaration of war, brought these five future presidents into the Pacific Theater of War. On December 7, 1941, two were in the Naval Reserve and three were civilians. Lieutenant Commander Lyndon Johnson, USNR, was a representative of the Tenth District of Texas in Congress, and Lieutenant (jg) John Kennedy, USNR, was working in Naval Intelligence in Washington, D.C. Richard Nixon was a lawyer in Yorba Linda, California; Gerald Ford was a lawyer in Grand

Rapids, Michigan; and George Bush was a high school student in Andover, Massachusetts. All served with distinction, and three were decorated for bravery. Kennedy and Nixon served at overlapping times in the South Pacific islands. Ford and Bush served at overlapping times in preflight training school and on aircraft carriers. None knew of the others.

Presidents who were in the military in World War II but did not serve in the Pacific are not included in this book. Dwight Eisenhower was commanding general of all Allied forces in the European Theater. From 1936 to 1939 he was chief of staff to Douglas MacArthur in the Philippines. Jimmy Carter graduated from the Naval Academy after the war. Carter served aboard the battleships *Wyoming* and *Mississippi*, the submarine *Pomfret*, and the nuclear submarine *K-1*. Ronald Reagan entered the United States Army as a second lieutenant during the spring of 1942. Because of poor eyesight, he was assigned to the Army Air Corps motion picture unit to make training films. Reagan was discharged from active duty in late 1945 as a captain.

Japan's attack on Pearl Harbor was a calculated risk. In the decade prior to World War II, Japan was the dominant power in the Pacific. She had subjugated Korea, Formosa, and much of China and was a major international diplomatic and commercial player. Antagonism flowed between Japan and the United States regarding international disputes and mutual racial mistrust. Japan hardly seemed in a position to quarrel with the United States, which supplied the vast majority of Japan's oil, gasoline, scrap iron, and machine tools, but, in many ways, war with the United States was inevitable. Japan's national needs and desires, coupled with her cultural differences with Western nations, led to a clash of wills, which ultimately could not be settled at the negotiating table. Japanese forces attacked the American Pacific Fleet at Pearl Harbor to allow their military time to conquer and defend oil- and mineral-rich Pacific nations. However militarily logical, Japanese leaders underestimated the tremendous outpouring of public support for war with Japan.

Sixteen million Americans served in the military during World War II. Of these, more than four million served in the navy, primarily in the Pacific Theater. Five of those navy men are the subject of this book. Lyndon Johnson came to the Pacific Theater first in June 1942 on an inspection trip to Australia and New Guinea. John Kennedy arrived in the Solomon Islands in April 1943 to join PT boat Squadron 2. Richard Nixon reported to the South Pacific Combat Air Transportation Command on New Caledonia in June 1943. Gerald Ford reached the Gilbert Islands in November 1943 onboard the light aircraft carrier USS *Monterey*, and George Bush arrived at the Marcus and Wake Islands in May 1944 on board the light aircraft carrier USS *San Jacinto*. Each would face danger and eventually return to civilian life...and politics.

Acknowledgments

I wish to express my deep appreciation to the Johnson, Kennedy, Nixon, Ford, and Bush Presidential Libraries, the United States National Archives, the Naval Historical Center, the WW II PT Boats Museum and Archives, and the Admiral Nimitz Foundation. Their research staffs were uniformly helpful. In particular, I wish to acknowledge the unqualified support of Alyce Guthrie from the WW II PT Boats Museum and Archives and of Barry Zerby from the National Archives Modern Military Records Section. I also wish to thank Henry Sakaida who generously shared his research materials on Lyndon Johnson's flight over New Guinea. Veterans Kenneth Prescott, Alvin Cluster, Glen Christiansen, Dick Keresey, William Liebenow, Le Roy Taylor, Warner Bigger, Harry Towne, Albert Stanwood, Howard Nielson, and Jack Guy patiently endured endless discussions. Presidents Ford and Bush promptly answered questions submitted in writing.

Manuscript drafts were reviewed by James Darr, Donald Jacobson, Henry Doscher, and Fern Marks. James Reed and Alvin Cluster reviewed a draft of the chapter on John Kennedy. Howard Nielson reviewed a draft of the chapter on Richard Nixon, and Jack Guy reviewed a draft of the chapter on George Bush. The reviewers' comments and suggestions greatly assisted in the book's preparation. Any errors are mine alone.

A special word of thanks to Captain J. Henry Doscher, USNR (Ret.), for his unceasing interest and support throughout the preparation of this book. Captain Doscher's book *Subchaser in the South Pacific* presents a dynamic account of life aboard ship during the Solomon Islands campaign, and his *Little Wolf at Leyte* captures the bravery exhibited by the crew of a destroyer escort in the Second Battle of the Philippine Sea.

Finally, my profound gratitude goes to the staff at White Mane Publishing Company. Without them, my manuscript would be gathering dust in a file cabinet.

Chapter 1
Lyndon B. Johnson
President's Representative

President Franklin Delano Roosevelt was vacationing on a fishing trip in the Gulf of Mexico in 1937. Ever the politician, he invited the newly elected Texas Representative Lyndon Baines Johnson to join him in Galveston, where he would dock and transfer to a special train. Johnson came aboard the ship, met Roosevelt, and was invited to ride through Texas with the president.[1] Johnson came away deeply impressed. Roosevelt, sensing an ally on the Hill, arranged for Johnson to be appointed to the House Committee on Naval Affairs.[2]

When it appeared that America was headed into war in Europe, Johnson sought a naval officer's commission. Although he had no direct military service, Johnson was appointed a lieutenant commander in the Naval Reserve during June 1940. Adlai Ewing Stevenson, civilian assistant to Secretary of the Navy William Franklin Knox, was instrumental in arranging Johnson's commission.[3] Because Johnson was not immediately assigned duty, he returned to his congressional seat.

Having worked in Washington for three years as an aide to Texas Representative Richard Miflin Kleberg prior to his election, Johnson knew how to cultivate the system. During his first two years in the House, he secured more federal funding for his Tenth District than any other congressman that year.[4] Johnson's influence on the Naval Affairs Committee grew, and he was able to garner an important naval air training base at Corpus Christi, as well as shipbuilding yards in Houston and Orange.

During his 1941 reelection campaign, Johnson promised his constituents that if he was responsible for sending men into battle, he would join them. On December 8, 1942, when Congress declared war against Japan, Johnson volunteered for active duty. Three days later, Congress also declared war against Germany. Johnson asked for and received an indefinite leave of absence to join the war effort.

Congressman Johnson had become acquainted with Bureau of Naval Personnel director Rear Admiral Chester William Nimitz during his Naval Affairs Committee work. Nimitz, who was born and raised less than 20 miles from Johnson's birthplace, often testified before the committee on behalf of the ongoing naval buildup. At their personal request, Nimitz signed the orders activating Johnson and fellow Naval Affairs Committee member Warren Grant Magnuson.[5] With the help of Committee Chairman Carl Vinson, Magnuson arranged to be temporarily assigned to the aircraft carrier USS *Enterprise*. He was on board the *Enterprise* when Vice Admiral William Frederick Halsey Jr.'s carrier group launched the Doolittle raid on Tokyo. Shortly thereafter, just before *Enterprise* left for the Coral Sea, Magnuson was transferred to duty in the Bureau of Navigation on the West Coast.[6]

Navy Undersecretary James Vincent Forrestal assigned Johnson to carry out an inspection tour of defense plants in Texas and on the West Coast, and then to report to the United States-New Zealand Joint Naval Command in San Francisco as a liaison officer. Johnson visited Houston, Corpus Christi, Los Angeles, San Francisco, San Diego, and Seattle before assuming his duties in San Francisco. His former congressional assistant—now Ensign USNR—John Bowden Connally Jr. joined him in San Francisco.[7] Johnson spent two days there and promptly wrangled a trip back to Washington, D.C., to plead for another position. Forrestal reassigned Johnson and Connally to Columbia University Professor J. W. Barker, who was in charge of industrial mobilization. Barker dispatched Johnson and Connally to navy shipyards on the West Coast to investigate labor problems. For 10 weeks, from the end of January to mid-April, the two navy officers visited shipyards from Seattle to San Diego, implementing navy training programs and explaining training manuals. Johnson and Connally visited San Francisco several times, finally taking up residence in San Francisco's Empire Hotel.[8]

Johnson yearned for greater responsibilities or to be assigned to a combat area. His political advisors informed him that Roosevelt was contemplating ordering congressmen in the military back to their duties, and time was running out on his promise to join the troops. In April, Johnson arranged another trip back to Washington, D.C., and personally presented his case to Roosevelt. Roosevelt responded:

> Will send you to Southwest Pacific on job for me re our men there. We may need to take additional steps for their health and happiness. You won't need to stay at Pearl Harbor but a couple of days then you can go to Australia, New Zealand, etc.[9]

At last, 33-year-old Johnson was assigned to a combat area—and as a representative of the president of the United States. Connally was reassigned to Forrestal's office, where he could keep abreast of Johnson's congressional affairs. While Johnson was away, his wife, Claudia "Ladybird" Johnson, kept up day-to-day communications with his constituents.

Johnson's mission has been criticized as politically motivated. It is undeniable that combat exposure would fatten his political resume. But Roosevelt faced real problems in the Pacific, as the war was not going well. Supplies and manpower were woefully short; General Douglas MacArthur had just been spirited out of the Philippines to take over an almost nonexistent army; interservice rivalries were rampant; and American relations with local Pacific island governments were rocky. The smooth-talking, ambitious, confident, hard-working Johnson was probably the ideal man to dissect the politicized reports that wound their way through the military chain of command to the commander in chief. At the same time, Johnson's visit would help assure the temperamental MacArthur of his commander's keen interest.

Three months before Johnson's arrival in Australia, MacArthur, his wife, Jean, their son, Arthur, and 17 top-level staff departed from the embattled island of Corregidor aboard four PT boats. Three of the officers skippering these boats—Lieutenants John Duncan Bulkeley, Robert B. Kelly, and Henry J. Branting-ham—would come to play a major role in the military career of future president John Fitzgerald Kennedy. For his actions in leading the escape, Bulkeley was awarded the Congressional Medal of Honor.

After a harrowing trip through enemy-controlled waters, MacArthur arrived at the Philippine island of Mindanao, where only one war-weary B-17 was available to fly the party to Australia. MacArthur contacted the commanding officer of the Allied Air Forces in Australia, Lieutenant General George H. Brett, and demanded three airworthy aircraft. Brett dispatched three B-17s from Townsville, of which two arrived safely. Leaving baggage behind, MacArthur departed for Australia. When the two B-17s reached Darwin, a Japanese air raid was under way, and the aircraft were directed to nearby Batchelor Field. MacArthur was met by two Douglas C-47s and ferried a thousand miles to Alice Springs where his party boarded a train to Adelaide. When he arrived, MacArthur delivered his famous "I shall return" speech and continued on by railroad to Melbourne to establish his headquarters.

MacArthur's impassioned oration implied that sufficient forces awaited him in Australia, but fewer than 32,000 Allied troops were available. The Australian defenses were so weak that plans were made to fall back from the northern provinces. MacArthur, who assumed the position of commander of the Southwest Pacific Area on April 18, directed that the defense of Australia be moved north to New Guinea. He initiated actions to hold the southern half of the Papuan Peninsula, which included its major harbor

Johnson points to map of early Pacific bases.

Courtesy of Lyndon Baines Johnson Library

and airfields at Port Moresby. With few troops, limited supplies, and a shortage of weapons, MacArthur was determined to build an army capable of returning to the Philippines. Rumors about the sorry state of affairs in the Southwest Pacific reached Washington, and Roosevelt dispatched Johnson to investigate and provide a first-hand account.

Johnson departed from Washington, D.C., on May 2, 1942, on the long trip to Australia.[10] His orders read in part:

> ...you will proceed to San Francisco, Calif. and report to Vice Admiral Robert L. Ghormley, U.S.N., thence when directed by him proceed via such transportation, including air, as may be available to Honolulu, T. H., and thence proceed via such transportation including via air, as may be available to such places in the South and Southwest Pacific as Vice Admiral

Robert L. Ghormley, U.S.N., may designate and report to
General Douglas MacArthur, U. S. A. for temporary duty.[11]

Robert Lee Ghormley was assigned to lead the South Pacific
naval forces and was flying to Auckland, New Zealand, to establish his headquarters. Included in his staff was Rear Admiral John
Sidney McCain, director of Air Operations.[12]

Johnson's itinerary included stopovers in Houston, Austin,
Los Angeles, and Portland, before he arrived in San Francisco.[13]
On May 7, Johnson flew to Hawaii and reported as ordered. Ad-
miral Ghormley's party left Hawaii on May 13 aboard a PB2Y
Coronado flying boat.

After refueling on Palmyra Island, Canton Island, and at Suva
in the Fiji Islands, Ghormley's aircraft reached Noumea, New
Caledonia, on May 18. Here, Johnson met Lieutenant Colonel
Samuel E. Anderson and Lieutenant Colonel Francis R. Stevens,

**Johnson listens to Admiral McCain on
a stopover at Suva, Fiji Islands.**

who were on an inspection tour for the War Department. Anderson and Stevens had been unable to proceed to Sydney, Australia, for eight days due to lack of air transportation and gratefully hitched a ride on Ghormley's aircraft. After delivering Ghormley to Auckland on May 21, the Coronado arrived in Sydney on May 23. During their brief stopover in Auckland, Johnson, Anderson, and Stevens agreed to conduct their inspection tours together.

The three officers flew to Melbourne, Australia, by commercial carrier to confer with MacArthur and begin their inspection tour. It has been reported that MacArthur was surprised and somewhat upset at Johnson's showing up in his theater of war. This thought is completely contrary to Johnson's meeting notes:

> He looked much younger than his years; he was extremely cordial and, I think, glad that we came. Immaculately attired—medals and all—plus a half-smoked cigar, we were seated and offered a cigarette. "Delighted to see you and I shall see that you see all."[14]

Further, MacArthur had a copy of Johnson's orders, so he would not have been surprised at Johnson's arrival.

MacArthur provided Johnson, Anderson, and Stevens with a detailed description of the theater including the Australian continent, its government, its military status, and the United States' military status in the Southwest Pacific. He then outlined a tour that included the east coast of Australia, the south coast of New Guinea, the north coast of Australia, and a return to Melbourne. MacArthur's staff followed with a series of briefings on intelligence, operations, and communications.

MacArthur assigned Brigadier General William Frederic Marquat as an escort to Johnson, Anderson, and Stevens to assure access to whatever areas the three officers wished to visit. Marquat had been an antiaircraft officer in the Philippines and was one of the 17 officers who accompanied MacArthur in his escape from Corregidor.[15] Marquat served under MacArthur throughout the war and became head of the Economic and Scientific Section of occupation headquarters in postwar Japan.

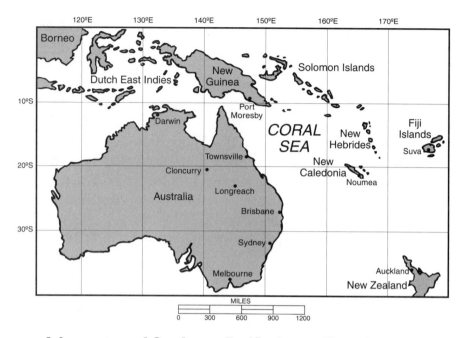

Johnson toured Southwest Pacific Area military bases in May–June 1942 on assignment from President Roosevelt.

General Brett loaned Johnson's party his personal aircraft, a B-17 nicknamed the *Swoose*—half swan, half goose. The *Swoose* was piloted by Major Frank Kurtz, a highly decorated veteran of the Philippine and Java battles. The aircraft was frequently unavailable due to a lack of parts—a common malady in 1942 Australia. When necessary, the officers took commercial flights or hitched a ride on military aircraft.

Johnson, Anderson, and Stevens visited production and training facilities in Melbourne. They flew to Sydney on June 3, where they spent one day visiting army headquarters, and then flew to Brisbane for more inspections. Johnson's party departed Brisbane on June 6 for Townsville on the barren northeast coast of Australia.[16] A month before the Japanese attacked Pearl Harbor, the Allies began constructing airfields at Townsville, Cairns, and Charters Towers to facilitate delivery of B-17s to the Philippine Islands.[17]

Johnson's party arrived at Garbutt Field, Townsville—home of the headquarters of the 22nd Army Air Force Bomb Group and its Martin B-26 Marauders. The 22nd had been ordered to Australia from Langley Field, Virginia, in February to help stem the Japanese advance. It was the first air group to reach Australia from America. After assembling in Brisbane, the 22nd moved to Townsville and flew its first mission over Rabaul, New Britain, via Port Moresby, New Guinea, on April 5, 1942. The bombers were based in the Townsville area rather than Port Moresby to avoid the almost daily raids by Japanese aircraft from Lae and Salamaua on the north coast of New Guinea. Townsville aircraft were dispersed to a number of local fields for protection from Japanese air attack. Headquarters Squadron was stationed at Garbutt Field, the 2nd and 408th Squadrons were at Reid River, and the 33rd Squadron was at Antil Plains. The 19th Squadron aircraft were dispersed to Stock Route. Since the airstrip only had a 3,600-foot runway, the aircraft taxied over to Garbutt Field for takeoff.[18]

While touring air bases at Torrens Creek, 200 miles southwest of Townsville, and Charters Towers, 80 miles southwest of Townsville, Johnson, Anderson, and Stevens learned that 50 percent of the aircraft were out of service.[19] Supplies were short, and support equipment was dearly needed. Spare parts were a particular problem; aircraft were often cannibalized to repair less-damaged aircraft.

Conditions were even worse at Seven Mile Airdrome, one of several airstrips around Port Moresby, New Guinea, and Johnson's next stop. Seven Mile was also known as Jackson Airstrip, named after RAAF Squadron 75's commanding officer, John Jackson, who had been shot down on April 28, 1942.[20] Nestled in a ring of hills, Seven Mile's runway was sloped, which made the direction of the wind and departure time important. Ground crews had little sleep, poor food, almost nonexistent shelter, minimal equipment, hordes of mosquitoes, and were under frequent attack from Japanese aircraft. Bomber crews staging overnight from Australia slept under the aircraft wings or in the fuselage on bedding and in mosquito nets brought with them. Fighter crews stationed at the base lived in native-built grass shacks. Provisions consisted primarily of Australian rations, which included mutton, bully beef, dried potatoes, and dried milk.[21]

Port Moresby's air bases suffered from inadequate warning of air attacks. The approach of Japanese aircraft was masked by the Owen Stanley Mountains, and the few operating radar sets only had a 75-mile range.[22] If forward spotters phoned in contacts, the alert might be as much as an hour. More often, Japanese aircraft were overhead when an alert was sounded.[23] During May, the Port Moresby area was attacked 21 times.

The Australian air force sent a squadron of P-40 fighter aircraft to Port Moresby in March 1942.[24] On April 30, the 35th and 36th Fighter Squadrons of the U.S. 8th Fighter Group flying P-39 Airacobras relieved the Australian unit. In their two-month stay, operating out of primitive conditions, the two U.S. squadrons downed 45 Japanese aircraft, while losing 13 pilots and 26 aircraft.[25]

In early June, the 39th and 40th Fighter Squadrons of the 35th Fighter Group replaced the 8th Fighter Group. Half of the aircraft flown by the new squadrons were P-39 Airacobras and half were P-400s, the RAF version of the P-39. Many U.S. pilots preferred the P-400 because its 20 millimeter cannon was more reliable than the P-39's 37 millimeter cannon.[26] It also had 60 rounds of ammunition compared to the 37 millimeter cannon's 15 rounds. Otherwise, the performance of the two aircraft was virtually identical. Their primary limitation was the lack of a supercharger, which restricted their effective operation to less than 17,000 feet altitude even though they had a ceiling of 35,000 feet. The P-39s and P-400s did have some advantageous characteristics over the Japanese Zeroes, such as firepower, rugged construction, and leakproof fuel tanks. The Zeroes had better maneuverability, acceleration, and a higher ceiling. Prior to June, 35 Allied fighter aircraft were lost.[27]

The 39th Squadron fighters operated out of Twelve Mile Airdrome and, eventually, the Fourteen Mile Airdrome. Fighters from the 40th Squadron operated out of Seven Mile Airdrome, where the previous fighter squadrons had been based.[28] Aircraft had to be parked among the trees for protection as only a few revetments were available. The airstrips were surfaced with gravel and pierced steel planking in an attempt to overcome the ever-present mud. Daylight heat and humidity were replaced by nighttime mosquitoes and humidity.

Johnson's party learned that on a typical mission, the bombers based in Northern Australia would fly six hundred miles to one of the airfields at Port Moresby, refuel, head out to bomb the Japanese airfields, and return. Bombing runs were unescorted because the fighters stationed at Port Moresby simply didn't have the range to escort the bombers and loiter over the target. They did meet returning flights and provide protection for a portion of the flight. After two months of flying extended missions over Rabaul, the bombers were directed toward the Japanese airstrips at Lae and Salamaua, 180 miles from Port Moresby. Lae was home to the Japanese Tainan Air Group, which included ace pilots Hiroyoshi Nishizawa, Saburo Sakai, and Satoshi Yoshino.[29]

Bombing runs were scheduled in the morning—even though it meant leaving Townsville during the previous day—because clouds and fog shrouded the New Guinea mountains in the afternoon. These missions required the aircraft and crew to be away from Townsville for 24 to 36 hours.

On June 8, Lieutenant Colonel Dwight D. Divine II informed the three officers that he was planning a major air raid for the next day, and they decided to ride along as observers. The mission, designated TOW 9, would attack Lae with multiple waves of bombers. If Lae was unsuitable, the alternate target was Salamaua. This was to be Divine's first combat mission since he assumed command of the 22nd Bomb Group.[30] Johnson's participation in the raid has been alternately reported as minimal and as one fraught with danger during intense air combat.

**B-26 Marauder aircraft of the type Lyndon Johnson boarded
for a mission to Lae, New Guinea, on June 9, 1942**

Courtesy of Michael Smith of B26.com

The mission planned for June 9 was the first coordinated bombing attack on the north coast of New Guinea. Three B-17s from the 19th Bomb Group's 435th Squadron stationed in Townsville were to bomb the Lae Airdrome from 30,000 feet at 9:30 A.M (2330 ZULU/8/6).[31] The B-17s were to draw the Japanese Zeroes up the Markham Valley northwest of Lae. Six B-25s from the 3rd Bomb Group stationed at Charters Towers were to follow at 9:45 A.M., bomb Lae from 18,000 feet, and lead any remaining Zeroes to the west.[32] The B-25s were to return via the mouth of the Lakekamu River, on the south shore of Papua, where fighter aircraft from the 35th Fighter Group would intercept any trailing Zeroes.[33] Finally, 11 B-26s from the 22nd Bomb Group were to follow at 9:59 A.M., bomb and strafe Lae from low altitude, and head east out to sea before returning along New Guinea's north coast. Fighter aircraft from the 35th Fighter Group were to meet the B-26s at Cape Ward Hunt to intercept any remaining Zeroes.[34]

The 11 B-26s were the mission's knockout punch. If the plan worked to perfection, the Zeroes would be caught on the ground while refueling or would be intercepted by the fighter aircraft. At the very least, aircraft ground facilities, ammunition dumps, fuel

```
US TWN NR 18
NEA  IMMEDIATE OPERATIONAL  SECRET NOT BY W/T  GREEN CONTROL
PASS TO 19 AND 22 BOMB GROUPS
GR 92 TO 19BOMB GR REPEAT MORESBY CWR  3 BOMB GR 22 BOMB GR
ACH TOWNSVILLE
TO /9HX7  7/6  11 (C)  TOW /8  8/9 JUNE (.)  THREE B17S TO ATTACK LAE
FROM MAXIMUM ALTITUDE AT 2330Z/8/6 (.) SELECT (A) DISPERSAL BAYS ON
N.E. SIDE OF RUNWAY (B)  DUMP AREA AT CONAELLS HOUSE (.)  AIRCRAFT TO
DRAW ZEROS  UP MARKHAM VALLEY AND AWAY FROM TARGET AREA (.)  THIS
THIS ACTION IS TO BE OF IMPORTANCE  (.)  SOME INCENDIARIES MAY BE
CARRIED (.)  THIS ATTACK TO BE COORDINATED WITH 1 B25S AND B26S '(.)
RETURN TO BASE AT CONCLUSION OF OPERATION
TOO 1114Z/7
```

19th Bomb Group orders

```
4 7 USATWN NR 17
  NEA
  IMMEDIATE OPERATIONAL SECRET NOT W/R GREEN CONTROL
  PASS TO   19 BOMB GROUP  22 BOMB GROUP


  GR  64 TO 3 BOMGR (R) CWR MORESBY  19 BOM GR 22 BOMGR
  FROM ACH TOWNSVILLE
  TO:G6/7  7/6  (C) TOW/10  8/9 JUNE (.) SEND SIX B25S TO BOMB LAE AT
  2345Z/8/6  FROM APPROX 18000 FEET (.)  TARGET (A) LARGE BUILDINGS IN WHARF
  AREA (B) CHINATOWN AREA (.) AIRCRAFT ENDEAVOUR DRAW ZEROS TO THE WEST
  FROM LAE (.) SOME INCEDIARIES TO BE USED (.) THIS ATTACK TO BE CORDINATED
  WITH B17S AND B26S (.
                  XX (.) RETURN TO BASE AT CONCLUSION OF
  OPERATION
  TO  12XX TOO  1122Z//7
```

3rd Bomb Group orders

```
L  USA TWN NR 16

   NEA  IMMEDIATE OPERATIONAL SECRET NOT BY W/T  GREEN  CONTROL

   PASS TO 22 BOMB GROUP AND 19THBOMB GROUPP

   GR 63 TO 22 BOMB GROUP REPEAT CWR MORESBY  19B G  3 BOMB GR

   FROM ACH TOWNSVILLE

   TO/95/7  7/6  (C) TOW/9  8/9 JUNE (.)  THE 22 BOMB GR WILL ATTACK LAE

   COMMENCING AT 2359Z/8/6 (.)  OBJECT DESTROY AIRCRAFT AND SUPPORTING

   GROUND FACILITIES FROM WHARF AREA TO CONAELLS HOUSE (.)  MAXIMUM LOAD

   100 POUND BOMBS TO ØØ  CARRIED (.)  TARGET AND BUILDING AREA TO BE T///

   THOROUGHLY STRAFFED DURING BOMBING  RUN (.)   AIRCRAFT TO RETURN MAZMZXND

   MAINLAND ON COMPLETION OF MISSION (.)

   TOO 1118/Z/7

   FG  VA

   USATWN NR16 R1200/7 LGC
```

22nd Bomb Group orders

```
   USA TWN NR22

   NEA  IMPORTANT OPERATIONAL SECRET  NOT BY W/T  GREEN CONTROL

   PASS TO 19   AND 22 BOMB GROUP

   GR 65 TO MORESBY REPEAT CWR  3BOMB GR 19 BOM GR  22 BOMB GR

   FROM ACH TOWNSVILLE

   TO/G8/7  7/6  REFER MY TO/G4/7 TO/G5/7  TO/G6/7

   (.)  SUFFICIENT FIGHTER SCREEN TO BE MAINTAINED TO PROTECT BOMBER FORCE

   ON RETURN FROM MISSION (.)  RESERVE OF FIGHTERS TO BE ON GROUND AT READY

   READY (.)  ONE FLIGHT FIGHTERS TO RENDEZVOUS WITH RETURNING B26'S AT CAPE

   CAPE WARD HUNT   ONE FLIGHT TO RENDEZVOUS WITH B25'S NEAR MOUTH LAKE-

   KAMU RIVER OR SOME SUCH PLACE ARRANGED IN THAT AREA

   C    DELETE LAST GROUPS ON LINES  2 AND 3

   TOO 1218/"Z/7
```

35th Fighter Group orders

depots, and wharf facilities would be laid waste, while the Zeroes were off chasing the B-17s and B-25s. It was a perfect chance to show the visiting dignitaries what combined air power could do.

Three B-17s, flown by Captains Theodore Faulkner, Maurice Horgan, and Wallace Fields, left Townsville at 1:00 P.M. on June 8 and staged up to Horn Island.[35] The B-17s' two-thousand-mile range would have permitted a round trip flight from Townsville to Lae, but it was prudent to shorten the trip to allow for contingencies. The aircraft arrived at Horn Island in just under four hours. Ground personnel refueled the aircraft, and the pilots and crew bedded down for the night. They could hardly have looked forward to the stopover. Horn Island was an inhospitable place with no conveniences, a short runway that ended at a cliff overlooking the ocean, and occasional treacherous wind conditions.

Similarly, B-25 and B-26 bombers staged up to Port Moresby to prepare for the mission. Six B-25s from the 90th Squadron of the 3rd Bomb Group at Charters Towers flew to Three Mile Airdrome.[36] Eleven 22nd Bomb Group B-26s flew to Seven Mile Airdrome.[37] Three B-26s were from the Headquarters Squadron, five were from the 19th Squadron, and three were from the 2nd Squadron. Divine assigned Lieutenant Walter A. Krell to lead the B-26 flight. As with the B-17s, the bombers arrived at their designated airstrips in just under four hours; ground personnel refueled the aircraft; and the men bedded down for the night.

Johnson, Anderson, and Stevens remained in Townsville until the early morning hours of June 9, when they departed for Seven Mile Airdrome in a B-17. The aircraft, flown by 435th Squadron commanding officer Major William Lewis, carried General Ralph Royce, who was commander of Australia's North Eastern Area and previously Chief of Staff to General Brett. Three reporters were also aboard the B-17: *Time*'s Robert Sherrod, *Collier*'s W. B. Courtney, and International News Service's Pat Robinson. Due to a navigational error, Royce's B-17 didn't land until 8:00 A.M.— nearly five hours after departing Townsville.[38]

Notified that an important congressman would be coming, Seven Mile Airdrome's commanding officer, General Martin Francis Scanlon, held the B-26s until the B-17 carrying the VIPs arrived. Five officers—Johnson, Anderson, Stevens, Marquat, and Divine—each boarded separate bombers to ride along as observers. This delay created a potential difficulty as the wind direction shifted at this time of day.

Johnson found a ride on B-26 aircraft #1488, known as the *Heckling Hare*—also known as the *Arkansas Traveler*—and piloted by Lieutenant Walter Greer. The crew included Australian copilot Flight Sergeant G. A. McMullin, top turret gunner Private First Class Robert Marshall, tail gunner and flight engineer Private First Class Harry Baren, bombardier and nose gunner Sergeant Claude McCredie, radioman Sergeant Lillis Walker, and navigator Lieutenant Billy Boothe. Marshall replaced Sergeant B. E. Newhouse who was incorrectly listed on the flight manifest.[39]

The 11 B-26s took off from Seven Mile Airdrome by 8:51 A.M.[40] In 1984 and again in 1985, aviation author Henry Sakaida contacted B-26 flight leader Krell who explained how their mission began:

> On the June 9th mission, I led the 22nd Bomb Group aircraft from Port Moresby in a north north westerly direction somewhat paralleling the westerly aspect of the Owen-Stanley Range and heading for Lae. There was a dense cloud cover overlaying the mountains and I kept the formation in a steady climb at about 190 MPH which I had hoped would give us enough altitude to clear the mountain and cloud tops by the time it became necessary to level off and attack Lae.[41]

Generals Scanlon and Royce, on the ground at Port Moresby, soon learned that the TOW 9 mission was not proceeding smoothly. On the previous day, Captain Fred Eaton of the 435th Bomb Squadron, 19th Bomb Group, flew a B-17 reconnaissance mission over Salamaua and Lae.[42] Salamaua was clear, but heavy clouds covered Lae in the early afternoon. Eaton landed at Port

**Seven Mile Airdrome commander, General Scanlon,
greets Johnson upon arrival from Garbutt Field
as General Ralph Royce looks on.**

COMBAT CREWS

MISSION: TOW 9   June 8 & 9, 1942.

#1516   #1508   #1437

P   2nd Lt. Flint, D. C.   2nd Lt. Bench,   2nd Lt. Hayes, H. A.
CP   2nd Lt. Curry, W. L.   P/O Passmore, (RAAF)   S/P Reed, (RAAF)
N   2nd Lt. Ammons, V. B.   2nd Lt. Beck,   2nd Lt. Winchester, J. R.
B   Sgt. Culbertson, N. C.   Corp. MaKuch,   Corp. Cunningham, T. W.
* E Sgt. Kaplan, I.   Corp. Miles,   Corp. Rio, D. J.
* R Corp. Hamilton, W. M.   S/Sgt. Siegel,   Sgt. Collins, C. M.
  G Corp. Tompkins, R. E.   Corp. Rockefeller,   *Corp. Westmoreland, B. O.
                              X Lt. Col. Stevens,
*--Destroyed one enemy A/C   (Down in sea off Lae)   *--Destroyed one enemy A/C

#1392   #1422   #1480

P   Capt. Ewbank, J. N.   1st Lt. Crosson, G. J.   1st Lt. McIver, O. B.
CP   2nd Lt. Brown, J. L.   2nd Lt. Rath, G. E.   2nd Lt. Anderson, F. J.
N   2nd Lt. Marshall, R. A.   2nd Lt. Grant, C. S.   2nd Lt. Wallace, G. B.
B   2nd Lt. Hansen, E. H.   T/Sgt. Smith, J. T.   Sgt. Primrose, W. E.
E   Sgt. Price, W. J.   Corp. Steslow, L. S.   Corp. McLean, J. H.
R   Sgt. Levendusky, E. F.   Corp. McCaskey, M. V.   S/Sgt. Powell, T. R.
G   Sgt. Marker, D. W.   Corp. Johnston, A. R.   Corp. Whitley, G. W.

#1488   #1496   #1536

P   1st Lt. Greer, W.H.   *½2nd Lt. Hatch, R. R.   2nd Lt. Stanwood, A. H.
CP   S/P McMullin, G.A (RAAF)   2nd Lt. Seffern, C. A.   2nd Lt. Markley, E. V.
N   2nd Lt. Boothe, B. B.   1st Lt. Wright, N. A.   2nd Lt. Kenyon, R. O.
B   Sgt. McCredie, C. A.   *½2nd Lt. Barnhill, G. D. 2nd Lt. Johnson, L. A.
E   Pfc. Baren, H. G.   Corp. Slater, R. I.   Pvt. Cleary, J. J.
R   Sgt. Walker, L. M.   *Corp. Robinson, L. G.   S/Sgt. Tyree, A. T.
G   Sgt. Newhouse, B. E.   Corp. Shemberger, J. F.   *Corp. Hyde, M. R.
X   Com. Johnson, L.B. (USN) X Gen Marquat, W. F.
                                 *--Destroyed one enemy A/C *--Destroyed one enemy A/C

#1433   #1363

P   1st Lt. Krell, W. A.   1st Lt. Powell, P. G.
CP   P/O Robertson, G.B. (RAAF) 2nd Lt. Ogonowski, E. P.
N   2nd Lt. Grauer, E. A.   2nd Lt. Casteel, C. W.
B   Corp. Darden, W. R.   Sgt. Ramsey, P. L.
* E Sgt. Engleman, J. W.   Sgt. Rickman, G. T.
* R Sgt. Norton, P. H.   *Sgt. Gundling, K. R.
* G Corp. Foley, J. D.   *Sgt. Riley, T. C.
X   Col. Anderson, G. (Gen Staff) Lt. Col. Divine, D. II
*--Destroyed one enemy A/C   *--Destroyed one enemy A/C
                                 (Crash landed Moresby)

**Flight manifest for the 22nd Bomb Group's June 9, 1942,
attack on Lae/Salamaua, New Guinea. Robert Marshall
replaced Sgt. B. E. Newhouse on Aircraft #1488.**

Moresby in the late afternoon and spent the night. On the morning of the raid, Eaton returned to Lae. At 9:00 A.M., the entire area was completely overcast at 19,000 feet, with a low overcast at 10,000 feet, and scattered clouds at 4,000 to 5,000 feet. The overcast would prove to undo the carefully laid plan.

About 40 minutes into the flight, the *Heckling Hare,* carrying Johnson, experienced engine problems. The right engine's electrical generator failed, disabling the right engine propellers' automatic pitch control and the top gun turret's azimuthal power drive. Greer salvoed his bomb load and returned to base at 10:08 A.M.[43] No mention of any combat damage was noted in the Action Report, which commented in detail on damage received by other aircraft. Albert Tyree, radioman and waist gunner on Albert Stanwood's B-26, confirmed that Greer's aircraft turned back:

> I saw Greer's plane leave formation. We were about 20 minutes from Port Moresby and had not crossed the mountains or engaged the Japanese aircraft. Greer's aircraft was not shot full of holes, but the aircraft that Lt. Col. Divine crash landed was.[44]

Robert Marshall, turret gunner for Greer's aircraft, remembered slightly differently:

> We had crossed over the Owen Stanley mountains before experiencing the generator failure. I could see Lae some 40 to 50 miles away from my turret gun position. Our aircraft was not under attack when the pilot salvoed the bombs and returned to base. We were on the ground and unloaded when the other planes returned. Although I didn't see Johnson on the aircraft in flight, I did see him leave the plane after we landed.[45]

Had Greer continued on, he would have had a difficult time evading Japanese Zero fighters with his top turret out of action and one of his two engines without automatic pitch control.

More trouble was in line for the mission. After the B-17s climbed to 27,000 feet altitude, Fields ordered his gunners to fire

MISSION:		TO.7 9	June 8 & 9, 1942.

AIRCRAFT & PILOTS: Hq. Sq., 1437 Lt. Hayes, 1516 Lt. Flint, 1508 Lt. Bench, 2nd Sq; 1392 Capt. Ewbank, 1422 Lt. Crosson, 1480 Lt. McIver, 19th Sq., 1488 Lt. Greer, 1363 Lt. Powell, 1496 Lt. Match, 1433 Lt. Krell, 1536 Lt. Stanwood.

DEPARTED TOWNSVILLE: By 1330L/8. Ship 1516 returned due to mechanical trouble, departed again by 1445L/8.

ARRIVED MORESBY : Eleven ships arrived by 1746L/8.

TARGET : Destroy aircraft and supporting ground facilities from wharf area to Connells house Lae aerodrome. Attack to be at 1000L/9 after B-17 and B-25 attack.

BOMB LOAD : Thirty 100lb demolition instantaneous fuze.

TAKE OFF MORESBY : By 0851L/9.

SHIPS RETURNED & REASON : 1488 by 1008 engine trouble.

TIME OVER TARGET : 1002L/9.

RESULTS : Three hundred fifty four 100lb demolition instantaneous from five to eleven thousand feet on Salamaua. 1422 dropped 28 bombs on Isthmus. 1392 dropped 24 bombs on native buildings in trees balance in sea at Salamaua. 1480 most of bombs on runway. 1437 bombs on native buildings in trees and some in sea. 1516 b from edge timber along edge of Isthmus last four in sea. 1363 all bombs in water. 1496 some in sea most on bungalows on Isthmus. Results large fires seen eastern half of Isthmus. Military intelligence later reported schooner sunk just off Salamaua.

INTERCEPTION : B-25's pursued by ten zeros met flight on way to target. B-25's were south east of intended course. Zeros left B-25's and attacked flight. Later number of zero's increased to twenty. Attacked from front sides and rear. One zero down in flames. One had prop shot off another probable. Ship 1363 left wing shot up hydraulic system out crash landed 7 mile. Aircraft repairable. Ship 1508 Lt. Bench seen to crash in sea thirty miles from coast south of Salamaua. Ship 1422 large hole tip of port wing. Ship 1516 twenty mm cannon shell in wing and seven point seven bullet holes in prop and fuselage. Ship 1480 cannon shell in elevator. Ship 1433 two holes in tail. Tail gunner Gundling bullet wound in right shoulder, not serious. P-t fighter escort at Cape ...rd Hunt took zero's off.

A/A: Heavy and accurate.

WEATHER: Not reported.

LANDED MORESBY: By 1147L/9.

RETURNED TOWNSVILLE: By 1552L/10.

Action Report for the 22nd Bomb Group's
June 9, 1942, attack on Lae/Salamaua, New Guinea

bursts to warm up their guns.[46] The overhead turret gun was inoperable, so the gunner stored the guns in an aft-facing position. The electrical safety solenoid should have locked the guns out. Unfortunately, the solenoid malfunctioned and triggered a burst into the B-17's own tail. The .50 caliber slugs severely damaged the vertical tail surface and split the rudder in two. Fields jettisoned his bomb load and made an emergency landing at Seven Mile Airdrome. When he arrived at 9:52 A.M., Generals Scanlon and Royce raced over to Fields' aircraft in a jeep, thinking the aircraft had been attacked by Japanese fighters. Fields explained the turret gun malfunction, and they left disgusted.[47] In addition to the adverse weather over the target, the mission had lost the use of a B-26 and a B-17.

Faulkner and Horgan arrived over Lae at 9:30 A.M. to find the target completely cloud covered.[48] The B-17s circled out to sea and returned 10 minutes later. When they arrived, the B-25s were bombing from a lower altitude. The two B-17 pilots waited for the B-25s to clear, and then bombed through the overcast at 9:55 A.M. They were 25 minutes late and were undetected, as the Zeroes had scrambled to take on the B-25s.

After striking the target, the six B-25s sped west, trailed by attacking Zeroes. Their route took them to the northern end of the 35-mile-wide, 7,000-foot-high pass between the Owen Stanley Mountains and the Kratke Mountains. The B-25 pilots knew that 40th Fighter Squadron fighters were waiting to ambush the Zeroes at the Lakekamu River mouth on the southern end of the pass. The B-25s, under attack by as many as several dozen Zeroes, headed in that direction. Unfortunately, the B-26s were northbound through that same narrow mountain pass. The Zeroes abandoned the outbound B-25s to attack the inbound B-26s. The American fighters—which staged up to Thirty Mile Airdrome on the morning of the raid—had little to do beyond guarding the area until the B-25s landed.[49]

The B-26s continued on their mission—now dogged by hordes of Zeroes—arriving over the target area at 10:02 A.M. Albert Stanwood, who was piloting B-26 #1536 that day, recalls:

I flew in the first flight of aircraft with Krell, Hatch, and Powell. Krell was leading, I was on the right, Hatch was on the left, and Powell was in the rear position. This was the first mission to have coordinated planning with the other airfields. I think the mission commanders were trying to put on a show for the VIP guests as the Zeros were supposed to have been grounded by the time our B-26s got over the target. We did not use our radios so as to not alert the Japanese and did not get a weather report or further directions during the flight. There was no briefing on the morning of the flight, so we were operating under whatever orders had been issued originally. In general, we never saw the official orders. We were told what our target was and when to leave—no more.

The B-17s and B-25s were supposed to suppress the Japanese fighters, but actually stirred up a hornets' nest. The B-25s must have been returning to base when we arrived because they dragged the Zeros right into us just after we got over a pass in the Owen Stanley Mountains. We were still climbing at the time, and they were about 3,000 feet above us. Krell diverted our course to Salamaua, because it was closer than Lae. We bombed from 8,000 to 10,000 feet altitude.[50]

After dropping their bombs, the B-26s dived and headed out to sea to escape the Zeroes. Lieutenant Willis Bench's aircraft, carrying Stevens, was attacked and shot down as it skimmed the ocean's surface 30 miles off Salamaua.[51] The remaining B-26s raced down the north coast of New Guinea, chased by the Zeroes.

Precisely as planned, eight fighters from the 39th Fighter Squadron met the flight north of Cape Ward Hunt and intercepted the Zeroes. Seven of the eight pursuit pilots were on their first combat mission; Donald J. Green was the only pilot with combat experience. Lieutenant Curran L. Jones describes the intense combat action:

Our eight fighters left Twelve Mile Airdrome at 9:00 A.M. with Donald Green leading. I was flying a P-400 and leading a four-plane flight element comprising McMahan, Bartlett and Price. Green took our flight over the Owen Stanley Mountains and up to 13,000 feet. As we approached the coast, I spotted the bombers off to the left over the water and on the deck about where they were expected. I could see Zeroes like flies around the bombers. The bombers were calling "Charlie," which was our call sign. I called Green and told him, but he kept going straight. So I radioed that I was taking my flight down. Green said he would cover. My flight element attacked a Zero that was going into a steep climb—the Zeroes' typical combat tactic designed to get the American aircraft to stall. All four of my flight's fighters fired on him. He must have gone down, but we were too busy with the Zeroes to watch him.

We were strung out in a line after the attack. Then I heard a radio call from my fourth pilot, John C. Price. I did a 180 degree turn and flew down the line. There was a Zero on Price's tail. The Zero went into a vertical climb just like the first one. I climbed farther than the Zero expected because I had the speed from coming down from altitude. I fired on him with all of my guns and saw two or three 20 millimeter cannon shells strike just forward of the cockpit. I could see movement in the cockpit, and then the pilot climbed out. I went by him on my left. He was hanging onto the cockpit and not wearing a parachute. After clearing my own tail, I followed the Zero down and saw him crash into the water. There were no witnesses at the time to my knowledge, but I found out later, based on the stripes on his fuselage, that the pilot was Satoshi Yoshino, a Japanese ace with 15 victories.

After the Zero crashed in the water, I looked for the bombers. When I spotted them, they were flying over land and climbing for their return over the mountains. I headed their way and came up on five bombers in a 3 + 2 formation. I called them on the radio to be sure they didn't mistake me for a Japanese fighter, flew to their left, did a slow roll, and escorted them to

Port Moresby. They landed at Seven Mile Airdrome, while I landed at Twelve Mile Airdrome.[52]

The B-26s were on the ground at Seven Mile Airdrome by 11:47 A.M. The last B-26 to land was piloted by Divine, who brought in Lieutenant Pierre Powell's crippled aircraft in an engine-off, wheels-up landing. The dead stick landing was observed by Johnson, who had been on the ground for over an hour, and was independently reported by Pat Robinson in *The Fight for New Guinea*. In fact, an existing film of the landing shows that the propellers were not turning, so that the impact on the ground did not damage the engines themselves.[53] Divine was awarded the Distinguished Flying Cross for his skillful landing.[54]

Most of the aircraft simply refueled at Seven Mile Airdrome and returned to Townsville on the day of the raid. Flint's aircraft developed fuel pump trouble and returned on June 10, along with Powell's hurriedly patched-up aircraft.[55]

A few days after the flight, the *New York Times'* Byron Darnton, who was on the ground at Seven Mile Airdrome, reported that Johnson's plane was forced to return without reaching Lae.[56]

Thirty-four-year old Johnson described the entire episode in his diary:

> Got up at 2 AM. Left for airport at 2:30 after having tea and toast. Got in air at 3:15. Generals Marquat, Royce, Colonel Anderson, Stevens. Arrived Moresby. 7 of 8 pursuit on 1st mission says Wagner. Almost froze for 3 hours. Stood up beat my legs, stomped my feet, put on windbreak sweater, fur coat, etc.—to no avail. Hit tree. Immediately left on mission to attack Lae. Andy with Krell. Marquat with Hatch. Stevens with Lt. Bench and me with Greer. After we were off field with Krell and Greer leading, Greer's generator went out; crew begged him to go on. For next 30 minutes we flew on one generator. Due to drop bombs at 10:10 having supposedly sucked zeroes up to 17,000 and 12,000 by B17 and B25 respectively.

Plan did not work. At 9:55 we turned. At 9:58 Zeroes intercepted—Andy leader got 3 and probably another. B-25 got 2
more and fighters got 4. Total 9 Zeroes. One B-26 shot down.
I lost my friend Steve—One fighter down. Another P-39 lands
with wind and only 2 gallons gas. Devine brings B-26 down on
belly wonderful—Boys unshaven, breath smells, they haven't
bathed but Crockett, Bowie, Bonham and Travis had nothing
on them in guts. Buzz Wagner takes me to 3 Mile field in jeep.
He should design our new fighters. He knows what it takes.
To bed at 8:30 after bath and shave and scotch. Couldn't get
my mind off Steve, Lt. Bench and other fine boys.[57]

Johnson never says that he was over Lae, nor does he describe
the fighters' encounter with the Zeroes north of Cape Ward Hunt.
In fact, he simply states that the aircraft flew on for 30 minutes.
Thirty minutes would have been just enough time to get back to
Seven Mile Airdrome for the officially reported 10:08 A.M. landing,
if the *Heckling Hare* aborted the flight about 40 minutes into the
flight. Turning at 9:55 A.M. and being intercepted by Zeroes at
9:58 A.M. is clearly a reference to the remaining B-26s.

Buzz Wagner, referred to by Johnson, is Lieutenant Colonel
Boyd Wagner—director of Fighter Aircraft in what would become
V Fighter Command. His headquarters were at Townsville, but he
spent a good deal of time at Port Moresby.[58] The 26-year-old
Wagner, commander of the 17th Fighter Squadron in the Philippines prior to the war, was the Army Air Corps' first World War II
ace.[59] Wagner lent stability to the inexperienced fighter pilots and
was instrumental in organizing and training the early arrivals. He
was not flying in early June because an enemy shell shattered
the windscreen of his P-39, showering his face and upper torso
with glass shards.

Johnson's account of nine Zeroes shot down is overstated.
Aviation author Frank J. Olynyk reports five Zeroes downed, based
on claims filed by 39th Squadron pilots Donald J. Green, Curran
L. Jones, Robert F. McMahon, John C. Price, and Richard C.
Suehr.[60] Green, Jones, and Suehr are quite certain, to this day,

that they each did shoot down a Zero.[61] Postwar accounts confirmed that Yoshino and Petty Officer First Class Sakio Kikuchi were shot down that day.[62]

The 39th Fighter Squadron Diary puts the action 15 miles east of Morobe, while the 22nd Bomb Group Action Report states that the air battle took place 40 miles southeast of Morobe over Cape Word Hunt.[63] This minor discrepancy is not surprising, given that a fierce battle was under way.

The seemingly well-planned TOW 9 mission turned into a disappointment that cost a B-26 and a P-39 aircraft along with the lives of their crews.[64] The plan seemed sound, and everything was clear in the operations orders. The overcast delayed the B-17s' bombing, and these aircraft were not noticed by the Zeroes in time to react. The B-25s were on time over the target and headed west to meet the 40th Squadron fighters as planned. The B-26s arrived over the target nearly on time but on a route apparently not anticipated by the planners. Krell stated that he chose the route to confuse Japanese spotters.[65] It appears that the mission was not as well coordinated at the pilot level as thought by the planners. Stanwood, for example, made it clear that he never saw the orders directing the B-25s to head west.

Johnson and Anderson spent the night at Port Moresby. General Royce returned to Townsville in the B-17 that brought the VIP party to Port Moresby.[66] Early in the morning of June 10, Johnson and his fellow travelers boarded the *Swoose*, which Kurtz brought up from Townsville, and headed for Melbourne via Darwin. It was not to be a smooth flight.

The *Swoose* reached Darwin after a three-hour stopover at what remained of Batchelor Field.[67] The base, located 45 miles south of Darwin, was almost totally destroyed in mid-February by Japanese air attacks from Admiral Chuichi Nagumo's carrier aircraft stationed in the Banda Sea and by land-based aircraft from Kendari and Ambon in the Celebes. All told, more than one hundred Japanese aircraft attacked the city of Darwin, its harbor, and Batchelor Field. Six ships were sunk and 20 aircraft destroyed.

Darwin civilians virtually abandoned the city for fear of invasion when the Japanese occupied the island of Timor—only four hundred miles to the west. Not satisfied with their success, Japanese aircraft raided Darwin 15 times between mid-February and early June.

The *Swoose* and its cargo of VIPs—including reporters W. B. Courtney and Lee Van Atta, who would later publish articles about the flight—began a 2,600-mile flight across central Australia to Melbourne via the aircraft refueling base at Charleville.[68] Midway through the first leg of the flight, navigator Harry Schreiber informed Kurtz that *Swoose*'s navigational octant was malfunctioning. Kurtz believed that he was near Cloncurry, an aircraft dispersal base for the 19th Bomb Group, and flew box car patterns searching for the airbase. Rather than risk a night landing with important passengers on board, Kurtz decided to land before daylight ran out. He chose a relatively flat pasture near several houses, ordered the passengers into the tail section, and

Johnson prepares to board the *Swoose* for a June 10, 1942, flight from Port Moresby to Darwin.

Courtesy of Lyndon Baines Johnson Library

landed the *Swoose* near the Carisbrooke sheep station at 3:30 P.M.[69] Johnson vividly described the adventure:

> We are going through the middle of Australia en route to Charleyville—At 11:00 we discover that we are lost due to arrive Cloncurry but can't find it. Then 4 hours of roaming—from 2:30 to 3:30 very tense. 3 generals in pilot's cabin Andy and I look at each other. We circle pasture and take bearings. We climb and circle, Now we are looking at parachutes—now place to land—select windmill and pasture. Kurtz then moves all to tail. Down we come bump bomb bum. We made it. All out doors. Flies by the million, beer, maps, natives and then a telephone. 5 hours wait, wrecks pick us up. Terrible ride 48 long miles to Winton & North Gregory Hotel (Adams Hotel) Ham and Eggs & Drink to bed at 12 up at 6. What a day—gen says he is...navigator. Tough shaving no bath—plenty mosquitoes—off to Longreach—Hope this is better day.[70]

Without navigation aides, Kurtz overshot Cloncurry by nearly two hundred miles and landed near the small town of Winton. At dawn, the crew added automobile gasoline to the *Swoose*'s tanks. Kurtz flew the *Swoose* to a dirt road at Winton, picked up his passengers, and flew on to the airbase at Longreach, where the ground crew refueled the aircraft.[71] Longreach was the home base of the 19th Bomb Group's 28th and 93rd Squadrons.[72] Johnson continued his account:

> Up at 6. Shaved, breakfast and off to plane which had gotten gas at 5 o'clock. Off to Longreach at 8. Fine flying still desert. Talk to Commodore Blayden about Australia and Congress. Land at Longreach....Gen. Royce leaves us at 11.[73]

The 435th Squadron History has General Royce returning from Port Moresby to Townsville on June 9. Johnson's diary entry regarding Royce's departure is consistent with White's account.[74] Royce must have come back to Port Moresby when Kurtz brought the *Swoose* up from Townsville.

After refueling, the party continued to Melbourne, arriving in the late afternoon of June 12. Johnson and Anderson spent the following five days briefing military officials and resting from their exhausting journey. On the sixth day in Melbourne, MacArthur summoned Johnson and Anderson to his office for a debriefing. He listened to their report for an hour, and then announced that he was decorating Johnson, Anderson, and posthumously, Stevens. Johnson quotes MacArthur in his diary:

> Thursday, June 18: Saw MacArthur at 11:45 AM. Ver sad—head down—low voice "glad to see you two fellows here where three were last. It was a mistake of the head to go on combat mission but it did justice to your heart. It was just what I would have done. I'm giving you Silver Heart [*sic*]. Gave Stevens DSC because he was your leader and gave his life. Such is war."[75]

Johnson and Anderson left Melbourne that same day for Sydney, where Johnson came down with the flu.[76] The two men departed Sydney on June 21 for Noumea, New Caledonia. Although Johnson was still suffering from a fever, he and Anderson continued their journey home the next day. By the time they reached the Fiji Islands, Johnson had become seriously ill and was hospitalized with a high fever. Anderson continued on to Hawaii, while Johnson remained hospitalized for three days. Johnson arrived in Pearl Harbor on June 26 and was well enough to fly to San Francisco on July 6. He reached Washington, D.C., on July 10.[77]

While Johnson was on his inspection tour, Roosevelt issued an Executive Order stating that all members of Congress serving in the military were to either return to their congressional duties or resign their seats. Johnson returned to Congress on July 16.

Johnson remained in the House of Representatives throughout the rest of the war. He served on the Naval Affairs Committee and chaired a subcommittee which investigated navy procurement and management. In the summer of 1945, as the war was drawing to a close, Johnson visited Admiral Nimitz at his advanced headquarters in Guam.

Johnson's political career continued with a succession of unbroken election victories. In 1948, 39-year-old Johnson narrowly won the Senate nomination in Texas's Democratic primary. Johnson's opponent, Governor Coke Robert Stevenson, contested the outcome of the primary election in Federal Court. Johnson prevailed, due in large part to the able support of his lawyer, future Supreme Court Justice Abe Fortas. Johnson easily won the Senate seat in the general election and was granted membership in the Senate Armed Services Committee. He gained national recognition by chairing the Preparedness Investigating Subcommittee, the same committee that propelled Harry S. Truman into the vice presidency. In 1949, he was promoted to commander in the Naval Reserve.

Johnson was elected party whip by his fellow Democratic Senators in 1951 after only three years in the Senate. This role put Johnson in frequent contact with his fellow Democrats as he corralled members for crucial votes. When Barry Morris Goldwater defeated Democratic Minority Leader Ernest MacFarland of Arizona in 1952, Johnson was elected to the position. Two years later, the Democrats gained control of the Senate, and Johnson became the majority leader. At age 46, he was the youngest man ever to serve in that position.

As majority leader, Johnson exercised control of the Senate for five years and built a reputation for hard work and effectiveness within the Democratic Party. He suffered a heart attack in 1955 and returned to the Senate in 1956. Johnson championed bills that established the National Aeronautics and Space Administration and the Civil Rights Acts of 1957 and 1960.

Yearning for higher office, Johnson threw his hat in the presidential ring in 1960. His power in the Senate could do him little good, however. In the months before the Democratic National Convention, Senator Kennedy swept through the primary states collecting delegates. Kennedy had enough votes to win on the first ballot, and Johnson accepted Kennedy's offer to campaign as his vice president. The Kennedy-Johnson ticket prevailed in a close election. Johnson was also elected to his third term in the Senate, an office which he resigned after his swearing-in ceremony.

As vice president, Johnson chaired the National Aeronautics and Space Council, the President's Committee on Equal Employment Opportunity, and the Peace Corps Advisory Council, in addition to his duties as president of the Senate. He traveled abroad extensively representing the United States. On November 22, 1963, Johnson became the 36th President of the United States following Kennedy's assassination. Johnson signed into law the Civil Rights Act of 1964 and the Economic Opportunity Act. He resigned from the Naval Reserve in January 1964.

Johnson selected Hubert Horatio Humphrey to be his running mate in the 1964 presidential elections. They faced the Republican ticket of Goldwater and William Edward Miller and won by the largest margin to date with a popular vote of 43,129,484 to 27,178,188 votes. The Electoral College vote was 486 to 52. During his four-year term, Johnson signed multiple laws that are generally referred to as the Great Society. Included were the Elementary and Secondary Education Act, the Voting Rights Act, the Civil Rights Act of 1968, and Medicare/Medicaid. Johnson nominated Abe Fortas and Thurgood Marshall to serve on the Supreme Court. The cabinet posts of Housing and Urban Development and the Department of Transportation were created during his term. America's direct military involvement in Vietnam originated while Johnson was president. Air attacks began after the Gulf of Tonkin incident in August 1964, and ground troops were dispatched in June 1965. Domestic violence and the assassinations of Martin Luther King and Robert Francis Kennedy tarnished Johnson's legislative accomplishments.

After completing his full term, Johnson chose not to run for reelection and retired to his ranch in Johnson City, Texas. He died in 1973 at the age of 64 and is buried in the Johnson family cemetery.

Johnson held elective office for 32 years. His active military career spanned eight months when on leave from Congress, of which two months were in the Pacific Theater. He remained in the Naval Reserve for 22 years after leaving active duty. For his service in the Pacific Theater, Johnson was awarded the Asiatic-Pacific Campaign Medal and the World War II Victory Medal in addition to the Army Silver Star. His citation reads:

LYNDON B. JOHNSON, Lieutenant Commander, United States Naval Reserve,

For gallantry in action in the vicinity of Port Moresby and Salamaua, New Guinea on June 9, 1942. While on a mission of obtaining information in the Southwest Pacific area, Lieutenant Commander Johnson, in order to obtain personal knowledge of combat conditions, volunteered as an observer on a hazardous aerial combat mission over hostile positions in New Guinea. As our planes neared the target area they were intercepted by eight hostile fighters. When, at this time, the plane in which Lieutenant Commander Johnson was an observer, developed mechanical trouble and was forced to turn back alone, presenting a favorable target to the enemy fighters, he evidenced marked coolness in spite of the hazards involved. His gallant action enabled him to obtain and return with valuable information.

By command of General MacArthur[78]

Chapter 2

John F. Kennedy
PT Boat Skipper

With his older brother already in the navy and the threat of war growing, John Fitzgerald Kennedy, a Harvard graduate, volunteered in mid-1942 for the Army's Officer Candidate School. He was rejected due to a previous back injury. Undaunted, Kennedy volunteered for the navy, and was again rejected.[1] He persisted and, with a bit of help from Navy Captain Alan Kirk, was directly commissioned as an ensign on September 25, 1941.[2] Kirk arranged for Kennedy to be assigned to the Office of Naval Intelligence in Washington, D.C., and he reported on October 26. Kennedy worked in the Foreign Intelligence Branch, helping with the preparation of daily security bulletins.[3] In his Officer's Fitness Report for the period October 27, 1941, to January 19, 1942, Rear Admiral Theodore Starke Wilkinson rated Kennedy 3.8 out of 4.0 in his Present assignment and gave him the highest possible marks in Intelligence, Moral Courage, Cooperation, and Loyalty. Wilkinson remarked: "This Officer's services were eminently satisfactory in every respect. His cheerful attention to duty materially aided the morale of his Section."[4]

Despite these high marks, Kennedy was reassigned to the Sixth Naval District Headquarters in Charleston, South Carolina.[5] He languished there for six months, instructing defense plant workers how to defend against enemy attack. During this time, he made several trips to hospitals in Charleston and Boston to treat his back injury.

With the war in the Pacific heating up, Kennedy requested sea duty. He was ordered to the Naval Reserve Midshipmen's School at Northwestern University in late July.[6] Students learned seamanship the navy way in an accelerated course designed to produce seagoing officers in sixty days.[7] Instruction included navigation, seamanship, gunnery, and naval regulations.

Kennedy was at Northwestern when Medal of Honor winner Lieutenant Commander (later Vice Admiral) John Duncan Bulkeley came to recruit officers for the Motor Torpedo Boat Squadrons Training Center he established at Melville, Rhode Island. Motor Torpedo Boat is the official name for the small wooden craft commonly known as PT boats. Bulkeley commanded the detachment of four Squadron Three PT boats that spirited General Douglas MacArthur out of Corregidor. MacArthur saw the value of the nimble, shallow-draft boats in South Pacific island waters and sent Bulkeley to the States to lobby for two hundred more PT boats. Having been successful in obtaining the boats, it was up to Bulkeley to train officers and crews to operate them. Bulkeley chose experienced PT boat officers as instructors, including Squadron Three veteran Lieutenant (jg) Henry J. Brantingham. Brantingham would come to mean a great deal to Kennedy during his service in the South Pacific.[8]

The Training Center was located on Naragansett Bay. Melville, as it was known, began operations in March 1942 under the direction of Lieutenant Commander William C. Specht. The first class had 51 officers and 177 enlisted men. Eventually, Melville handled 90 officers and 860 enlisted men in each eight-week class. Facilities included 34 classrooms, 42 maintenance buildings, and 197 Quonset huts for living quarters.[9]

Kennedy was an experienced seaman in small boats and applied for this branch of the navy known for its daring and independent PT boat captains. After he completed his midshipman training in September, Kennedy was ordered to Melville.[10] Students took courses in gunnery, navigation, and seamanship and participated in rigorous exercise and athletic competition. In October, Kennedy was promoted to lieutenant (jg), having served a full year. His prowess with watercraft was apparent to Melville executive officer Lieutenant Commander (later Rear Admiral) John Harlee. Upon completing his training on December 2, Harlee assigned Kennedy to Squadron Four for duty as an instructor and skipper of the Melville training boat PT 101. Despite his vehement protests that he preferred a combat assignment, Kennedy took command of PT 101 on December 7, one year after the bombing of Pearl Harbor.[11]

The assignment did not last long. In January 1943 Specht directed Kennedy to take PT 101 to Jacksonville, Florida, to join Squadron Fourteen, which was to be stationed at the Panama Canal.[12] Five of Squadron Four's PT boats left Melville for Jacksonville. Four days later, Kennedy was hospitalized with a stomach ailment in Morehead City, North Carolina. He rejoined the boats in Jacksonville.[13] Before he left Melville, Kennedy realized that Squadron Fourteen might spend the entire war guarding the Canal and requested duty in the South Pacific. He enlisted the aid of Massachusetts Senator David Walsh, chairman of the Senate Naval Affairs Committee, to be certain that he got his way.[14]

In mid-February, the Bureau of Naval Personnel ordered Kennedy to the Solomon Islands as a Squadron Two replacement officer.[15] Six days later, he handed over his command and headed west.[16] Kennedy's transport ship, SS *Rochambeau* (AP 63), left San Francisco on March 6, 1943. *Rochambeau* was converted from the French liner *Marechal Joffre*. The ship was in the Philippines when the American Pacific Fleet at Pearl Harbor was attacked, and she departed for the United States under the command of Navy Lieutenant Thomas G. Warfield.[17] This officer would also loom large in Kennedy's future. After a two-day stop in San Diego to pick up 1,500 navy men, *Rochambeau* sailed westward.[18]

During the long voyage across the Pacific, Kennedy met and befriended Ensign James A. Reed who would remain close for the rest of Kennedy's life.[19] *Rochambeau* entered the port of Santo (now Lugainville) on Espiritu Santo Island on March 28 and proceeded up the Segond Channel to the well-protected harbor.[20] Reed remembers:

> We sailed by the remains of a transport ship the SS *Coolidge* and traveled through a narrow channel. Then we entered a large harbor. Jack and I were standing at the rail when the South Pacific Fleet came into view. The fleet made an impressive sight, and Jack made some exclamation to that effect.
>
> I was assigned to PT boat headquarters in Noumea, New Caledonia, and reported there. Before we parted, Jack convinced me that I should try to get assigned with him. When the opportunity presented itself a few months later, I volunteered to move up to Tulagi.[21]

After docking in Santo, Kennedy transferred to LST 449 anchored at Berth 32 in the Segond Channel.[22] The 4,000-ton ship departed Espiritu Santo on April 4 for Guadalcanal transporting several hundred servicemen.[23] Passengers included PT boat officers and men bound for nearby Tulagi Island. Tulagi was the home port of Motor Torpedo Boat Flotilla One, the parent organization of Squadron Two to which Kennedy was to report. Lying just south of the larger Florida Island, Tulagi is two miles long and half a mile wide.

Japanese troops seized Tulagi from the Australians on May 3, 1942, and established a float plane base at the nearby island of Gavutu. These two islands were invaded by U.S. Marines on August 7 and were secured in two days.[24] Seabees from Guadalcanal built a small PT boat base at the native village of Sesape. PT boats first arrived on October 12, 1942, while the fight for Guadalcanal was raging some 20 miles across the Sealark Channel.

Tulagi Island in the foreground with Florida Island in the background. The mouth of the Maliali River is in the upper left.

Courtesy of United States
Naval Historical Center

Four Squadron Three (2) PT boats were transported from Panama to Noumea, New Caledonia, by two cargo ships. Squadron Three (2) was so named because the original Squadron Three had been decimated in the Philippine action. After unloading and checking out the boats, the skippers of the four boats and their squadron commanding officer, Lieutenant Commander Alan Montgomery, paid a call on Admiral Robert Ghormley. He wanted the PT boats to harass the Japanese ships that were shelling the marines on Guadalcanal at night. In addition to the damage, the marines were kept awake by the constant bombardment.[25]

The PT boats were towed to within three hundred miles of Tulagi and then proceeded under their own power. Part of the PT base force came along to expand the facilities at Sesape.[26] A storehouse and base headquarters were soon established. Dr. Emilio Lastreto set up a small infirmary in an abandoned native hut on a point of land near the entrance to Tulagi Harbor.[27] Thirty-six hours after arriving, the four boats went into action against eight Japanese destroyers, three cruisers, and a battleship that were bombarding Guadalcanal.[28] Stunned by the sudden attack out of the dark, the Japanese force retired without battle.

The PT boat tender USS *Jamestown* (AGP 3), a converted 1,780-ton yacht, arrived on October 23 bringing precious food and supplies along with the rest of the base force personnel. *Jamestown* moored along the west bank of the Maliali River on Florida Island across the bay from Tulagi.[29] The tender provided welcome relief to the PT boat crews as fuel could be pumped rather than manually handling 55-gallon drums. *Jamestown* also provided lodging for the PT boat officers.

A second group of four Squadron Three (2) PT boats arrived on October 25 under command of executive officer, Lieutenant Hugh M. Robinson. More confrontations with Japanese surface ships ensued. Lester H. Gamble in PT 37 scored two torpedo hits on a Japanese destroyer on November 11, for which he was awarded a Silver Star. On December 9, John M. Searles in PT 59 stalked and sank the two-thousand-ton Japanese submarine I-3 while it was attempting to deliver supplies to Guadalcanal. Searles was awarded a Navy Cross for his actions, and the crew were awarded Silver Stars. Two days later, Gamble sank the 2,700-ton Japanese destroyer *Teruzuki*. For this action, and two additional attacks on destroyers in January, Gamble was awarded the Navy Cross.[30] Lieutenant Clark W. Faulkner in PT 40 torpedoed another Japanese destroyer and also received the Navy Cross.[31]

Because *Jamestown* quarters were hot and overcrowded, some of the officers moved to thatched huts in the native village located in a clearing east of the Maliali River. The base force converted an old church into a recreation hall to provide some distraction from the pressures of combat.[32]

Food was always a difficulty at the PT boat base. Staple items included rice and Spam, which became tiresome. The military-issued Spam is similar to SPAM®, a canned spiced-ham product made by the Hormel Company.[33] To add variety, cooks experimented with fish gathered by throwing hand grenades into the water and, although somewhat repulsive sounding, with the meat of large fruit bats.[34] Mutton obtained from New Zealand in gallon cans was greasy and foul smelling.

Motor Torpedo Boat Flotilla One was established on December 15, 1942, to coordinate the multiple squadrons operating out of Tulagi. Commander Alvin P. Calvert, the flotilla's first commanding officer, established his headquarters in Sesape. Robinson became Calvert's material officer in February 1943, turning command of Squadron Three (2) over to Searles. Squadron Two reached Tulagi in late November 1942 and provided some relief for the beleaguered Squadron Three (2) veterans. Lieutenant Allen H. Harris replaced Lieutenant Rollin E. Westholm, the Squadron Two commander, who was promoted to Flotilla One's chief of staff.

More officers saw the benefits of living in the native village. One group moved into a former native boat shop, and the base force installed such improvements as windows and a wooden deck. The village even boasted a nearby waterfall where the men could bathe.[35] Before long, a dock was built with Marston mat laid over cross beams attached to bollards; this is the dock often seen in base pictures. Somewhere along the line, the little village acquired the name Calvertville after the Flotilla One commander.

With Guadalcanal in American hands, Squadron Three (2) personnel left for Noumea on February 18 aboard the *Jamestown* for some much needed rest and recreation. Their PT boats had engaged the Japanese on 35 nights, denying the Japanese the ability to supply their troops on Guadalcanal at will and providing a bit of comfort to the American troops by disrupting the nightly Japanese bombardment.[36]

USS *Niagara* (AGP 1), a 1,920-ton yacht converted to a PT boat tender, arrived in Tulagi Harbor on February 17, 1943, one day before the *Jamestown* left for Noumea. She took *Jamestown*'s mooring on the west bank of the Maliali River. Additional PT base force personnel arrived in March 1943 and expanded the facility.[37] Fueling and repair facilities were constructed on Macambo Island in Tulagi Harbor, and housing at Calvertville was upgraded. Personnel were able to move from native huts to screened-in tents with elevated wooden floors.

Calvertville, Florida Island

Courtesy of David M. Levy

When LST 449, with Kennedy on board, reached Guadalcanal at mid-day on April 7, a Japanese air raid was under way. The Japanese command sent 67 Val dive bombers and 110 Zero fighters against Guadalcanal and Tulagi.[38] Several of the Vals attacked the LST and the destroyer *Aaron Ward* (DD 483). LST 449 experienced several near misses and was partially disabled. *Aaron Ward* took a bomb in her aft engine room and sank before she could be towed to Tulagi.[39] After repairing some battle damage, LST 449 headed south to escape further air attacks. She cruised about for five days before returning on the night of April 12 to unload army troops and supplies at Lunga Point, Guadalcanal.[40] Early the next morning, LST 449 ferried the PT boat men across Skylark Channel to the Government Wharf on Tulagi Island. The wharf was located near the PT boat base at Sesape on the southern end of Tulagi. Sesape was not much of a base—a few Quonset huts, some makeshift docks, an abandoned marine railway, and several machine shops. At first the railway was used to pull the boats partway out of the water for repair, but this was ineffective. Later, pontoon cradles were used to lift PT boats out of the water similar to floating dry docks.[41]

Kennedy moved into a native hut in Calvertville, now vastly improved from the original native village. His roommate, John Iles, remembers:

> I bunked next to Kennedy in Melville, probably because of alphabetical order. I arrived in Tulagi in February 1943 and remember seeing Kennedy walk up the pier when he arrived in April. Four of us lived in a one-room native hut in Calvertville. It was located close to the landing and behind some refrigerators. We cleaned up the hut and had a wood floor put in. The hut was furnished with four cots and some orange crates for storage. Kennedy and I were first, then came Gene Foncannon and Lenny Thom.[42]

PT boat base at Sesape, Tulagi Island.
Several floating dry docks are visible.

Courtesy of the Admiral Nimitz Museum of
the Pacific War, Fredericksburg, Texas

Tulagi's harbor was also home to nine submarine chasers. SC 761 Executive Officer J. Henry Doscher recalls:

> There were several large mooring buoys permanently anchored in the wide area of Tulagi's harbor. These buoys were used by the submarine chasers and occasional other ships. Every two or three days, we moved alongside the water dock at the mouth of the Maliali River on Florida Island to replenish our supply of water. The Seabees built a pipeline to an underground spring high in the hills, and fresh water was plentiful. We stayed alongside that dock as long as possible because showers were not restricted.[43]

Squadron Two commander Harris assigned Kennedy as the executive officer of PT 47 to learn the ropes from its skipper George Wright. On April 25, Kennedy took command of PT 109. The ship's log read:

0830 Underway for Sesape
1100 Lt. (jg) J. F. Kennedy assumed command of boat
1145 Moored at the usual berth in bushes
1500 L. E. Drewitch F 1/c L. E. Drawdy F 1/c, C. A. Harris GM
3/c reported aboard

and was signed by Ensign L. J. Thom, Exec.[44] It was common practice to moor the PT boats under the bushes, largely mangrove trees, to hide them from enemy aircraft.[45]

PT 109 was built by Elco Naval Division of the Electric Boat Company in Bayonne, New Jersey. The wooden hulled craft was 80 feet long, had a 21-foot beam with a draft of five feet, and displaced 50 tons fully loaded. Three 12-cylinder Packard engines producing 3,600 HP powered the early 80-foot Elcos which were capable of 40+ knots. Later the Packard engines were improved to deliver 4,500 HP. The boats carried three thousand gallons of 100-octane gasoline, making them extremely vulnerable to enemy fire. Consequently, the PT boats operated almost exclusively at night and, as much as possible, remained out of sight during

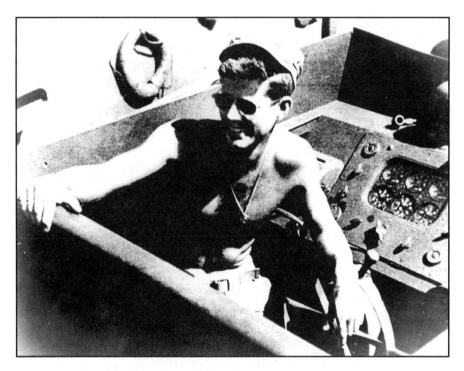

Kennedy in PT 109's cockpit

Courtesy of John Fitzgerald Kennedy Library

the day. Three officers and a crew of 12 to 14 men could be accommodated on board.

PT 109 had a 20 millimeter Oerlikon cannon, two twin .50 caliber Browning machine gun turrets, and four 21-inch torpedo tubes. The Mark VIII torpedoes used early in the war were ineffective due their slow speed, short range, and a tendency of the warhead not to detonate on impact. They were eventually replaced by the much-improved Mark XIII torpedoes. Smoke generators were an important part of the defensive system. The PT boats raced away from an attacker in a zigzag pattern, laying down smoke to throw off the gunners' aim.

Although still in combat status, PT 109 was in need of refurbishing and restaffing. Lieutenant Bryant L. Larson explains:

> I took over command of PT 109 in Panama, and we were
> shipped to the Solomon Islands in November 1942. There were

about a dozen PT boats at Tulagi then. We were assigned to Squadron Two commanded by Rollin Westholm, and he rode on the 109 when we went on patrol. By April 1943, when I turned command of PT 109 over to Kennedy, her engines were tired from five months of patrolling. The ship was not in disarray as was portrayed in the movie *PT 109.*[46]

Bryant had taken command of PT 109 from her first skipper, Jack J. Kempner. After a three-month mission to the Galapagos Islands, Squadron 5 Commanding Officer Henry Farrow assigned Kempner to the Elco plant to oversee the construction of six PT boats to replace those transferred to Squadron 2. PT 109 was one of the boats transferred.

Kennedy retained Leonard Jay Thom, a former Ohio State football player, as executive officer, and picked up Gunner's Mate 2/c Charles Albert Harris, Motor Machinist's Mate 2/c Leon E. Drawdy, and Motor Machinist's Mate 2/c Edmund T. Drewitch from the new-replacement crew. Six days later, Gunner's Mate 3/c Maurice L. Kowal and Torpedoman 2/c Andrew Jackson Kirksey reported aboard. In the following week, Radioman 2/c John E.

**Part of the PT 109 crew. Kennedy is on the right
and the officer on the left is Alan Webb.**

Courtesy of John Fitzgerald Kennedy Library

Maguire arrived. PT 109 was put in drydock, and the crew set to work scraping, sanding, and painting while the engines were being overhauled. Routine night patrols began on April 29. Alan W. Webb recalls:

> I arrived in the Solomons in February 1943 with the Melville class that included Lenny Thom, John Iles, and Joe Atkinson. We were replacement officers. My first assignment was as executive officer for Les Gamble. I often went out with Iles and with Kennedy. I'm the officer on the left in the widely-distributed picture of the PT 109 crew.[47]

Lieutenant Alvin Peyton Cluster, a Naval Academy graduate, replaced Squadron Two commander Harris in May. Cluster had been stationed at Funafuti in the Ellice Islands and was involved in the remarkable rescue of World War I fighter ace Eddie Rickenbacker. Rickenbacker and the crew of a B-17 had been adrift for 23 days after crashing at sea.

Kennedy impressed Harris in the short time Harris was his squadron commander. He gave Kennedy the highest possible rating in Moral Courage and in Reactions in Emergencies, as well as rating him Outstanding in comparison with other officers of his rank and approximate length of service.[48]

During the month of May, PT 109 carried out routine patrols and experienced occasional aircraft raids.[49] PT 109 took on fresh water alongside *Niagara* and refueled at Mocambo Island in Tulagi's harbor. Tulagi had grown considerably by this time with more than 50 PT boats and one hundred officers.[50]

Niagara departed for New Guinea on May 23 in the company of six PT boats being transferred to the Southwest Pacific Theater. PT 110 skipper Pat Munroe recalls how Kennedy could have been in that group:

> I was in the Russell Islands in charge of the base area but returned to Tulagi with PT 110. Six boats were designated by Commander Calvert to transfer to New Guinea, but one of

them was destroyed by air attack. Kennedy's PT 109 and my
PT 110 were the only boats available to fill in for the lost boat.
Calvert had no particular preference between the two of us so
flipped a coin. I won the coin toss and set out for New Guinea
with the *Niagara.*[51]

Along the way, a high altitude Japanese bomber attack seriously
damaged *Niagara*. After the crew were taken off, PT 147 sank
her with a single torpedo. The PT boats then returned the crew to
Tulagi. Six days later, *Niagara* Seaman 1/c Edgar E. Mauer reported to PT 109, having lost all of his personal possessions.

PT 109 departed Tulagi for the Russell Islands on May 30,
joining 11 PT boats. An amphibious force invaded the Russells on
February 21 with virtually no Japanese resistance. Seabees built
a PT boat base in Wernham Cove at the south end of the island of
Banika. The base, made operational on February 25, was more
rudimentary than Sesape. There was no deep water harbor or
repair facility. PT boats were simply moored under mangrove trees
along the shoreline of the Sunlight Channel between the major
islands of Pavuvu and Banika. Pavuvu, although larger than Banika,
was rugged and densely wooded and was never developed.[52]

The Russell Islands PT boat base was first occupied in April
by Squadron Two. Squadron Six, commanded by Lieutenant
Faulkner, and Squadron Nine, commanded by Lieutenant Commander Robert B. Kelly, took their turns. Kelly was executive officer of Squadron Three in the Philippines and participated in the
evacuation of MacArthur's staff. Kelly's squadron was recalled
from the Russells to move up to Rendova Island in support of the
New Georgia invasion and was replaced by Squadron Three (2).
Searles explains:

> I was assigned to develop the base to assist in the inva-
> sion of Bougainville and to train junior officers. Fuel was stored
> on one island and torpedoes were stored on a second island.
> Admiral Halsey visited for several hours on July 1, 1943, and
> he named the base Searlesville.[53]

The torpedoes were stored on the island of Hoi in the mouth of the Sunlight Channel just outside Wernham cove. A dock built of boulders and palm trees accommodated the unwieldy weapons.[54]

Officers lived in an abandoned Lever Brothers plantation house on Banika. The house, on a hill overlooking Sunlight Channel, consisted of a kitchen and officers' mess hall surrounded on three sides by a large veranda. Officers slept on cots on the veranda with mosquito nets draped from the ceiling. After a few bites from roving rats, the officers learned to tuck the nets under their mattress to keep their hands and arms from trailing down to the floor.[55] On alternate nights, many officers not on patrol played card games indoors with the windows covered by blankets. Kennedy was neither a good poker or bridge player and spent much of his spare time talking with fellow officers.[56]

A small dock was located on Wernham Cove just down the hill from the plantation house. The dock was used to unload crew members brought from their boats to eat at the mess tent, as well as to fuel the PT boats. The boats were refueled one at a time with a hand pump after wrestling 55-gallon fuel drums from storage under the mangrove trees.[57] The dock was parallel to shore and had a small tool shed on its end. This was the scene in the movie *PT 109* of Kennedy's crash when racing another PT boat. PT 40 captain John F. Kearny tells the story:

> One day Kennedy and I were arguing whether a 77-foot Elco or an 80-foot Elco was faster. We agreed to race when returning home from patrol the next morning. The race started out side by side and was quite even; we were neck to neck entering Sunlight Channel. I pulled back on my throttles, but Kennedy didn't. He hit the pier and shook the dust off the shed on the end of the pier. Kennedy's boat suffered a small hole, but nothing that couldn't be fixed.[58]

PT 61 skipper Kenneth W. Prescott explains:

> Jack was always running into things. He was in a hurry whatever he did, and he always wanted to be first. It wasn't

that Jack was a poor sailor, but that PT 109's engines always needed fixing and didn't respond well to sudden changes.[59]

Searles acknowledged that the PT boats would race home from night patrols to be first to fuel.[60] A gasoline tanker, YOG 49, supplied by Admiral Halsey greatly eased the refueling burden.[61]

From May 31 to June 12, PT 109 went on patrol from the Russell Islands five times with no enemy sighted. PT 109 departed for Tulagi on June 13 to have her engines repaired, and returned to the Russell Islands on June 16. Between June 17 and June 30, PT 109 went on a single patrol and otherwise remained moored. Searles explains the relative inaction:

> Our patrols out of the Russell Islands were canceled by Admiral Halsey. There just weren't all that many targets. More important, the patrols were becoming very risky due to the Japanese float planes. The planes would spot our phosphorescent wakes at night, cut their engines, and come in silently to bomb us.[62]

Japanese float plane pilots were expert at spotting a PT boat's bright phosphorescent wakes at night. The wakes literally glowed due to the wake's turbulence exciting small animal and plant life in the rich, warm waters.[63] Float plane pilots would simply attack the location at the head of the wake. The PT boats' best solution was to cruise at low speed to keep the wake signature down.

Searles' explanation is supported by an Air Solomons intelligence report of that period:

> In order to intensify their night searches, the Japanese have returned to the practice of bringing float planes into Rekata Bay at dusk and sending them out on night search or attack missions. Four or five float planes were reported as landing at Rekata Bay at dusk several nights during the week, and planes three times during the week ending June 25, 1943, attacked shipping between Guadalcanal and the Russells.[64]

Rekata Bay is located on the northeast coast of Santa Isabel Island 60 miles from the Russell Islands.

Unfortunately, the quarterly log book for PT 109 ends on June 30, and the new log book was lost at sea. Therefore, the record of what happened next must come from other sources. Motor Machinist's Mate 2/c William N. Johnston and Motor Machinists's Mate 1/c Patrick Henry McMahon reported aboard in early July.

In mid-July, PT 109 was ordered to Rendova Harbor to provide assistance in the New Georgia invasion. Kennedy wanted to join Rendova's commanding officer Robert Kelly.[65] Kelly was reassigned to open a new PT boat base at Lever Harbor on New Georgia before Kennedy arrived.[66] The new commanding officer at Rendova was Commander Thomas G. Warfield, an Annapolis graduate, former captain of the troopship *Rochambeau*, and commanding officer of Squadron Ten. As Rendova base commander, Warfield had overall command of elements of Squadrons Five, Nine, Ten and Eleven. PT 109 was the lone representative of Squadron Two.

Warfield was a stern man who brooked no nonsense from his independent PT boat captains. He believed in doing things by the book. His operating procedure was to send large numbers of PT boats into the patrol area and to restrict radio transmissions to contact reports. When a division commander executed a maneuver, the other PT boats were to react by visual sighting—not by radio command. Warfield kept his distance from the men and operated out of a reinforced command bunker with a radio transmitter. Kennedy was now serving with unfamiliar PT boat captains and taking orders from a base commander very different from Squadron Two commanding officer Cluster.

The Rendova PT boat base headquarters were on the island of Lumbari near the western entrance to Rendova Harbor. Lumbari was two hundred yards wide by four hundred yards long. In addition to Warfield's bunker, the island contained an intelligence unit, a mess hall, and a small repair shop. The PT boat fuel depot was on a separate island. Unlike Tulagi, Rendova Harbor's beaches had a shallow slope, so the PT boats had to be moored in the open. Typically, the boats were moored in threes around buoys anchored in the harbor.[67] Officers and crew lived on their PT boats at first. Later, officers moved to tents on shore. Rations obtained from the army included powdered eggs, powdered milk, Spam, Vienna sausages, dehydrated potatoes, and pancake mix.[68]

Japanese troops at nearby Munda, New Georgia, were being resupplied and reinforced at night from the Japanese base at Vila on the southern tip of Kolombangara Island. Supplies and troops were off-loaded there and transported to New Georgia by

Rendova Harbor. Bau Island is in the foreground, Rendova Island is on the upper left, and Lumbari Island is on the upper right inside the western entrance.

Courtesy of WWII PT Boats Museum and Archives,
Germantown, Tennessee

barge. On the night of July 21, a Japanese supply convoy successfully transited Blackett Strait between the islands of Gizo and Kolombangara, thereby avoiding the more heavily patrolled Kula Gulf. Kolombangara is a foreboding island dominated by a rain forest and a six-thousand-foot-high extinct volcano. With the island as a background, ships were virtually undetectable by eye, a fact that would prove crucial on the Stygian night of August 1, 1943.

The primary mission of the Rendova PT boats was to disrupt the Japanese nighttime supply convoys and to warn of any attempted seaborne attack on the New Georgia assault troops. Warfield received his orders from the Task Force 31 commander, Rear Admiral Richmond K. Turner, who directed the battle for New Georgia from his headquarters on Guadalcanal. It was up to Warfield to determine how to carry out those orders.

PT 109 was on routine patrol in Blackett Strait on July 19, 1943, when it was attacked by a Japanese float plane. Crew members Kowal and Drawdy were hit by shrapnel from the exploding bombs. PT 109 sustained significant damage, including a large hole near the waterline. When PT 109 returned to Rendova at the end of its patrol, Kowal and Drawdy were sent to a hospital in Tulagi.[69] They were replaced by Torpedoman 2/c Raymond L. Starkey and Motor Machinist's Mate 1/c Gerard E. Zinser. Also added were Motor Machinist's Mate 2/c Harold W. Marney and Seaman 2/c Raymond Albert. Zinser was an experienced PT boat machinery service man who normally worked in the base force, but was pressed into service because of the wounding of Drawdy.[70] He was the last living survivor of the crash of PT 109.[71]

PT 109 was patrolling off Gizo Island on July 24 with four PT boats when another float plane attacked; this time there were no casualties. The following night, PT 109 was patrolling off Wana Wana with five PT boats. Japanese float planes attacked, and the executive officer of PT 105 was killed by shrapnel from a near miss. PT 109 patrolled off the northwest tip of Gizo with four PT boats on July 27 without incident. On July 30, while patrolling off

Makuti Island at the lower edge of Blackett Strait, PT 109's rudder failed, and she returned to base for repairs.[72]

Japanese supplies were generally transported to Vila by Daihatsu barges, which hugged the Kolombangara coastline to escape detection. Typically, the barges were diesel-powered craft, 40 to 50 feet long, and capable of making eight knots while carrying one hundred men or 10 tons of cargo. Occasionally the Japanese command reverted to the use of destroyers when the need was great. On July 30 the commanders of the Japanese destroyers *Amagiri, Hagikaze, Arashi*, and *Shigure* received orders to convoy 120 tons of supplies and nine hundred troops from the Japanese base at Rabaul to Vila via Blackett Strait. The convoy was to sail on the night of August 1, in part because the moonless night would help conceal the convoy against the blackness of Kolombangara Island.

While PT 109 was undergoing rudder repairs, Kennedy decided to install a single-shot, breech-loading 37 millimeter tank gun on PT 109's foredeck for use against the armored barges. PT 109's crew removed the boat's life raft and bolted the gun's frame to the foredeck. A large timber (variously reported to be 4x4, 2x6 or 2x8 planks or coconut tree logs) was lashed in place to absorb the gun's recoil. PT 109 was ordered out on an important mission before the gun could be further secured and the life raft remounted.

Headquarters sent a secret message to Warfield informing him that a Japanese convoy would run down Blackett Strait on the night of August 1–2. The Task Force commander directed Warfield to operate all the PT boats he could muster to intercept the convoy and warned that Japanese aircraft would attempt to stop the PTs.

On the afternoon of August 1, Rendova was suddenly attacked by Japanese bombers. PT boat crews scrambled to their weapons and fired back. Then, just as suddenly, the air attack was over. PT 117 was sunk, and PT 164 was heavily damaged with two men killed. Fifteen boats remained seaworthy, only four of which had radar sets.

Kennedy and the other PT boat captains reported ashore to Warfield's operations dugout to receive their instructions for the night patrol. Warfield briefed the men that the Japanese convoy was expected in the Kula Gulf at half past midnight. Their job was to patrol Blackett Strait and intercept the Japanese convoy if it came that way. Warfield created four PT boat divisions around the PT boats with radars:

North end of Blackett Strait (Off Vanga Vanga)

Lt. Henry Brantingham in PT 159 with

> Lt. (jg) William Liebenow in PT 157
>
> Lt. (jg) John Lowrey in PT 162
>
> Lt. (jg) John Kennedy in PT 109.

Middle of Blackett Strait (Off Gatere)

Lt. Arthur Berndtson in PT 171 with

> Lt. (jg) Philip Potter in PT 169
>
> Lt. (jg) Stuart Hamilton in PT 172
>
> Lt. (jg) Edward Kruse in PT 163

South end of Blackett Strait (Off Makuti Island)

Lt. Russel Rome in PT 174 with

> Lt. (jg) Richard Keresey in PT 105
>
> Lt. (jg) Joseph Roberts in PT 103

South of Ferguson Passage

Lt. George Cookman in PT 107 with

> Lt. (jg) Robert Shearer in PT 104
>
> Lt. (jg) David Payne in PT 106
>
> Lt. (jg) Sidney Hix in PT 108.[73]

The latter division was meant both as a reserve unit and to cover if the Japanese left Blackett Strait to attack the American forces on New Georgia.[74]

Brantingham, having fought in the Philippines with Bulkeley and Kelly, was the most experienced of the PT boat captains, and Warfield placed him in command of the four divisions.[75] Unfortunately, Brantingham's charges consisted of PT boats from four separate squadrons. Three were from Squadron 9, five were

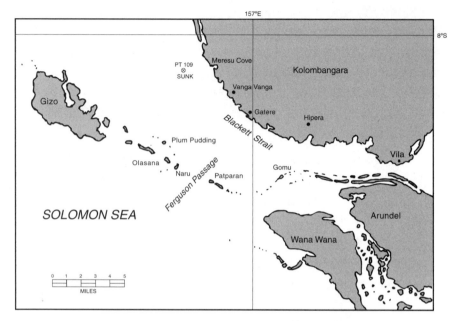

**Scene of PT boat engagement with Japanese
destroyers and rescue of the PT 109 crew**

from Squadron 10, six were from Squadron 5, and one (Kennedy's)
was from Squadron 2.

When the conference was concluded, Kennedy returned to
PT 109 to make preparations to get under way at sundown. Along
the way, he encountered an old friend, Ensign George H. R. Ross,
who asked to go along on the patrol. Ross was executive officer
of PT 166 which was sunk by B-25s on July 20,1943, although
Ross was not on board at the time. Kennedy decided he could
use Ross to man the 37 millimeter antitank gun, so he agreed.

The sun was setting as the PT boats pulled out. By 9:30 P.M.
the PT boats were on station conducting their patrols. It was a
moonless night and an overcast blocked the customary Southern
Hemisphere stars. In short, it was pitch-black.

The battle action that follows is abstracted from Warfield's
action reports (with some exceptions noted).[76]

At midnight, Brantingham's radar detected four ships heading south off Vanga Vanga on Kolombangara Island. Thinking the

contacts were barges moving near shore, Brantingham immediately attacked with guns. When Japanese destroyers responded with search lights and large caliber fire, Brantingham launched four torpedoes from 1,800 yards. None of them hit, but one started a fire in its launch tube, illuminating PT 159. Lieutenant (jg) William F. Liebenow in PT 157 fired two torpedoes, which also missed. Both PT boats then left the scene at high speed. Lieutenant (jg) John R. Lowrey and Kennedy saw the enemy gun flashes but thought that shore batteries must be firing on the first two PT boats. Brantingham ordered Lowrey and Kennedy to lay to prior to his attack. (Brantingham states that he told Kennedy before the mission to attack when he did.[77] Liebenow states that Kennedy and Lowrey simply got separated in the dark.[78])

As the Japanese destroyers continued south, they were picked up on Lieutenant Arthur H. Berndtson's radar. He correctly assessed that the blips on the screen were from destroyers, closed to 1,500 yards, and fired four torpedoes. When Berndtson's torpedo tubes caught fire, he raced out of the area, leaving his division's other three PT boats behind. Lieutenant (jg) Stuart Hamilton and Lieutenant (jg) Edward H. Kruse retired through Ferguson passage, where they were attacked by Japanese float planes. Lieutenant (jg) Philip A. Potter, having lost contact with the rest of Berndtson's division, headed northwest away from the Kolombangara shoreline and encountered Kennedy and Lowrey. After radioing Rendova for instructions, these boats resumed patrolling off Vanga Vanga. (Apparently, they were closer to Meresu Cove north of Vanga Vanga.[79])

Lieutenant George E. Cookman, patrolling south of Ferguson passage, could also see the searchlight and gun flashes. He entered Blackett Strait, fired four torpedoes in the direction of his radar sighting, and retired to base. Lieutenant (jg) Robert D. Shearer, Lieutenant (jg) David M. Payne, and Lieutenant (jg) Sidney D. Hix entered Blackett Strait and patrolled there until Warfield ordered them to return to their assigned patrol area south of Ferguson Passage.

Lieutenant Richard E. Keresey, in Lieutenant Russel W. Rome's Division, seeing gun flashes to the northwest from Brantingham's, Berndtson's, and Cookman's encounters, was well aware that a battle was under way. When the destroyers entered the southern area of Blackett Strait, Rome closed to one thousand yards (Keresey says it was more like 3,500 yards.[80]), fired four torpedoes, and headed for Ferguson Passage. Roberts also fired four torpedoes and headed home. Keresey saw a destroyer turn on a search light. (Keresey states he only saw Rome and Roberts fire their torpedoes.) Unwilling to retreat, Keresey maintained his station until his lookout spotted a destroyer one thousand yards off his port bow. He fired two torpedoes, then turned to find Rome.

This completes Warfield's account of the PT boat action on the inbound leg of the Japanese destroyers' mission.

During the destroyers' run to Vila, all four PT boat division commanders attacked and left the area without further orders to their accompanying PT boats. Brantingham states that they were ordered home by Commander Warfield, which is consistent with Keresey's account. The remaining PT boat captains had virtually no knowledge of what had happened. Berndtson recalls that radio blackouts, caused by atmospheric conditions, were frequent in various areas of Blackett Strait.[81] Further, the pounding the boats took at high speed in choppy waters often knocked the radios off frequency. If contact reports were sent, they could easily have been missed. As for the surprise upon encountering the destroyers, PT 157 Gunner's Mate Raymond A. Macht recalls:

> We were the second boat in our Division. Radio transmission was poor. We made visual contact with a target near shore and were very surprised when it opened fire with heavy weapons. We had been briefed that only barges would be inside our patrol station because the water was too shallow for destroyers.[82]

The four Japanese destroyers arrived at Vila at 10:30 P.M. and began unloading supplies and troops into barges and landing craft.[83] Within an hour, all 70 tons of supplies and nine hundred troops were debarked. Led by the *Amagiri*, the destroyers immediately left for the return trip to Rabaul under the cover of darkness. They wanted to clear the area fast, so the destroyers headed northwest into Blackett Strait at 30 knots. A high-speed dash was no simple task, as the waters near Vila were narrow, full of reefs, and poorly charted.

Warfield's action report on the battle picks up when the four destroyers reentered the southern end of Blackett Strait.

Keresey in PT 105 was still on station, but had only two torpedoes remaining. At 2:30 A.M. he saw a destroyer outlined by an explosion to the northwest and fired his last two torpedoes. (Keresey states that his lookout spotted the destroyer as it entered Blackett Strait at 2:00 A.M., that PT 105 was fired upon by the destroyer, and that Keresey then fired his remaining two torpedoes.[84]) Ten minutes later, Keresey saw what he thought was a distant flare to the northwest. Keresey returned to base through Ferguson Passage, where he encountered three PT boats heading into Blackett Strait.

Shearer, Payne, and Hix saw the explosion and gun flashes to the northwest and reentered Blackett Strait. They did not locate the convoy, which had already passed by. Hamilton and Kruse returned to their station in the middle of Blackett Strait by 2:55 A.M. and began to patrol off Gatere. They also arrived too late to see or hear anything.

Kennedy, Lowrey, and Potter were patrolling east of Gizo Island in right-echelon formation. Kennedy was leading, followed by Lowrey and Potter, each about a mile apart. Lowrey spotted a warship traveling at 40 knots some seven hundred yards from PT 162 and turned to avoid a collision.[85] The crew saw the warship collide with PT 109, causing it to explode and burn for 10 to 15 minutes. Potter also saw the ship coming, fired two torpedoes from 150 yards, and retired to the southeast. Along the way, Potter encountered a second warship and fired his remaining two torpedoes before heading for home.

Liebenow, having returned to the area, saw a ship close to Kolombangara's shore and fired two torpedoes without result.

(Liebenow says he returned to base with two torpedoes remaining.[86]) No other contact was made with the destroyers, and all remaining boats returned to Rendova at 4:00 A.M.

So ends Warfield's account.

PT 109 radioman Maguire sheds light on why the speedy and nimble boat was unable to avoid a collision with the *Amagiri*:

> We were patrolling on our center engine, going along quietly. The wing engines were running but not engaged. All three engines were muffled. We must have been doing about six or seven knots. When the forward lookout shouted "Ship at two o'clock," Kennedy signaled the engine room to put the wing engines in gear. But we were going so slow that he never got the boat turned to make a torpedo run. The Japanese ship made a starboard turn toward us, and we couldn't get out of the way in time.[87]

PT 109 was idling to keep its phosphorescent wake and engine noise down. Idling on one engine was the problem. It would take some time to engage the other two engines, and the engines could not just be slammed into full throttle when they were idling. Keresey estimates it took thirty seconds to get a PT boat up to speed if all three engines were idling in gear.[88] PT 109 only had about 10 seconds from the time the lookouts spotted the *Amagiri* at several hundred yards until the collision occurred.[89]

The night of August 1–2, 1943, saw the last large engagement of PT boats with the enemy. Thirty torpedoes had been fired without a hit, and one PT boat was sunk. The battle is described by Captain Robert J. Bulkley in *At Close Quarters: PT Boats in the United States Navy* as "...perhaps the most confused and least effectively executed action the PTs had been in."[90] Kennedy used a little stronger language to express similar feelings.[91]

Even the Japanese officers couldn't agree on what happened. Convoy commander Captain Katsumori Yamashiro believed that the *Amagiri*'s ramming of PT 109 was accidental.[92] *Amagiri* captain Lieutenant Commander Kohei Hanami stated that *Amagiri* maneuvered to strike PT 109:

About two o'clock in the morning of the August 2nd, we discovered the ship rushing forward at one thousand meters ahead. At once we judged that it was the torpedo-boat. We decided to carry out the ramming, considered to be the only one tactic for the torpedo-boat at that time. We turned the head and instantly ran into the boat.[93]

This version of events on the bridge is supported by navigation officer Goro Nakajima.[94] Searles, a veteran of two tours of duty in PT boats, explains:

After the war, I learned that it was Japanese destroyer policy to turn toward a PT boat and pick up speed. This was done to present a minimum frontal area to the torpedo spread. Therefore, there is no doubt that is what the captain of the *Amagiri* did. The ramming of PT 109 may or may not have been intentional, but turning toward the PT boat definitely was.[95]

No mention was made in Warfield's report of any attempt to rescue the crew of PT 109. Potter later said that he had circled back to look for PT 109 survivors, but by that time the fire was out, and he could see nothing in the dark.[96] Liebenow, patrolling miles away, saw the flash and headed toward the area but couldn't find anything in the blackness of the night.[97] William C. Battle, skipper of PT 171 in which Berndtson was riding, saw an explosion on the horizon but thought it was due to a hit on a destroyer.[98] Battle and Liebenow, among others, did not learn of the 109's loss until the next morning. Several skippers wanted to go back to the area in the morning to search for the 109 crew, but Warfield denied them permission because of a lack of air superiority.

What happened on board PT 109, and in the subsequent days until rescue, is taken largely from the account of Flotilla One Intelligence Officers Lieutenant (jg) Byron R. White and Lieutenant (jg) J. C. McClure, written after interviewing the survivors, and from a 1943 *New Yorker* article, written by John Hersey, after interviewing Kennedy, Johnston, McMahon, and Maguire.[99] Kennedy was acquainted with future Supreme Court Justice White, having met him during Kennedy's sabbatical from Harvard in the spring semester of his junior year.[100] White, a Rhodes Scholar at Oxford University, attended a 1939 London reception given by Ambassador Joseph Patrick Kennedy whom Kennedy was visiting. White and Kennedy met again that summer, while White was studying in Munich.[101] When White volunteered for service in the navy, he was selected for Naval Intelligence and assigned to PT Boat Flotilla One.

About 2:30 A.M. on August 2, PT 109 was moving slowly and quietly over the calm waters. Barely a sound could be heard, and the pitch-black night was nearly impenetrable to the human eye. A terse radio message came across alerting the crew of PT 109 to trouble: "Am being chased through Ferguson Passage. Have fired fish."

Potter came alongside in PT 169 asking about the gun flashes and indicating he had lost contact with his division. When radio instructions came from Warfield to resume patrolling, Kennedy was in the eastern-most PT boat off Vanga Vanga, with Lowrey and Potter trailing. From time to time, the three boats would lose contact with each other because of the darkness and the enforced radio silence.

The PT 109 crew were at various positions. Kennedy was at the wheel. Ross was on the bow as a lookout. Thom was standing beside the cockpit. Maguire was in the cockpit. Marney was in the forward turret. Mauer was standing beside Thom. Zinser was standing by the hatch. Starkey was at the 20 millimeter gun. Kirksey was at the starboard aft torpedo. Albert was in the aft turret. Johnston was asleep on deck. McMahon was in the engine room. Harris's location was not recorded.

Several authors report that PT 109's crew were not alert, but Zinser insists that they were:

> I had just come topside from my watch in the engine room and was near the hatch. We were definitely on alert because there was talk that destroyers might be there, and we had seen flashes to the south. It was a moonless night and so dark out

that you could hardly see your hand in front of your face. I neither heard nor saw the destroyer approach.[102]

Marney shouted "Ship at two o'clock!" Ross spotted the ship's phosphorescent bow wave and tried unsuccessfully to load the 37 millimeter gun. Kennedy attempted to turn toward the *Amagiri,* but could not maneuver quickly at low speed. Within 10 to 15 seconds from sighting, the *Amagiri* struck PT 109, slicing diagonally through the boat, just aft of the cockpit.

PT 109's stern section containing the engines sank quickly, but the bow section remained afloat. Escaping 100-octane gasoline burned on the water's surface 20 yards from the bow section, and fumes were all around. Marney and Kirksey were apparently killed in the collision, as they were never seen again. Kennedy ordered everyone not already knocked into the water to get overboard, in case the flames spread to the bow section and the gas tank exploded.

When the flames subsided some 10 to 15 minutes later, Maguire, Mauer, and Kennedy swam to the bow section. The first order of business was to locate PT 109's remaining crew. From the shouting, Kennedy determined that Harris, McMahon, and Starkey were in the water one hundred yards to the southwest while Zinser and Johnston were one hundred yards to the southeast.

Maguire and Mauer heard Zinser, who was burned on the arms and chest, call out, and Maguire went to help. Ross regained consciousness after fainting from the gasoline fumes and went to Thom's assistance. Maguire, Zinser, Ross, and Thom swam to the bow section, following blinker-light flashes from Mauer. Albert joined them. In the meantime, Harris located McMahon, who was badly burned. After hearing Harris's calls for help, Kennedy swam to the three crewmen and towed McMahon back to the bow section. He then returned and assisted Harris in removing his waterlogged jacket and sweater. Now recovered, Thom swam to Johnston, who also fainted from gasoline fumes, and helped him reach the bow section. Starkey, although burned on his face and hands, was able to swim to the bow section on his own.

The crew members climbed onto the bow section and spent the rest of the night believing they would be rescued in the morning. They did not fire their Very pistol for fear of attracting enemy attention. At dawn the crew could see Rendova Peak and took comfort in the fact that it was only 38 miles to the south. It was discomforting that the crew could see Japanese settlements on Kolombangara, two miles to the east, and on Gizo Island, three and one half miles to the west. If the crew could see the buildings, then Japanese spotters with binoculars certainly were able to see the remains of PT 109. Kennedy and his men had to decide whether to wait for rescue near the bow section or to strike out for shore. With PT 109 in precarious shape, Kennedy ordered eight of the crew into the water, leaving the injured McMahon and Johnston on the bow section.

At 10:00 A.M. the bow section turned over and seemed to be settling in the water. With no rescue craft in sight, Kennedy decided to set out for land. Kolombangara was closest, but was occupied by enemy troops, as was Gizo. Kennedy chose to strike out for safer ground. At 1:00 P.M. the survivors headed for the apparently uninhabited Plum Pudding Island, about four miles southeast of Gizo Harbor. The PT 109 crew were unaware that Australian Coastwatcher Arthur Reginald Evans of the Royal Australian Naval Volunteer Reserve and his assistant, U.S. Army Corporal Benjamin Franklin Nash, were secreted at Hipera in the hills of Kolombangara about a mile from the coast.[103] Evans and Nash saw the flames from the collision during the night and spotted the drifting bow section in the morning. Evans radioed this information to Coastwatcher headquarters. At 9:30 A.M. he received a reply that PT 109 was lost in action. At 1:12 P.M. headquarters asked him to be on the lookout for survivors.[104] Cluster and PT 153 captain Stanmore B. Marshall recall that an air search was initiated, but the crew was not spotted.[105]

Kennedy ordered nine men to cluster around the timber that had been lashed to the deck and put Thom in charge. This would keep them together and assist the injured Johnston, Starkey, and

Zinser. The men tied their shoes to the timber, hung onto the timber with one arm, and stroked with the other arm. Kennedy clamped the loose end of a strap on McMahon's life vest in his teeth and towed him along while swimming a breast stroke. He swam in spurts, pausing to rest when necessary.

Kennedy reached Plum Pudding first, with McMahon in tow. Plum Pudding was a small island, 40 yards in diameter, but it offered good cover of casuarina and kerosene wood trees.[106] There were a few coconut trees, but the coconuts were green and inedible.[107] Kennedy and McMahon came ashore on the southeast tip of the island, collapsed on the sandy beach, rested momentarily, and crawled to the bushes to get out of sight. It had taken nearly four hours from the time they left PT 109's bow section. The nine men grouped around the timber had slower going as they tried to stay together and work as an unrehearsed team. They reached Plum Pudding, brought the timber through the coral, and collapsed on the beach. When they took stock, the survivors found that they had six .45s, one .38, one large knife, one light knife, and one pocketknife between them. But no food or water.

Aircraft flew over, possibly on a search mission. Kennedy ordered the men to remain hidden because they could not be certain of the planes' identity until they were overhead. By the time the aircraft arrived, it was too late to signal them.

Kennedy decided to swim out into Ferguson Passage at dusk to flag down passing PT boats with the ship's lantern. Kennedy left Plum Pudding Island wearing only his shorts and shoes. After walking on the coral reef, pulling himself along, and finally swimming in deeper water, he reached Ferguson Passage and began treading water. His rubber life belt helped keep him afloat, and he had wrapped the ship's lantern in kapok. Unfortunately, Warfield sent the PT boats to Gizo Strait on the northwest end of the island—not through Ferguson Passage.

As the hours wore on and he saw aerial flares to the northwest, Kennedy realized what was happening and decided to return to Plum Pudding. He lightened his load by dumping his shoes

Plum Pudding Island where the PT 109 crew first came ashore

Courtesy of Jimmy Evas

and the now inoperable lantern, but strong currents kept him from swimming directly to the island. As dawn broke on August 3, Kennedy reached Three Palm Island, an islet south of Plum Pudding, crawled into the bushes, and went to sleep. Hours later he awoke and swam the last half mile to Plum Pudding, collapsing on the beach. Kennedy asked Ross to make a similar attempt at Ferguson Passage that night and went to sleep.

On the evening of August 3, Ross swam out to the edge of Ferguson Passage and treaded water. He saw and heard nothing, so he fired Kennedy's .38 revolver three times with no answer. On his return Ross encountered the same islet as Kennedy had and went ashore to sleep for the rest of the night. On the morning of August 4, he swam back to Plum Pudding and reported his lack of success to Kennedy.

Kennedy decided the survivors would move 2,300 yards southwest to Olasana Island to be closer to Ferguson Passage and to obtain food and water. Olasana is a somewhat larger island about six hundred yards long and 130 yards wide.[108] Abundant vegetation provided ample places to hide from Japanese patrols, and a generous supply of coconuts was available to nourish the hungry and thirsty men.

After a three-hour swim, the men reached the eastern tip of Olasana but were too exhausted to go out into Ferguson

Passage on the evening of August 4.[109] Too bad. PT boats ran through Ferguson Passage that night. On the morning of August 5, Kennedy and Ross swam to nearby Naru Island (also known as Gross or Cross Island). They cautiously crossed the island under cover of trees and bushes. On the far shore the two men discovered a Japanese crate containing crackers and hard candy. Nearby they discovered a native lean-to with a one-man canoe and a barrel of water.

Kennedy and Ross then spotted a Japanese ship aground on a distant reef and crept along the shore to investigate. Two natives were examining the shipwreck. Thinking that the natives could help contact authorities, Kennedy and Ross tried to attract their attention. The natives were startled by the bedraggled white men and hurriedly paddled off in their two-man canoe.

The two natives were 19-year-old Biuku Gasa and Aaron Kumana. They lived on Sepo Island, four miles north of Gizo Harbor, and worked for Evans. On August 2, the night that Kennedy first swam into Ferguson Passage, Gasa and Kumana observed the Japanese landing troops on the northern coast of Gizo. They left the next morning by canoe to inform Evans. The two natives paddled down Blackett Strait, stopped overnight on Wana Wana, and then crossed over to Kolombangara. When Gasa and Kumana reached Evans at his outpost in Hipera on August 4, they told him about the Japanese troops. Evans asked if they knew of any PT boat survivors around Gizo, but they could only report that they had not seen any.

Gasa and Kumana returned to Wana Wana, where they spent the night with friends. The two natives left on August 5 to return to Sepo Island. Their trip took a slight detour when they noticed a ship stranded on a reef off Naru. Gasa and Kumana pulled their canoe up on the reef, swam to the ship, and began rummaging through its contents.[110] While searching the ship's stores, they saw Kennedy and Ross across the lagoon and took them to be shipwrecked Japanese.[111] Frightened by the encounter, the two natives quickly abandoned their search, swam to their canoe, and paddled furiously away.

Gasa and Kumana then headed for home. Becoming thirsty along the way, they turned toward Olasana Island to pick up some coconuts. As they neared shore, the two natives saw a giant of a man with white skin, blond hair, and a blond beard coming out of the brush. Thinking he must be German, and an ally of the Japanese, they paddled backwards quickly to a safe distance and stopped to listen to his shouts. The man, six-foot, two-inch Thom, was shouting words in English. At first, the natives were suspicious that such a large man could be an American. Gasa described the original encounter:

> He said "I'm an American." I said "No you are Japs." He said "Are you two scouts?" I said "No." He said something about a PT boat but I did not understand him. So I said to Kumana "We have to be very careful." Then I said "If you are Americans, what is the symbol on your plane?" He replied "If you see the big white star, I belong to that star." Then he pulled up his sleeve and said "See my skin. Jap skin is red. My skin is white." I said "I don't care what color your skin is, you are Jap."[112]

Then a second crew member, who was not nearly as tall, joined Thom in trying to convince the natives that they were Americans. He asked Gasa if he knew John Kari, and Gasa replied that he did. Gasa and Kumana gradually overcame their doubts, paddled ashore, and gave the Americans what little food (sweet potatoes) and cigarettes they had.[113]

After paddling the canoe found on Naru into Ferguson Passage to search for PT boats, Kennedy returned to Olasana late at night on August 5 to divide up the crackers, candy, and water among the men. The food was like manna from heaven, and the water supplemented the meager amounts they had collected during rainfalls. Kennedy met the two natives, and together they determined that it was each other they had seen on Naru.[114]

The next day, August 6, Kennedy, Gasa, and Kumana returned to Naru by canoe, meeting Ross on the way. Ross turned around and joined the three men in searching the island. Satisfied that there were no Japanese there, the natives showed Kennedy a hidden two-man canoe. Gasa and Kumana were very familiar with Naru as they often stood watches there.[115]

Kennedy decided to send Gasa and Kumana to Rendova with a message. Using his sheath knife, he carved a crude message on a piece of coconut shell which read:

> NAURO ISL
> NATIVE KNOWS POSIT
> HE CAN PILOT 11 ALIVE NEED
> SMALL BOAT
> KENNEDY[116]

Back on Olasana, Thom arrived at the same conclusion. Maguire located a blank invoice from the Burns Philp Company, and Thom wrote a more detailed message on the back.[117] Thom entrusted the note to the natives when they stopped by Olasana to tell the men that they were on their way to Rendova. Kennedy and Ross did not return to Olasana that night.

After they paddled across Ferguson Passage, Gasa and Kumana stopped at Wana Wana to inform Benjamin Kevu, another of Evans' scouts, that there were survivors on Olasana. They picked up John Kari, the English-speaking scout, and continued on their journey to deliver the two messages to the PT boat base on Rendova.

In the meantime, Evans moved his headquarters from the hills of Kolombangara to the small island of Gomu in Blackett Strait to be more centrally located.[118] Nash remained on Kolombangara, and communicated with Evans by walkie-talkie.[119] Kevu sent a messenger to Gomu to inform Evans of the survivors. Evans' radio equipment was not yet set up, so he did not immediately notify Rendova. Instead he penciled a message requesting that Kennedy come to Gomu to plan the rescue of the PT 109 officers and crew.[120]

On the night of August 6, Kennedy and Ross left Naru and headed out into Ferguson Passage in the two-man canoe for

another attempt at flagging down a PT boat. High waves capsized the canoe and hurled the canoe, Kennedy, and Ross back
over the reef. The two men made their way ashore across the
coral and fell asleep on Naru's beach.

On the morning of August 7, Evans sent Rendova a secret
radio message via the Coastwatcher organization stating that the
PT 109 men were on Gross Island.[121] Gross Island was the name
by which Evans knew Naru Island, and Kennedy had written his
message when he was there.

Evans dispatched seven of his scouts under the leadership
of the English-speaking Kevu to deliver his written message to
Kennedy, to bring food to the stranded men, and to return Kennedy
to Gomu. The scouts arrived on Naru during the morning and
handed Evans' message to Kennedy. The natives then paddled
Kennedy and Ross to Olasana, where they set up kerosene stoves
and cooked a meal of C rations and yams.[122] C rations consisted
of a meat and vegetable hash, biscuits, fruit juice powder, and
the all-important coffee and cigarettes.

The natives scaled coconut trees to fetch additional coconuts and green palm fronds, making dishes from the coconuts
and spoons from the palm fronds. They also built a wind- and
rain-proof shelter for McMahon from the green palm fronds. The
109 crew had tried to do so unsuccessfully with dried palm
fronds.[123]

While Evans' scouts were headed to Naru, Gasa, Kumana,
and Kari reached the Blanche Channel east of Rendova. Rather
than paddle on, they stopped at an American army base at Nusa
on the northwest tip of Roviana Island. There they showed the
messages to several U.S. Army officers. Colonel George M. Hill
wrote to Kennedy fourteen years later:

> ...Early on the morning in question, a native landed at Roviana,
> in spite of your instruction to go to Rendova, and contacted men
> of my Service Battery, which because of supply, were located
> near the landing point....(We) were able to understand partially
> what the native was trying to explain; namely, (1) Americans
> stranded on island behind the Japs. (2) One man with feet badly

burned or injured and needs help. (3) That I as "Chief of the Americans" could give him rescue boat immediately.[124]

The native was John Kari.

Hill contacted the army ammunition supply base on Kokrana Island by radio, and a message was sent to the nearby PT boat base on Lumbari. Hill then sent the three natives to a navy base on the adjoining Sasavele Island for pick-up.[125]

When the men had been seen to, Kennedy got into the natives' canoe to return to Gomu. Kevu instructed Kennedy to lie down under some palm fronds to hide from Japanese aircraft, and the natives paddled out into Blackett Strait. Kennedy arrived on Gomu at 3:00 P.M. on August 7 and was met by Evans. Evans had received a message from Rendova that three PT boats would go to Gross Island at 10:00 P.M. Had they done so, they would not have found the survivors.

After some discussion over tea, Kennedy and Evans settled on a different rescue plan, which Evans radioed to Rendova. Kennedy would meet the PT boats at Patparan Island and personally guide them to the location of the survivors.[126] The scouts paddled Kennedy out to Patparan (actually Patuparao, but Evans' spelling will be used to minimize confusion) at 10:00 P.M. and settled down to wait for the PT boats.

PT 157, skippered by William Liebenow, retrieved the natives from Sasavele Island at 5:30 on the afternoon of August 7 and brought them to Rendova.[127] With the coconut and letter in hand, Warfield now had confirming evidence of the Evans' radio message.

Warfield ordered Brantingham to form a rescue party. Brantingham chose to ride in Liebenow's PT 157, as he had great confidence in her skipper and crew. Along for the rescue mission were Cluster, Gasa, Kumana, Kari, Chief Pharmacist Mate Fred T. Ratchford, and two newspaper reporters: Leif Erickson of API and Frank Hewlett of UPI. Cluster came to Rendova from the Russell Islands in the afternoon of August 7 to assist in the rescue.

PT 157 skippered by Lieutenant William Liebenow seen with binoculars. Gunner's Mate James Smith is in the starboard gun turret. Torpedoman Welford West is second from right.

Courtesy of William Liebenow

Warfield, still fearing a trap, was expecting Kennedy to radio in from Evans' location and wanted Cluster on hand to recognize Kennedy's voice.[128]

Berndtson, riding in Battle's PT 171, was scheduled to command a patrol in the Vella Gulf with seven other PT boats. Brantingham directed Berndtson to accompany PT 157 on the rescue mission and to rejoin the patrol when the rescue mission was completed. PT 171's radar could be used to detect Japanese traffic in the area and, if necessary, could assist in locating a passage through the reef east of Olasana. Walkie-talkies were brought along to communicate between boats. Walkie-talkie signals did not travel as far as the boat radios, so would minimize the chance of interception.[129] Battle remembers the mission:

We first heard of the PT 109 survivors from coastwatcher Evans' message. The natives arrived about the same time with Kennedy's coconut. Our orders were specific from the beginning. There was no doubt where we were going to go, because Evans' message was very precise.[130]

The two PT boats left Rendova at 8:30 P.M. on August 7. Liebenow recalls:

We traveled at eight to ten knots to keep our wake down so we wouldn't be spotted by Japanese float planes. I was not told that there was any particular schedule such as indicated in Evans' message, so we were not in any particular hurry. When we got to the appointed place, we were able to contact Kennedy almost immediately.

We knew before we left Rendova that we were supposed to pick up Kennedy first. We did not set out to rescue the PT 109 crew by ourselves as has been reported, and we did not receive a message while underway to change our plans.[131]

The PT boats reached the vicinity of Patparan Island just before midnight. Liebenow fired four shots with his .45 caliber service revolver as previously arranged. Kennedy fired three shots from his service revolver and one shot from a Japanese rifle borrowed from Evans. Torpedoman Raymond E. Laflin, a PT 157 lookout that night, definitely remembers hearing four shots.[132] Brantingham and Liebenow remember that it was three shots, but this is a minor discrepancy.

With Kennedy on board, Liebenow headed PT 157 across Ferguson Passage and skirted the coral reef a mile east of Olasana Island. As the outline of Olasana came into view, Kennedy pointed it out to Liebenow and told him where to look for a deep water passage through the reef. PT 157 gunner's mate James S. Smith remembers:

I was in my gun turret on the starboard side of the cockpit. The three natives were in the cockpit with Liebenow giving him directions as to how to get through the passage. We were very concerned about getting hung up on the reef. Liebenow posted Welford West on the bow with a lead line. He didn't trust the natives to know the depth of the water, since they traveled in shallow-draft canoes. Our PT boat had a six-foot draft so we did not want to go inside a water depth of seven feet.[133]

PT 157 skipper Liebenow recalls the night:

> Kennedy and two natives were in the cockpit with me. We could see the partially submerged reef quite well due to phosphorescence from the breaking waves, and I simply stayed 25 to 30 yards outside of it. The natives helped find the reef passage, mostly by pointing, but one of them spoke some English. I sent West up to the bow to take depth measurements with a lead line, and I slowed a bit when we were passing through the reef. I don't recall Brantingham being in touch with Berndtson, but it's entirely possible, since Brantingham was stationed on the bow. He did not pass any instructions on to me, probably because we could see the reef's outline quite well. As senior officer on the mission, Brantingham could have countermanded any order I gave or any decision I made. He never did.[134]

Motor Machinist's Mate Theodore P. Aust concurs that a native could see the coral reefs due to the phosphorescence in the breaking waves.[135]

Berndtson recalls his role:

> We used the 171's radar to help locate the passage in the reef. As the 157 was transiting the passage, I gave directions to Brantingham by walkie talkie. Then we lay to about a half mile off the reef, while the 157 carried out the rescue. We were guarding against armed Japanese barges, as they had a route right by the reef. Brantingham informed me by walkie talkie when the PT 109 crew were on board. Once we saw PT157 clear the reef and head for Rendova, we continued on to the Vella Gulf.[136]

Torpedoman Welford H. West remembers the mission this way:

> The second PT boat gave Brantingham radar information
> when we were going through the reef. I was on the bow with a
> lead line giving Liebenow water depths. I didn't see the natives,
> but they were probably in the cockpit with Liebenow.[137]

Thus, West verifies that Brantingham was in communication with the second boat.

After clearing the reef, Liebenow headed for Olasana:

> It was a short distance to the island after we passed
> through the reef, and it probably only took 10 to 15 minutes to
> get there. Because West was indicating water depths greater
> than eight to ten fathoms, I returned to my patrol speed until
> we neared shore. I pulled PT 157 up close to shore, say 10 or
> 15 yards. We were a little to the left of the center of the island,
> where Kennedy and the native said we would find the PT 109
> crewmen. We did not drop anchor, in case we had to leave in
> a hurry. I kept the boat's bow toward the island so that the
> engines wouldn't get fouled. We were close enough to shore
> that Kennedy called out to the men, and we could hear their
> replies.

There is fair agreement how the rescue boat got to its position off Olasana. What happened next is the subject of far more disagreement.

Cluster describes how he went ashore in a dinghy to assist the survivors:

> After Liebenow lay to off Olasana, I made the first trip into
> the island with an eight-foot wooden dinghy. The dinghy had
> been stored on the stern, and we departed from there. One of
> the natives, Gasa, was in the bow and Kennedy was in the
> stern of the dinghy. I did the rowing. We took Gasa along
> because he knew best where the 109 crew were. Kennedy, of
> course, insisted on going, since he was PT 109's command-
> ing officer. He stood in the dinghy and shouted out "Lenny,

Lenny." I told Kennedy to pipe down because we were in Japanese territory, but he would have none of it.

Thom shouted something in return and stepped out of the bushes. Kennedy and Gasa stayed on the island, while I brought the most seriously injured crew man, McMahon, out. Several trips were made by small boat until all of the crew were off the island. I don't recall who made the successive trips or which boats they used. It is entirely possible that the healthy crew men waded and swam out. Once the injured men were retrieved, there would have been no reason to wait. They would simply have climbed up on the rowboat and stepped up onto the bow.[138]

West went ashore in PT 157's 12-foot rowboat:

> Ray Macht and I took the rowboat ashore to take out the wounded; I remember Starkey was one of them. The men were hiding in the bushes until we identified ourselves. Ray rowed once, and I rowed at least once. We finished up around 2:00 A.M. It was not unusual for gunner's mates and torpedo men to get this kind of assignment because we were designated as deck crew.[139]

Macht agrees:

> After we got through the reef, PT 157 lay to off the island. We lowered the boat's rowboat over the port bow, and I rowed ashore with West. We didn't come ashore exactly where the men were, but it was relatively easy to locate them. We gathered up five or six injured men and rowed them out to the PT boat. This all took about three quarters of an hour. I did not go back ashore again but returned to the gun turret as a lookout. We used to have an eight-foot dinghy on the PT boat, but I was not aware that it was along for the mission.[140]

Laflin remembers the rescue the same way:

> When we got inside the reef, we lay to off the island. I was posted as one of the lookouts, since we were in enemy

territory. We sent our dinghy, and possibly one more, ashore to retrieve the 109 crew. Because the dinghy was small, a number of trips were required. The injured came aboard first and were taken below to the crew's quarters for physical exams and first aid.[141]

Liebenow provides more details:

> I called Ratchford up from below and sent him up to Brantingham on the fo'c's'le. Brantingham may have sent him ashore to treat the injured, but that was up to him. The most seriously injured crewmen were placed in the rowboat, brought out, and helped aboard by Ratchford. This took about an hour. The rowboat may have made more than one trip, but I don't recall that. The healthy crewmen waded and swam out wearing life jackets. They used the rowboat to step up onto our PT boat. Upon returning to Rendova, we dropped the PT 109 crew off on Lumbari Island at a makeshift dock and returned PT 157 to its regular mooring.[142]

Brantingham apparently did not send the pharmacist ashore, as Zinser recalls that the burns on his arms were treated on board the PT boat.[143] Aust verifies that the PT 109 crew waded out to the boat and recalls seeing a "floating dock" alongside the PT boat when he took a break from the engine room.[144] Finally, Danny Kennedy, a local diver, confirms that seven feet of water is reached about 10 yards offshore, and by 15 yards, the sea floor drops away dramatically.[145]

PT 157's log was burned for security reasons before leaving Lever Harbor and was recreated from memory months later.[146] The new log describes the rescue:

> August 7, 1943
> ....1553 underway for Onaiavisa Inlet. 1630 lying to in Onaiavisa Inlet. 1730 3 native guides came aboard, underway for assigned birth and moored at 1755. 2030 underway for Ferguson Passage with Exec Officer MTB Ron 9, Com MTB Ron 2 and party aboard. 2330 lying to west of

Pailerongoso Island. 2345 Boat Captain PT 109 came aboard,
underway for northwest side of Cross Island.

August 8, 1943
Underway in Ferguson Passage. 0030 lying to 0.4 miles east
of Banini Island. Sent small boats to pick up survivors of PT
109. 0215 two officers and 8 men aboard and underway for
PT Base Rendova. 0515 moored in berth, survivors left
ship...[147]

A few words of explanation are in order. Onaiavisa Inlet is on the
northeast end of Sasavele Island. Exec Officer MTB Ron 9 is
Brantingham, and Com MTB Ron 2 is Cluster. Pailerongoso is a
small island two thousand yards southeast of Patparan.[148] Banini
may have been a native name for Olasana, or the log simply may
have gotten the name wrong. PT 157's log report that more than
one small boat went ashore lends credibility to Cluster's account.

What appear to be somewhat disparate accounts can, in
fact, be largely reconciled. A summary description of the rescue
follows that, while not satisfying everyone's view, is consistent
with a majority of the information at hand. The summary has ben-
efitted greatly from many discussions with Liebenow and Cluster.

After picking up Kennedy near Patparan Island, Liebenow
crossed Ferguson Passage about midnight, traveling at eight to
ten knots with muffled engines to keep his wake and engine
noise down. He skirted the coral reef east of Olasana with the
natives and Kennedy directing him to a deep water passage
just beyond Leorava Islet. Liebenow determined the reef's location from phosphorescence due to waves breaking over the partially submerged reef, so Brantingham never gave Liebenow any
additional guidance. As PT 157 slowed and traversed the passage, West made water depth measurements with a lead line.

Entering Olasana Lagoon, Liebenow headed straight for the
island. West's measurements enabled Liebenow to resume his
original speed until he neared shore. In 15 minutes, PT 157
reached a water depth of 10 feet and lay to 15 yards off shore.
While Liebenow held PT 157 steady with his bow toward shore,

Brantingham ordered West and Macht to lower the PT boat's row-boat over the port side of the bow. Meanwhile, not wishing to stand idly by, Cluster gathered up Kennedy and Gasa and launched the eight-foot dinghy over the stern.

As Cluster got the dinghy under way, Kennedy was shouting so that his voice, and that of the PT 109 crew's replies, could be heard on PT 157. When the eight-foot dinghy reached shore, Gasa and Kennedy got out and assisted the injured McMahon aboard. Cluster then rowed back to PT 157. Macht and West arrived at the island in the 12-foot rowboat and retrieved Johnston, Starkey, and Zinser who were also injured. They rowed back to PT 157 and assisted the injured men aboard. West then made a second trip to collect several more men. He pulled the rowboat alongside PT 157's port bow and held it there for the men to climb aboard. The remaining healthy men, including Kennedy and Gasa, waded and swam out to PT 157 using the rowboat as a floating dock to climb aboard. When all were accounted for, the rowboat was retrieved, and Liebenow headed PT 157 out to sea.

Quartermaster Waldo de Wilde plotted PT 157's course on the way into Olasana, and Liebenow carefully reversed that course on the way out of the lagoon. Then Liebenow set a bearing for Rendova, while Battle and Berndtson in PT 171 headed on to take up patrol in the Vella Gulf. During the three-hour voyage, PT 157's cook Stanley G. Kendall made sandwiches for the survivors and passed out medicinal brandy.[149] PT 157 arrived in Rendova early on Sunday morning, August 8, six days after the sinking of PT 109. Liebenow dropped his charges off on Lumbari Island, and returned PT 157 to its regular mooring.

Lumbari staff were delighted to see the PT 109 crew and gave them a rousing welcome home.[150] Gasa, Kumana, and Kari were given gifts of food and clothing.[151] They were taken to Nusa, Roviana, by barge, where they retrieved their three-man canoe. The three natives then paddled back to Wana Wana, where Gasa and Kumana retrieved their two-man canoe and returned to Sepo.[152]

The PT 109 survivor's burns, cuts, and abrasions were treated with simple first aid in the makeshift infirmary. That same day, August 8, they were sent to sick bay at Tulagi.[153] Kennedy acquaintance Paul B. Fay recalls meeting a PT boat ferrying the 109 crew to Tulagi, but does not recall which PT boat.[154] Liebenow and several of his crew remember it was the 157. Unfortunately, the 157's log (written months later) does not record that trip.

When the PT 109 survivors arrived at Tulagi, they were placed under the care of Dr. Joseph Wharton. Most of the crew were not seriously injured, although many had fungus and infected coral cuts. The most severe burn cases were sent to a larger hospital unit on Guadalcanal.[155]

Reed remembers Kennedy's return to Tulagi:

> The whole camp was elated when news came that Jack had been rescued. I saw him a lot when he was recuperating at Tulagi. Jack looked thin from his ordeal. He spent a great deal of time resting, reading, and enjoying the company of fellow officers. His favorite book was *Pilgrim's Way* by John Buchan, and he gave me a copy. Although Jack did not drink very much, he often came to the Officers' Club just to talk. The club was named The Royal Palms.[156]

Prescott explains:

> I was a charter member of the Officers' Club in Calvertville. The officers paid dues to operate it. The club was in a tent with a floor, tables, and a counter. The bar was tended by the senior officers' mess attendant, who could make many colorful drinks. He had been a bartender at a nightclub in Chicago before the war. I remember Jack coming around to visit.[157]

Kennedy spent three weeks recuperating on Tulagi before receiving his next assignment. He lived in a tent at the back of Calvertville and spent a great deal of time talking with a group of fellow officers.[158] The tents constructed by the base force were a far cry from the original native huts. They were elevated above the ground, had wooden floors, and included screened-in sides.

Cluster offered Kennedy the choice of going home or taking over PT 59, which, along with PT 60 and 61, was being converted into a gunboat to better deal with the Japanese barges. Torpedoes proved ineffective against the shallow-draft barges and were being replaced on the three gunboats. The barges were no pushovers; they were armed and armored.

PT 59 skipper David Levy began the task:

> When we started going after barges, we found that they often had as many as 30 soldiers on board with rifles. This was a serious problem since our boats were made out of wood. We experimented with several materials—even concrete—to protect ourselves. Eventually, we installed light armor with the work being done at Sesape. This early conversion was simply to stop rifle bullets; it would not stop heavy rounds.[159]

Twenty-six-year-old Kennedy had only been in the Solomons for five months and was not ready to return home. He took the command of the 77-foot Elco PT 59 on September 1 and began overseeing its five-week long conversion to heavy weapons.

Much of the heavy construction work on PT 59 was performed by the repair ship USS *Argonne* (AG 31) in Purvis Bay, Florida Island. Four torpedo tubes and two 20 millimeter antiaircraft guns were removed to make room for six additional .50 caliber machine guns and two 40 millimeter Bofors cannon. Also, 1/4-inch armor shields were added to the guns. The extra armor and guns made PT 59 bow heavy, but trim was not important for interdicting slow-moving barges.[160]

Thom was given command of PT 60, so Kennedy selected Reed as his new executive officer. Reed was reassigned to a secret project before he could come aboard PT 59. He participated in an experimental effort to adapt a PT boat to simulate the sounds of an invasion as a way of decoying Japanese troops.

Partial view of PT 59 weapons, crew, and radar mast

Courtesy of John Fitzgerald Kennedy Library

Speakers broadcast such sounds as cannon fire, anchor chains dropping, small boats getting under way, and orders being shouted. As far as Reed knows, the decoy was never used in combat.[161]

Donovan reports that PT 109 crew members Maguire, Mauer, Kowal, Drewitch, and Drawdy joined PT 59's crew.[162] Indeed, Kennedy wrote to his parents that he got most of his crew back.[163] By October 1, only Drewitch and Kowal remained on PT 59's roster, although Keresey indicates that Maguire was still on board.[164] Lieutenant (jg) Robert Rhoads joined Kennedy as his executive officer, and eight new crew members came aboard, including Ensign Isaac John Mitchell.[165] Kennedy also named Mitchell executive officer since Mitchell had commanded PT 21 before it was decommissioned due to wear and tear.

On October 8, PT 59 joined two PT boats in a photo identification mission. PT skipper Prescott flew over the boats in a B-24 and directed a photographer to take pictures that would be reproduced and given to Allied fighter and bomber pilots for friendly forces recognition.[166] A copy of one photo hung in Kennedy's Senate office and in the White House. Prescott marked the back of the photo "Made for Old Shafty," and that marking remains on the photo today.[167] Fellow PT boat officers assigned the sobriquet "Old Shafty" to Kennedy because he often expressed the opinion that he "was being shafted."

Kennedy took PT 59 up to Rendova via the Russell Islands. After a week of outfitting and training, including a visit to the airfield at Munda to have her compass compensated by technicians, PT 59 left for the new PT base at Lambu Lambu Cove on the northeast coast of Vella Lavella Island. The cove was four hundred yards long and one hundred yards wide, and the boats entered through a narrow passage in the reef that formed the outer boundary. Fifteen miles up the coast from the airstrip at Barakoma, the base was a primitive place with a few tents and a repair dock

PT boats under way for friendly craft identification photo. PT 59 is in the foreground.

Courtesy of John Fitzgerald Kennedy Library

left over from the previous trading post.[168] No native huts were available to occupy, and there was no fresh water spring to provide drinking water.

Lambu Lambu Cove was originally opened on September 25 by Squadron Eleven commander Lieutenant Commander LeRoy T. Taylor who brought up seven PT boats and an APc (a small coastal transport).[169] Taylor remembers:

> We set up tents on the left bank of the cove. The boats and the APc were moored near there under the overhanging trees. The APc carried the base force, equipment, and supplies. Our radio equipment was placed in a dry cave. Fuel was supplied in 55 gallon drums brought up by LSTs and stored on the right bank. Fueling was entirely by hand—one barrel at a time.[170]

When this arduous task was completed, the PT boats moored under the mangrove trees along the shore. PT 59 gunner's mate W. Glen Christiansen recalls:

> Because the boats were moored far apart and we were busy cleaning our guns and refueling, we really didn't get to know the other boat crews. In our gunboat, eight crew and two officers lived on board while seven crew and one officer lived ashore in tents. The tents were located on the left side of the cove along with the command post and first aid tent.[171]

In the two months since the rescue of the crew of PT 109, navy forces fought a decisive battle in Vella Gulf. *Arashi, Hagikaze,* and *Shigure,* three of the four Japanese destroyers that had run Blackett Strait on August 1, attempted a supply mission on August 6 with the destroyer *Kawakazi.* This time they were met by six American destroyers. Of the four Japanese destroyers, only *Shigure* survived. It was the last time Japanese destroyers would attempt to resupply Vila.[172] Subsequently, barges carried out the resupply task.

Upon arrival at Lambu Lambu Cove on October 18, PT 59 was sent on patrol across the New Georgia Sound to Choiseul

PT Boat at repair dock in Lambu Lambu Cove

Courtesy of Captain Le Roy Taylor

Island, a way station for the Japanese barge traffic. Six PT boats cruised off the northwest tip of Choiseul near Redman Island hunting for barges. Japanese float planes attacked but did not inflict any damage. Similar patrols occurred over the next week without incident.

Kennedy was promoted to lieutenant on October 22, 1943.[173] That day, PT 59 sailed down to the Naval Headquarters at Biloa just south of Barakoma airstrip to take on 1,800 gallons of fuel.[174] Certainly, the job was easier there. After several days of maintenance at Lambu Lambu Cove, PT 59 resumed patrolling. In a few days, the boat and crew would be involved in a daring mission at the mouth of Choiseul's Warrior River.

Just after dusk on October 27, 1943, seven hundred marines from the 2nd Parachute Battalion (Reinforced) of the I Marine Amphibious Corps left their base near the Juno River a few miles from Lambu Lambu Cove. The battalion, commanded by Lieutenant Colonel Victor H. Krulak (later Lieutenant General), consisted of companies E, F, and G, a communications platoon, a regimental weapons company, and a detachment from an experimental rocket platoon. Krulak's marines were armed with Johnson .30 caliber semi-automatic rifles and light machine guns, 60 millimeter mortars, and rocket launchers. Their mission was a feint designed to draw the Japanese military's attention away from the Allies' primary thrust at Empress Augusta Bay on Bougainville Island. The marines debarked in four destroyer transports designated APDs, each carrying along a personnel landing craft designated an LCP(R) for Landing Craft Personnel (Ramp).

Krulak remembers:

> I flew down to Guadalcanal with my regimental commander Lieutenant Colonel Roger Williams to receive our orders. General Vandegrift's staff at IMAC Headquarters informed us that our mission had to be started in 48 hours to divert Japanese military leaders' attention in a timely fashion. We were met at our camp by four APDs, and it took about 45 minutes to load the men and head out. There were about five thousand Japanese soldiers on Choiseul, but we had the advantage of a specific plan and the mobility provided by the four landing craft that we brought along. The coastwatcher on Choiseul, Carden Seton, was a big help in selecting our invasion point at Voza, north of the primary Japanese base at Kakasa. A Navy officer, Dick Keresey, was along with us to select possible locations for a PT boat base.[175]

A platoon from Company G led by Lieutenant Rea E. Duncan went ashore at 0:45 A.M. to scout the area and establish a perimeter defense. By 2:00 A.M. all personnel and supplies were ashore, and the APDs retired, leaving behind the four landing craft. With the help of natives organized by Seton, all supplies, ammunition, and material were moved inland 1,500 yards along a freshly cut trail.[176] A base camp was established on a mesa, which provided good security and fresh water from a nearby stream. Scouts at listening posts on the beach north and south of the village communicated with the base camp by a voice-powered telephone line.

**A Landing Craft Personnel (Ramp) has a crew of three
and can transport thirty-six armed troops.**

Cartwheel: The Reduction of Rabaul

The landing craft were taken to the small offshore island of Zinoa and camouflaged. These craft would be key to the marines' plans as the island was covered with dense vegetation and massive trees, all of which hindered overland movement.

Krulak led a 20-man patrol eight miles south from Voza to raid the Japanese barge staging area at Sangigai on the morning of October 29. When the patrol reached the Vagara River, it spotted and attacked a Japanese barge crew. Fresh with intelligence about the terrain, Krulak's marines returned to the base camp to plan their attack. The next morning, after an air attack on Sangigai, marines from Company E and F attacked Japanese positions, killing 72 Japanese troops, destroying material dumps, capturing vital charts of Japanese mine fields, sinking a barge, and generally making as much commotion as possible. Half of the marines returned to Voza by landing craft, and the rest of the marines dug in near the Vagara River as it was getting dark. The remaining marines were retrieved the following morning by the landing craft.

PT 59 was patrolling off Choiseul on October 31 and spotted a barge close to shore. Kennedy ordered the crew not to fire on the barge for fear of hitting American forces. Returning to Lambu Lambu Cove at 6:30 A.M., PT 59 left for Biloa at 11:00 A.M., picked up New Zealand officers, and returned to Lambu Lambu Cove at 3:00 P.M. PT 59's log book does not indicate that PT 59 was refueled at this time, a fact that was to play a major role in upcoming events.[177]

What followed next is reconstructed from the 2nd Parachute Battalion's War Diary and its Unit Journal, PT 59's log, and interviews with Krulak, Keresey, Battalion Executive Officer Major Warner T. Bigger, one officer and nine crew members who manned the two PT boats involved, and eight marines from Company G. Understandably, not everyone agrees on what happened nor was everyone in a position to witness various events.

Krulak sent out an 87-man task force led by Major Bigger in the early morning hours of November 1. Their mission was to carry out a day raid on the main Japanese shipping base in Choiseul Bay 20 miles northwest of the marines' camp at Voza. A secondary target was the Japanese barge replenishment and fueling center on Guppy Island. The task force consisted of Company G (less one platoon), a TBX radio team, a detachment from the Battalion Intelligence section led by Lieutenant Samuel Johnston, and two natives. They sailed northwest from Voza to the Warrior River in three of the landing craft. The task force left camp at 6:30 A.M., and at 8:00 A.M. Johnston, three marines, and two native guides began a reconnaissance of the coastal area south of the Warrior River.[178] Finding no evidence of Japanese troops, the landing craft turned upriver and debarked the marines at 11:30 A.M.[179] Bigger chose the southeast bank so that the river would cover his left flank against direct attack as he marched upriver.[180]

Expecting to proceed farther upriver, the landing craft traveled only two hundred yards before grounding on sand bars. After debarking the marines, the landing craft withdrew to a cove near the coastal village of Nukiki several miles southeast of the

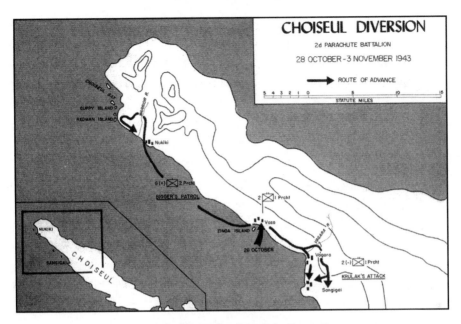

**Routes of the 2nd Marine Parachute
Battalion on Choiseul Island**

Silk Chutes and Hard Fighting

river to be hidden until the marines returned from their attack on Choiseul Bay.

Bigger ordered Sergeant Thomas D. Siefke's nine-man squad to bivouac one hundred yards southeast of the river to guard the TBX radio and its three-man crew.[181] He left the radio behind because it was unable to communicate with Krulak through the dense jungle.

The task force maneuvered up the southeast bank of the river. After crossing the river's headwaters, Bigger's task force became mired down in a dense swamp. The two native scouts, who were not from that area, admitted they were lost.

Bigger decided to bivouac for the night on a dry area when it became clear that the mission could not be completed in the remaining daylight hours. He sent Duncan and a marine squad back to notify Krulak of the change in plans, to send the landing craft back to Voza for the night as a safety precaution, and to return the landing craft to Nukiki in the morning.

The radio team was not able to reach Krulak throughout the day. Having encountered a Japanese patrol in the vicinity of the TBX radio camp, Duncan ordered the radio team to continue trying during the rest of the day, and then move overland with Siefke's squad to Nukiki to bivouac for the night. Duncan continued overland to Nukiki and took the three landing craft back to Voza as instructed by Bigger. That evening, Krulak informed Marine Headquarters by radio that the landing craft were in bad shape.

After trying unsuccessfully to reach Krulak, Siefke's squad and the radio team moved down to Nukiki, as ordered, and bivouacked on the northwestern bank of a small stream that ran through the village. At dawn on the morning of November 2, Siefke and Corporal Michael M. Vinich observed a Japanese patrol in the southeastern part of the village. Siefke rounded up his squad and brought them to the beach while Vinich, standing waist deep in water, signaled to the landing craft coming northwest from Voza.[182] One of the landing craft came ashore. As the marines waded out, Siefke and Private First Class James Moe opened up on Japanese soldiers advancing across the steam. The landing craft embarked the marine patrol, raked the Japanese position with machine gun fire, and returned to the base camp. Arriving at Voza at 9:00 A.M., Duncan and Siefke reported the encounter with the Japanese patrol to Krulak.[183]

It was clear to Krulak from the fire fight, and from Japanese landing craft spotted along the coast opposite Moli Island, that a Japanese force had moved in behind Bigger's task force. He was unable to get in touch with Bigger by radio to warn him.[184]

Unaware of these developments, PT 59 remained moored at Lambu Lambu Cove.

Bigger's task force resumed its march to Choiseul Bay at 6:30 A.M. on November 2. They were joined by a scout more familiar with the area and arrived at the coast by 11:30 A.M.[185] Heading northwest along a Japanese coastal trail toward Choiseul Bay, Bigger's task force came upon a five-man Japanese outpost opposite Taro Island. The marines quickly eliminated the outpost, but Bigger suspected that the Japanese base at Choiseul Bay was alerted by the sounds of gun fire. He exercised his option of attacking the closer Guppy Island. Proceeding to the water's edge 1,200 yards south of Guppy Island, the marines deployed 60 millimeter mortar tubes in the surf and pumped more than 120 rounds into the base. Several fires were ignited. Bigger then ordered his task force to return to the Warrior River along the narrow coastal trail.

The marines reached the river at 4:00 P.M. but found no landing craft there to take them off. They set up defensive positions along the river's northwestern bank and the seaside trail leading from Guppy Island. Bigger attempted to get in touch with the radio squadron, which he thought was still on the southeast side of the river, to request the boats come to the northwestern shore. The mouth of the Warrior River was one hundred yards wide, so he led a small patrol upriver where crossing would be easier. A Japanese patrol coming down the trail on the northwest river bank discovered Bigger's patrol and fired on them. Heavy fire from the marine defensive positions quickly routed the Japanese patrol.

Johnston then volunteered to swim the river at its mouth. He was accompanied by Platoon Sergeant Frank Muller and Corporal Paul Pare. When they approached the southeast bank, the three marines were fired on by Japanese troops emerging from the jungle. Johnston was wounded and taken captive; Muller was wounded and drowned trying to return; and Pare made it back to the northwest bank. A fire fight broke out across the river as the marines turned their weapons on the Japanese troops. Clearly, the enemy was there in force.

Krulak anticipated that Bigger could use some help extracting his task force. At 12:55 P.M. he radioed Marine Headquarters requesting fighter and PT boat cover for the three landing craft going to the Warrior River at 4:00 P.M.[186] Duncan and a marine squad accompanied the three landing craft to provide additional firepower.

When the urgent message for help came in to Lambu Lambu Cove, Lieutenant Commander Taylor had just left for Rendova, leaving Squadron Nineteen commander Lieutenant Commander Russell H. Smith in charge of the base. Only two PT boats were available. Kennedy's PT 59 was at the fueling dock being refueled and had only seven hundred gallons in its tanks. PT 236, a 78-foot Higgins boat skippered by Fred Crawford, was alongside fully fueled. Motor Machinist's Mate 2/c Charles Ridewood remembers:

> I was on watch in one of our gun turrets. Our skipper, Fred Crawford, came running down to the dock shouting that we had to leave right away. PT 59 was at the fueling dock along side us. I wasn't aware until later that the boat was not fully fueled.[187]

The officers agreed to send these two boats, and, if necessary, PT 236 would tow PT 59 when it ran out of fuel. The boats left Lambu Lambu Cove between 4:15 and 4:35 P.M.[188] They sped toward Voza some sixty miles away, trying to locate Krulak's position in the waning light of November 2.

Fighting was still under way when the three landing craft reached the Warrior River. Although a rain squall reduced visibility and the Japanese were firing haphazardly, Marine Corporal James Schnell was seriously wounded. The landing craft coxswains brought the boats close to shore, while Duncan's marines and the landing crafts' Lewis machine gun crews provided covering fire.

Two of the landing craft approached a barren spit of land on the northwest shore of the river mouth. Carrying their wounded, Bigger's marines retreated over the beach, waded out over the coral in shallow water, and scrambled over the sides of the landing craft. The landing crafts' ramps were not lowered because they were still offshore and were under fire. A third landing craft beached one hundred yards up the coast and deployed its ramp to pick up the task force's rear guard.[189] The three landing craft backed away under cover of the rain squall. The time was 6:35

P.M. At 6:37 P.M. Krulak radioed Headquarters that the task force was expected back by 8:00 P.M.[190] The landing craft had gotten under way successfully.

PT 59 and PT 236 reached Choiseul's coastline off Voza at 6:15 P.M. There at the prescribed meeting place was Keresey, Kennedy's fellow PT boat captain, waiting in a hastily repaired fourth landing craft. Keresey picks up the story here:

> I boarded PT 59 and told Kennedy that we needed to head north to support the landing craft going in to pick up the Marine Task Force. There were two PT boats, but I couldn't identify the second boat because it was dark. When we got to the Warrior River, one of the landing craft was towing another offshore.
>
> We came alongside the landing craft and took the Marines aboard the PT boats. I thought about ordering the gunners to fire on the enemy but did not do so because I was afraid we would hit our own boats on the way in and the Marines on the way out. The landing craft and PT boats were very crowded.[191]

Keresey confirms that he was thinking of the .50 caliber guns along the side of PT 59 when he said they didn't fire on the enemy. Christiansen recalls that he did fire:

> I was stationed at the forward gun position on the bow of PT 59. When we arrived at Warrior River, a Marine officer pointed out where the Japanese were, and I fired my 40 millimeter cannon at their position. My ammunition consisted of a mix of high-explosive and armor-piercing projectiles as well as tracer rounds so was more powerful than the .50 caliber guns. Being stationed forward, I could fire without endangering our own forces.[192]

PT 236 Gunner's Mate Leo Campbell remembers the mission:

> We arrived at Warrior River just before dark. A rain squall made it difficult for the Japanese troops to see us. We made

several passes by the shore and fired into the Japanese positions. That suppressed their fire. Some of the Marines were
in the water and some were on the Higgins boats. When we
hove to three hundred yards off shore, we threw a cargo net
over the side to help the Marines board. One of the Higgins
boats pulled up to us, and we unloaded the Marines.[193]

Bigger recalls the evacuation this way:

The fire fight lasted about an hour before the landing craft
came. It was getting dark, and a rain squall had started. Two
landing craft came ashore on a barren spit of land at the mouth
of the Warrior River. We had to wade out to the boats over a
coral reef into chest-deep water 20 yards out. We handed up
our wounded and scrambled in over the sides of the boats. The
landing craft I was on backed off and then its engine quit. There
was danger of being blown ashore on the southeastern river
bank. Then a PT boat came along and offloaded our men. I
climbed up onto the PT boat about midships with a helping
hand from the crew and went below with Dr. Stevens to see to
the wounded. Corporal Schnell died that night.[194]

Sergeant Edward Elexander Thomas was another of the marines
present:

We marched back from the Guppy Island raid to the Warrior River bank and were waiting in the jungle for the landing
craft. Johnston, Muller, and Pare started to swim across the
river, and the Japanese opened fire from the east bank. We
were worried that the Japanese might attack from the Guppy
Island area too, but that didn't happen. The fight lasted about
fifteen minutes. Then several landing craft appeared one hundred yards northwest of the river mouth. Two landing craft
pulled up to shore—maybe we had to wade out, but no more
than 10 or 15 feet in shallow water. Japanese fire ceased
because of a heavy rainfall, but several Marines had been
wounded. I got on the landing craft on the right. It was very

crowded. Our landing craft pulled up to a PT boat, and we scrambled up a cargo net on its stern.[195]

Marine Private First Class Harry Towne describes the evacuation:

> I saw the landing craft circling offshore near the mouth of the Warrior River. Two came in together, loaded, and backed off. The third approached the beach farther north. The sea was getting a bit rough. I was part of the rear guard and one of the last to climb aboard. It was early evening as darkness was rapidly approaching. We were aware there was some difficulty with one of the first two landing craft and were worried that the wind might blow the disabled boat ashore. Fortunately, we were well beyond enemy fire at the time. Then two PT boats appeared. As they got closer, the PT boats stopped and took aboard the Marines from the two landing craft. The landing craft I was on moved up to one of them, and we boarded. The PT boats then took us down to Voza, where we debarked and spent the night in the little native village.[196]

Already battered from previous trips, the disabled landing craft sprang a leak when encountering coral during the squall. As the water rose in the boat, marines bailed with their helmets. The landing craft's engine sputtered and died, leaving the boat with no way to maneuver. The second landing craft got a line to the disabled boat and towed it several hundred yards out before the PT boats arrived. The situation was still precarious because the Japanese had troops and landing craft between the Warrior River and Voza, and could have brought vessels down from Choiseul Bay. The two PT boats hove to and proceeded to offload the marines from the two landing craft. Kennedy's PT 59 took the marines off the damaged landing craft while PT 236 took care of the other two landing craft. When all were clear, the damaged landing craft was scuttled.

There is disagreement among those present whether the second landing craft towed the disabled landing craft away from shore. This doubt can now be put to rest. Duncan states in a 1986 letter to Company G Marine Roy Philip Homerding:

> The coxswain was a very brave man. Without his repeated diving into the pitch black ocean to retrieve the tow line, we might still be there. I recommended him for a medal for his bravery.[197]

Estimates of the number of marines on PT 59 range from 15 to 50. Fifteen marines is probably low, but not out of the question. Fifty is high given that the 77-foot PT 59 gunboat was heavily armed with machine guns and cannon and carried a large crew. PT 59 radar operator Vivian Scribner recalls:

> We encountered the landing craft four hundred yards off shore. It was dark but not raining. They maneuvered up to our port stern, and the Marines scrambled aboard. I don't remember an accurate count of the number of Marines we took aboard, but they were all over the deck and below deck.[198]

Undoubledly, the 78-foot PT 236 took aboard a majority of the marines.

The two PT boats escorted the two operational landing craft back to Voza, arriving at 9:30 P.M. The landing craft ferried the marines ashore. Corporal Schnell was too badly wounded to be moved, so Dr. John Stevens remained on board PT 59 to tend to him. Keresey went ashore on one of the landing craft, conferred with Krulak, and returned to board PT 236 for the trip back.[199] He went below to sleep, so did not witness the remainder of the trip.[200]

Kennedy headed PT 59, now dangerously low on fuel, back to Lambu Lambu Cove. PT 59's engines, burning fuel at three hundred gallons per hour, ran out of fuel at 3:00 A.M., and the boat was towed the rest of the way by PT 236. They arrived in Lambu Lambu Cove at 8:00 A.M.[201]

The next night, PT 59 returned to Choiseul with four PT boats to escort three LCI transports (Landing Craft Infantry) embarking Krulak's marines and returning them to the marine base on Vella Lavella.

PT 59's laconic log entries regarding the incident read as follows:

> November 2, 1943: Moored at Lambu Lambu. 0800—Mustered, no absentees. 1635—Underway for patrol off Choiseul Isle. 1820—Arrived at Choiseul and met an invasion barge of ours, took aboard a marine officer to direct in the evacuation of marines from Virulato River Area—met marines in Higgins boats and took them aboard.

> November 3, 1943: Underway off coast of Choiseul Isle. Discharged marines as directed. One marine deceased and two wounded remained on board for medical attention at Lambu Lambu. 0300—exhausted gas supply and was towed by accompanying P.T.s. Moored at base. Said wounded marines and casualty removed to doctor's care. 10:00—Took aboard 2,000 gals. fuel at Lambu Lambu fuel dock. 1900—Underway to evacuate marines at Choiseul, accompanied by four PT's, met three L.C. I.'s and proceeded to Choiseul coast. Patrolled coast as L.C. I.'s beached and took aboard marines.

> November 4, 1943 0000—Underway screening L.C. I.'s who were beached taking aboard marines. 0100—Underway escorting L.C. I.'s to Vella Lavella. 0500—Left company of L.C. I.'s as directed by O.T.C. 0555—moored at base. 0900—Took aboard 900 gallons fuel.[202]

The log is incorrect in several minor details. First, the Virulato (actually Virulata) River is 40 miles south of the area for which PT 59 was headed. Virulata River was the originally targeted landing site, but Krulak redirected the landing to Voza when coastwatcher Seton informed Krulak that Voza was undefended. Second, the officer taken aboard was Keresey, not a marine. The latter discrepancy is easily explained as Keresey was wearing marine fatigues that night. Keresey was well known to Kennedy, so it is clear that Kennedy did not write or dictate the log entry.

With the marines safely back at their base on Vella Lavella, life returned to business as usual in Lambu Lambu Cove. For the next two weeks, PT 59 conducted patrols off Choiseul, searching for Japanese supply barges and shelling Japanese positions. On November 5, PT 59 participated in a barge hunting raid with PT 187 off northern Choiseul. The PT boats fired at two barges near Moli Island, but the barges eluded them. After patrolling Choiseul Bay, the PT boats returned to Moli Island, and in the early dawn light, spotted some beached barges. PT 59's log reports that hits were made on three barges.

Kennedy made four patrols to Choiseul between November 7 and November 16. On the third patrol, PT 59 strafed Guppy Island with 75 rounds of 40 millimeter ammunition.[203] The lack of action in these days was surely because the Japanese had withdrawn their troops from the Central Solomons. They were concentrating on defending Bougainville against the Allied forces at Empress Augusta Bay. Kennedy's last patrol was on the night of November 16, when PT 59 scouted Redman Island off the northwest tip of Choiseul.

Lambu Lambu Cove base physician Dr. E. Reid Bahnson observed that Kennedy was unable to keep meals down in the morning. Sensing that something more than the quality of the food was responsible, Bahnson ordered Kennedy to Tulagi for a more complete checkup.[204] On November 18, PT 59 traveled down Vella Lavella's coast to Biloa, whereupon Kennedy turned command of PT 59 over to Ensign Mitchell.[205] Within a month, Navy Lieutenant Richard Milhous Nixon would arrive at nearby Barakoma airstrip to command the local air cargo support detachment.

Kennedy underwent a medical exam at Tulagi where an X-ray taken on November 23 revealed an early duodenal ulcer.[206] He spent the next month in Calvertville with little to do but pass the time of day with his fellow officers. About this time, Kennedy was promoted to Squadron Two executive officer. On December 21 Cluster issued an order sending him home:

> In accordance with a dispatch dated 14 December 1943
> from Commander South Pacific, which cannot be quoted

herein, you will consider yourself detached from duty in Motor Torpedo Boat Squadron Two and from such other duties which may have been assigned to you.

You will proceed via first available air transportation, PRI-ORITY FOUR, to the United states, and report to the Commanding Officer, Motor Torpedo Boat Squadron Training Center, Portsmouth (Melville), Rhode Island for duty.[207]

Several of Kennedy's friends recalled that Kennedy was still on Tulagi at Christmas time looking for transportation home, but they are mistaken about the date.[208]

Prescott remembers:

I took Jack and his duffle bag to Guadalcanal in my PT boat. When we docked at the harbor, I got a jeep from the port authority and drove him to Henderson Field. He inquired about a flight and was told one would be arriving from Australia in an hour and a half. When Jack got back to Florida, he wrote to my father telling him of my well being, and that he

PT boat officers George Ross, John Kennedy, Paul Fay, and James Reed. Fay became undersecretary of the navy and Reed became assistant secretary of the treasury in the Kennedy administration.

Courtesy of John Fitzgerald Kennedy Library

had left me on December 19. I'm quite certain that he flew all the way home because the dispatcher told him he would be able to do so and, in our subsequent contacts, he never told me otherwise.[209]

Again there is a small mix-up in dates. Kennedy's orders were dated December 21 as was his Fitness Report. Cluster rated Kennedy 4.0 in Present assignment, 4.0 in Ability to command, 3.8 in Administration, 3.9 in Ship handling, and Outstanding in comparison to other officers of his rank and approximate length of service.[210]

Kennedy's flight apparently stopped in Espiritu Santo. According to the log of the escort carrier USS *Breton* (CVE 23), Kennedy boarded the ship at 9:20 A.M. December 23, 1943, shortly before *Breton* left for the United States.[211] With only a Priority Four classification, he must have been bumped from the aircraft. Like many returning veterans, he probably waited around a few days for a flight and then quickly decided to take a berth on a ship when one became available. *Breton*'s log entry states that Kennedy was under orders from the commanding officer of APO708, the post office address of the army base on Espiritu Santo.[212] Apparently, transportation was arranged at the last moment, and any authority was deemed acceptable. *Breton* officer Lester Sperberg verifies that Kennedy was on the voyage from Espiritu Santo to San Francisco:

> This was my last voyage on the *Breton*, as I had been transferred to the States for LST training. I recall meeting Kennedy in the ward room, where officers of the same rank were seated together. He had a distinctive Boston accent. Years later, I wrote to the Kennedy library to see if I was correct. They confirmed that Kennedy was on the *Breton*.[213]

Sidney Sherwin was returning from a tour of duty on the USS *Indiana*:

> I was rotating back to the States to help commission another battleship. My room mate on the *Breton* was Lt. John F.

Kennedy. Although I was senior, I gave him the lower bunk because of his bad back. I was aware that he was the son of the former Ambassador to Great Britain. All I knew of his military service was that he was in PT boats in the Solomons.[214]

The 7,800-ton *Breton* was one of the many escort carriers that was used to transport aircraft and personnel to and from the battle zone.[215]

Breton left Espiritu Santo harbor on the afternoon of December 23 bound for Tutuila Island, American Samoa, under escort by the destroyer USS *Warrington* (DD-383). She stopped at Tutuila to pick up personnel and disabled aircraft to be ferried back to the United States.[216] *Breton* reached San Francisco Bay on January 7, 1944, and moored at the Naval Air Station Alameda just after noon. Kennedy left the ship sometime before 4:00 P.M.[217]

After stops in Los Angeles to see friends and Rochester, Minnesota, to consult with physicians at the Mayo Clinic, Kennedy traveled to Florida to visit his parents and to recuperate. It was here that Kennedy wrote to Prescott's father:

> For the last eight months I had the pleasure of serving with your son in P. T.s in the Solomons area. I saw him last the 19th of December—when he took me over in his boat to Guadalcanal where I caught a plane to start my way home...[218]

Kennedy says "start" his way home. His trip by air was apparently interrupted, and he never bothered to inform Prescott of the change in plans.

Kennedy left for Rhode Island on February 5 and was briefly assigned to Melville.[219] He entered a hospital for treatment of a herniated disk. In March, he transferred to PT Boat Shakedown Detail at the Subchaser Training Center in Miami, Florida, to assist in training green PT boat squadrons. The commanding officer of the Shakedown Detail was Alan Montgomery, former commanding officer of Squadron Three (2) in the early days of Tulagi.[220] Squadron Six commanding officer Faulkner, who was executive officer of the Shakedown Detail between assignments in the Pacific, remembers:

> I hadn't known Jack Kennedy in the Solomons because I was on the Russell Islands when he was at Tulagi. I did know him when I was executive officer of the PT boat detachment at the Submarine Chaser Training Center in Miami. Jack was on limited duty there because of his bad back. When I left for New York to take over Squadron 37, Kennedy was still assigned to Miami.[221]

Although the duty was easy, in late May Kennedy departed for the Chelsea Naval Hospital in Boston and was admitted on June 11.[222] A month later, Kennedy underwent surgery on his spine at the New England Baptist Hospital. The operation was not successful, and Kennedy spent eight weeks in the hospital recuperating. He was also diagnosed with colitis, which explained the stomach problems Kennedy had been having over the past year. Kennedy returned to the Chelsea Naval Hospital, where he was treated as an outpatient. Chelsea doctors examining Kennedy confirmed that he had chronic colitis, and, in December, recommended he be retired from the service.[223] He appeared before a medical panel of the Naval Retiring Board on December 27, which found him incapacitated from the colitis.[224] Kennedy was subsequently discharged from the navy for physical disability, effective March 1, 1945.[225]

Kennedy traveled to an Arizona resort in January 1945 to recuperate. After three months of rest and physical therapy, he joined the Hearst newspaper syndicate to cover the United Nations Charter Conference in San Francisco. Upon completion of that assignment, he covered the British elections in which Churchill was defeated. While in Europe, Kennedy attended the Potsdam Conference as a guest of Secretary of the Navy James Vincent Forrestal. He returned to the United States in August.

Kennedy entered the race for United States Congressman from the Eleventh District of Massachusetts in April 1946. Centered at Beacon Hill in Boston, the district was overwhelmingly Democratic. The real challenge was to win the Democratic nomination. In a crowded campaign field, he garnered 40 percent of the vote, while other candidates split the remaining votes. True to form, when the election was over in November, Kennedy won the seat by a large margin. He entered the Eightieth Congress in January 1947 and was assigned to the Education and Labor Committee. Also joining the committee was freshman California Representative Richard Nixon. Kennedy was reelected to Congress in 1948 and 1950.

After three terms in the House of Representatives, 35-year-old Kennedy successfully campaigned for the Senate seat held by Henry Cabot Lodge Jr. He was sworn in as Massachusetts' junior Senator on January 3, 1953, and was assigned to the Labor and Public Welfare Committee, as well as the Government Operations Committee. Kennedy married Jacqueline Lee Bouvier in September 1953. While recovering from an October 1954 back surgery, he wrote the Pulitzer Prize-winning *Profiles in Courage*, a book about eight U.S. senators who risked their careers to fight for their beliefs. Kennedy returned to the Senate in May 1955.

During the 1956 Democratic Convention, presidential nominee Adlai Stevenson asked the delegates to choose the vice-presidential nominee rather than naming his own candidate. Thirteen names were put forward. On the second ballot, Kennedy came within a whisker of carrying the day, but Senator Albert A. Gore Sr.'s concession to fellow Tennessee Senator Carey Estes Kefauver put Kefauver over the top. Kennedy's strong showing put him on the road to the White House. In 1957 he gained a seat on the prestigious Senate Foreign Relations Committee. Up for reelection in 1958, Kennedy defeated his opponent by garnering 74 percent of the votes cast.

Kennedy campaigned in seven Democratic primary elections in1960 and won each of them. He was selected on the first convention ballot. Kennedy offered the vice-presidential nomination to Lyndon Johnson who, to the surprise of many, accepted. The 1960 Republican ticket consisted of Vice President Nixon and former Massachusetts Senator Lodge. In a hard-fought race, which saw the introduction of the Presidential Debates, Kennedy defeated Nixon by the slimmest of margins to date. He became the 35th President of the United States with a popular vote of 34,221,344 to 34,106,671 and an electoral vote of 303 to 219. Kennedy was 43 years old.

During Kennedy's presidency, he formed the Peace Corps, signed the Nuclear Test Ban Treaty, created the Alliance for Progress, and championed America's race to the moon. The Bay of Pigs invasion by Cuban exiles, the quarantine of Cuba to force the removal of Soviet missiles, and the Soviet erection of the Berlin wall occurred while Kennedy was in office. Kennedy proposed landmark legislation in the areas of poverty, civil rights, tax reform, aid to education, and medical aid for the aged, but the bills were not passed by Congress during his presidency. He nominated Byron R. White and Arthur J. Goldberg to serve on the Supreme Court.

Kennedy was assassinated on November 22, 1963, in Dallas, Texas, at the age of 46. He is buried at the Arlington National Cemetery.

Kennedy held elective office for 16 years. He served in the navy for three years of which eight months were in the Pacific Theater. Kennedy was awarded the Naval & Marine Corps Medal, the Purple Heart, the American Defense Service Medal, the American Campaign Medal, the Asiatic-Pacific Campaign Medal with three engagement stars, and the World War II Victory Medal. The Naval & Marine Corps Medal is awarded for heroism not involving actual conflict with the enemy; his citation reads:

TO
LIEUTENANT, JUNIOR GRADE,
JOHN FITZGERALD KENNEDY
UNITED STATES NAVY

For extremely heroic conduct as Commanding Officer of Motor Torpedo Boat 109 following the collision and sinking of that vessel in the Pacific War Theater on August 1-2, 1943. Unmindful of personal danger, Lieutenant (then Lieutenant, Junior Grade) Kennedy unhesitatingly braved the difficulties and hazards of darkness to direct rescue operations, swimming many hours to secure aid and food after he had succeeded in getting his crew ashore. His outstanding courage, endurance and leadership contributed to the saving of several lives and were in keeping with the highest traditions of the United States Naval Service.

James V. Forrestal
Secretary of the Navy
May 19, 1944[226]

Chapter 3
Richard M. Nixon
Ground Aviation Officer

Richard Milhous Nixon was a lawyer with the Whittier, California, law firm of Wingert and Bewley when he heard the announcement of the Japanese attack on the American Pacific Fleet at Pearl Harbor. He interviewed for a position with the Federal Office of Price Administration upon the recommendation of his Duke Law School instructor David F. Cavers.[1] On January 6, 1942, he received a telegram which read in part:

> Your appointment as Assistant Attorney $3200 per annum, in the Office for Emergency Management, Office of Price Administration has been approved. Please report January 15.[2]

Nixon and his wife Thelma Catherine Ryan Nixon, better known as Pat, drove from their home in Whittier to Washington, D.C., to begin his new job. They arrived on January 9.

Twenty-nine-year-old Nixon joined 177 attorneys who had the unenviable task of interpreting a dizzying array of war-rationing regulations. He worked in the tire rationing program, answering written inquiries regarding how to apply the regulations. The Japanese penetration of the Pacific Southwest threatened to cut off 90 percent of the United States' rubber supplies, so President Roosevelt issued an executive order halting domestic tire sales. A conscientious worker, Nixon rose to the position of acting chief of interpretations for the Rubber Branch in less than three months.[3]

In another three months, he became acting chief of the rationing coordination unit.

After several months of working in Washington, D.C., Nixon put aside his Quaker beliefs and volunteered for military service. Surely the presence of thousands of uniformed officers influenced his decision. Nixon applied to the navy in March 1942, which offered direct commissions to attorneys. The navy's cadet selection board accepted his application on May 8 and suggested an air intelligence or administration assignment.[4] A recommendation letter from Nixon's supervisor Jacob Beuscher smoothed the way.[5]

Nixon was commissioned a lieutenant (jg) in June and ordered to report for indoctrination in August. He arrived at the Naval Training School at Quonset Point, Rhode Island, on August 17 and was assigned to the Aviation Indoctrination Training Platoon 17, Class 4-1942. William Pierce Rogers was one of Nixon's classmates; Gerhard Mennen Williams was another.[6]

Upon completion of the 60-day course, in which he finished 96th out of 750 officer candidates, Nixon became a ground aviation officer.[7] He requested aircraft carrier duty, but on October 10, 1942, found himself assigned to the Naval Air Station being established in Ottumwa, Iowa.[8] Nixon was an administrative aide to the executive officer. For five months he carried out such mundane duties as writing the charter for the Officers' Club.

A bulletin from the Bureau of Naval Personnel posted in late March 1943 offered a way out. All able-bodied line officers under 30 years of age were to be ordered to duty afloat as the war required. Requests for sea duty could be initiated immediately.[9] Nixon applied, again with a preference for service on an aircraft carrier. The navy approved his application for change of duty, and he was ordered to San Francisco for transportation to Noumea, New Caledonia. Nixon's last day of service at Ottumwa was May 7,1943.[10] He and Pat drove to San Francisco, arriving on May 16.[11] Nixon reported for duty on May 19.[12]

Nixon sailed for Noumea on May 31,1943, aboard the 10,000-ton transport ship SS *President Monroe* (AP 104).[13] Cabin mate Lester Wroble recalls:

I was in Nixon's class at Quonset Point, Rhode Island, and was also designated as a ground aviation officer. We were transported to the South Pacific on the SS *Monroe*. There were nine officers in a cabin originally built for two people. The cabin had three triple bunks, and the shower stall was used for storage. We didn't have a shower in the 19 days it took to reach our destination. One day, about the time we crossed the equator, the swimming pool was filled with salt water, and we took a bath of sorts. I left the ship in Noumea, New Caledonia, and was sent to Guadalcanal as Officer in Charge of a Patrol Service Unit that maintained B-24s. I didn't see Nixon again until I rotated up to the Green Islands.[14]

The War Shipping Administration acquired the *Monroe*, a former American President Lines combination freighter-passenger vessel, at the outbreak of the war.[15] Previously configured for 13,000 tons of cargo and 96 passengers, *Monroe* now transported five thousand troops.

Nixon arrived in Noumea on June 17 and found that no assignment awaited him. He was ordered to the U.S. Naval Advance Base for quarters.[16] Eight days later Nixon reported back to the *Monroe* for a two-day trip to the Fleet Air Command South Pacific on Espiritu Santo in the New Hebrides Islands (now Vanuatu).[17] Fleet Air Command assigned him to the South Pacific Combat Air Transport Command, popularly known as SCAT, headquartered in Noumea.[18] The SCAT commanding officer subsequently assigned Nixon to the Passenger Division, Marine Aircraft Group 25 Headquarters, Tontouta, New Caledonia.[19] No Fitness Report exists in Nixon's navy jacket for the period May 7 to July 1 when he was in travel. The record simply states that Nixon was assigned to Transport Group Three, Amphibious Forces.[20]

SCAT's predecessor, Marine Utility Squadron 253 from Marine Air Group 25, was rushed to the South Pacific to supply the marines at Guadalcanal.[21] Fourteen R4D cargo aircraft, fitted out

**Lieutenant Nixon in Passenger Division, SCAT Headquarters,
Tontouta, New Caledonia, summer 1943**

Courtesy of Richard Nixon Library and
Birthplace and the Richard Nixon Estate

with neoprene fuel bladders holding an additional eight hundred
gallons of aviation fuel, were flown out to the Pacific by hopping
from island to island. The first leg from Naval Air Station San
Diego, California, to Marine Air Station Ewa on Oahu, Territory of
Hawaii, began on August 23, 1942. The flight required almost 16
hours and was the longest nonstop mass flight of twin-engine
aircraft on record.[22] Other stops were at Palmyra, Canton, and
Fiji, each about one thousand miles apart.

The Marine Air Group, known as MAG 25, set up headquarters at the existing air base near Tontouta, 30 miles northwest of
Noumea. Seventy-one officers and crew of MAG 25 bunked in
metal warehouses until a ground crew arrived and built a camp-
site along the Tontouta River. Initially, the men slept on folding

cots on the ground; eventually, the tents had wood floors and screened sides.

Three weeks after the marines invaded Guadalcanal in early August, SCAT aircraft began to arrive. MAG 25's squadron commander, Lieutenant Colonel Perry K. Smith, flew an unarmed SCAT R4D transport aircraft into Henderson Field carrying Marine Brigadier General Roy S. Geiger and key staff members. Geiger commanded the air units on Guadalcanal for two months before moving his Marine Air Wing Headquarters to the bomber base on Espiritu Santo. The second R4D flown into Henderson Field, piloted by MAG 25 executive officer Lieutenant Colonel Wyman F. Marshall, carried three thousand pounds of cargo. Both planes evacuated wounded and personnel sick with malaria and dengue fever on their return flights.

Malaria and dengue fever were serious business in the South Pacific. More than half of the soldiers transported by SCAT had the debilitating symptoms of headache, muscle ache, chills, fever, sweating, fatigue, and diarrhea. With an annual average temperature of 80 degrees Fahrenheit, an annual rainfall of 130 inches, a thick tropical rainforest, and rotting vegetation, the Solomon Islands were a natural breeding ground for the Anopheles mosquito, which spreads malaria, and the Aedes mosquito, which spreads dengue fever. Servicemen took Atabrine (a synthetic form of quinine) to relieve the symptoms. The only effective preventive measure was to avoid mosquito bites by sleeping under a net at night, when the mosquitoes were active.

A second MAG 25 squadron, VMJ-152, joined Squadron 253 at Tontouta. In August Admiral Halsey created the 50-plane SCAT command out of the two marine squadrons of R4Ds at Tontouta and the army air force 13th Troop Carrier Squadron of C-47s at Plaines des Gaiacs, New Caledonia. In addition to the pilots and flight crew, SCAT had 700 enlisted men and 150 officers.[23] In May 1943, SCAT added the Marine VMJ-153 Squadron and the Army 63rd Squadron.

SCAT was truly a multi-service outfit. The aircraft were flown and maintained by marine and army personnel, while the navy provided one third of the ground personnel and most of the ground aviation officers.[24]

R4Ds and C-47s were militarized DC-3s with enlarged cargo doors and a navigator's astrodome. The workhorse aircraft were known by the names Skytrain and Gooney Bird. Two Pratt and Whitney 1,200 horsepower engines powered the aircraft, which had a range of 1,500 miles at a cruising speed of 185 mph. DC-3s could carry eight thousand pounds of fuel and cargo, but SCAT crews often exceeded that limit. A typical load on a flight from Espiritu Santo to Guadalcanal was three thousand pounds of cargo—the eight hundred gallons of fuel weighed five thousand pounds. On the return trip, the aircraft evacuated 16 litter cases. The unarmed and unarmored DC-3 had a maximum speed of only 230 mph. Pilots simply ducked into the ever-present clouds to escape enemy fighter aircraft.

Nixon served as assistant operations officer (SCAT) and officer in charge SCAT Detachment from July 1 to September 30, 1943.[25] His Fitness Report, signed by the new commanding officer, Wyman Marshall, labeled Nixon's job performance Outstanding. During his stay at Tontouta, Nixon wrote to Pat that he worked every night from 5:30 on, but had his days free.[26] He undoubtedly had the night shift because of his lack of seniority. Nixon prepared manifests and supervised the loading and unloading of SCAT's cargo planes. The aircraft ferried ammunition, fuel, supplies, men, and mail to the combat areas and returned with sick or wounded soldiers. Ailing soldiers were brought back to New Caledonia because the hospital facilities were well developed and the climate was mild. Wounded soldiers were taken to the closer island of Efate for immediate care.[27]

In late August Nixon was driving a jeep from Noumea to Tontouta:

> I heard a siren and pulled over. Two Jeeps full of MPs were clearing the way for a motorcade. I thought it might be

**SCAT crew and R4D cargo aircraft at
Tontouta Air Base, summer 1943**

Courtesy of Richard Nixon Library and
Birthplace and the Richard Nixon Estate

some high ranking general. But when the Army weapons carrier sped past I was amazed to see that the passenger, wearing a big floppy hat to protect herself from the blistering sun,
was Eleanor Roosevelt. Since the battle for the Solomon Islands was still raging a few miles to the north, her visit made
a great impression on us all.[28]

Anna Eleanor Roosevelt was on a six-week goodwill tour. She
visited hospitals, mess halls, and outdoor theaters—talking with
soldiers and spreading her uplifting spirit. After her successful
stops in New Caledonia, New Zealand, and Australia, Halsey
agreed to let her fly to Efate, Espiritu Santo, and Guadalcanal.
The latter stop was a courageous move on her part, as
Guadalcanal was still under occasional fighter attack. Roosevelt
traveled on in a B-24 Liberator bomber, temporarily named *Our*

Eleanor, which was escorted by Cactus Air Force fighter aircraft. Pilot William Harris remembers:

> Our squadron of P-38 fighter aircraft met Eleanor Roosevelt's plane two hundred miles south of Guadalcanal early in the morning and escorted it into Henderson Field. The officers were anxious to make a good impression, and they went so far as to order the fighter and bomber pilots to paint over any insignia of questionable taste.[29]

Upon arrival on Guadalcanal, Roosevelt ate breakfast with the Thirteenth Air Force commander, General Nathan Farragut Twining. She toured hospitals and a cemetery, spoke to the troops, and met again with Halsey, who came up for dinner. Afterward, she talked at great length with an old friend, Joseph P. Lash, who was stationed on Guadalcanal as a meteorologist.[30] Lash would subsequently chronicle the Roosevelts' lives in a series of books.

The following morning, the American fighters escorted Roosevelt's aircraft back toward Espiritu Santo. Halsey would later state that Roosevelt's visit accomplished more good than that of any other dignitary who passed through the South Pacific.[31] Her experience with MacArthur was not so rewarding. He refused to see her when she visited Australia and would not allow her to travel to New Guinea.[32]

Thirty-year-old Nixon was promoted to lieutenant on October 1, 1943.[33] Shortly thereafter, he transferred to base ACID as officer in charge of the SCAT Unit. SCAT pilot Ellsworth Terrill "Terry" Nobles identified ACID as Bauer Field on Efate Island.[34] A letter from Pharmacist's Mate A. H. Patterson to Nixon confirms that Nixon was officer in charge there.[35]

Efate was not a choice assignment. Admiral Ernest Joseph King selected the island as a forward base in February 1942. A small army detachment from Noumea garrisoned Efate in March.[36] Seabees hacked out an air strip, and a marine air group began operations in late May. The airstrip was named after its former commander, Medal of Honor winner Lieutenant Colonel Harold

W. Bauer, who disappeared after a dogfight over Guadalcanal. Bauer Field was located 30 miles from the port city of Vila, but it might as well have been three hundred miles. The road to Vila was poorly constructed and strung over steep hills, creek beds, and mosquito-filled swamps.[37]

According to his Fitness Report, Nixon was officer in charge of the SCAT unit on Efate from October 10 to December 15.[38] The latter date is uncertain as Nixon was ordered to Espiritu Santo on November 16, 1943, for further assignment.[39] This was not the only time that Fitness Reports' dates and associated assignments differed from transfer orders. Surely, this disagreement has led to some confusion regarding Nixon's overseas service.

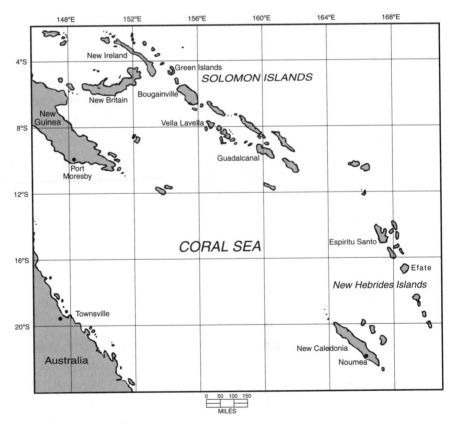

Nixon served at SCAT bases from Noumea to the Green Islands.

Nixon's assignments on Espiritu Santo are not specified in his orders. SCAT pilot William Kay Snyder remembers Nixon supervising the loading of SCAT aircraft:

> I met Nixon briefly when he was a Naval Loading Officer at Espiritu Santo. I also remember seeing pictures of him at the entrance of the cargo door on one of our R4Ds.[40]

During the next three weeks, Nixon probably carried out a number of short term assignments at various bases. SCAT pilot H. Jesse Walker remembers seeing Nixon playing poker in the rear of the dispatch building at Henderson Field, Guadalcanal.[41] Also, SCAT pilot Otis Carney remembers Nixon opening the cargo door several times on Guadalcanal during Carney's tour of duty from September 1943 to March 1944.[42] Although it is not mentioned in any of his Fitness Reports, Nixon's Guadalcanal service is confirmed by a navy-prepared summary of his service.[43] Nixon may have been temporarily stationed at the air strip at Munda, New Georgia, as well. Nobles remembers seeing him there several times in late 1943.[44]

Hundreds of thousands of American troops passed through Espiritu Santo during the war in the South Pacific. Among them was Navy Lieutenant James A. Michener, who was a publications and personnel officer for the Solomon Islands. He traveled extensively in the region visiting numerous islands.[45] Michener wrote *Tales of the South Pacific* while based in Espiritu Santo, and local legend has it that the model for Bali Hai was the nearby island of Ambae. Michener explained that the name Bali Hai came from a tiny, miserable village on the island of Mono in the Treasury Islands.[46]

On December 10 Nixon was ordered to base PYRE, where he took over as officer in charge of the SCAT unit.[47] SCAT navigator Clovis E. Davis identified PYRE as the Barakoma airstrip on Vella Lavella.[48] SCAT commanding officer Colonel Allen C. Koonce signed an abbreviated Fitness Report placing Nixon on Vella Lavella from December 16 to December 31, 1943.[49]

SCAT crew loading an R4D cargo aircraft on Espiritu Santo
Courtesy of DC-3 Memorial Web Site and Colonel William Snyder

American PT boats landed a six-man reconnaissance party near Barakoma on July 21. They returned with a 45-man pre-invasion force on August 12 to scout beach landing areas and to locate an area suitable for an airstrip. On August 15, a 4,600-man marine force landed on Barakoma beaches and drove the Japanese defenders north along the coastal plain. As with each of the Solomon Islands, the inland terrain is dominated by forest-covered mountains with several dormant volcanoes. Seabees constructed an airstrip on the plain near Barakoma and had the airstrip operational a little more than one month after the invasion. The strip was immediately put to use to stage fighter aircraft for flights over the Japanese-held island of Bougainville and the Japanese bastion at the port of Rabaul, New Britain.

On September 18, 3,700 New Zealand troops arrived at Barakoma to relieve the Americans and to clear the island of Japanese.[50] The 35th and 37th Battalions of the 3rd New Zealand Division conducted a pincer movement, moving around the sides of the island by small landing craft and leapfrogging from bay to bay. The New Zealanders had the Japanese trapped in the north-west corner of the island by the end of September. On the night of October 6, Japanese landing craft evacuated more than five hundred Japanese soldiers. The two New Zealander battalions linked up and secured the area shortly thereafter. Subsequently, a combined New Zealand and American force operated the Barakoma airstrip and built roads connecting the strip with naval facilities at Biloa.

Nixon moved from Barakoma to Piva Uncle airstrip on Bougainville about January 1, 1944. The date is not precise be-cause the telegram ordering his move is not dated.[51] Bougainville is a 130-mile-long by 30-mile-wide jungle-covered island with mountain ranges running along the center of the island. Several active volcanoes spewed steam and smoke into the already clouded skies. Virtually all of the civilization, if it can be called that, existed on the coastal plains because the mountain regions were steep and heavily forested. Daily rains turned its plains into jungles, swamps, and mud. Malaria and dengue fever were a constant concern.

Bougainville was originally occupied by the Japanese in March 1942 as a supply base and fueling depot for positions in the southern Solomon Islands. The United States 3rd Marine Di-vision landed at Empress Augusta Bay on November 1, 1943. The location was an inspired choice as five thousand Japanese troops from the 23rd Infantry Regiment were isolated on Buka Island in the north and fifteen thousand at Buin on the south ends of the mountainous island. There were few passable roads—more aptly described as trails—to the Bay's location halfway up the western side of the island. Fourteen thousand marines stormed ashore and cleared a beach head in an area defended by three hundred Japanese soldiers. The Japanese command rushed troops and ships from Rabaul but were repelled by American cruis-ers and destroyers in what came to be known as the Battle of Empress Augusta Bay. In mid-November, the marines reached the area of Piva Forks, several miles inland from the beach.

Nixon in typical Bougainville attire early 1944

Courtesy of Richard Nixon LIbrary and
Birthplace and the Richard Nixon Estate

Because the objective of the invasion was to establish airstrips, the marines simply pushed the Japanese troops back and
established a defensive perimeter. Beginning work five days after
the marines landed, Seabees completed a fighter airfield at Cape
Torokina on December 10. A SCAT R4D landed that day accompanied by 17 Chance Vought F4Us and six Douglas SBDs.[52]
Howard Krogh Nielson remembers his SCAT flights into Torokina:

> My early flights to Bougainville with troop replacements
> landed on the Torokina strip along the edge of Empress Au-
> gusta Bay. While we unloaded and took on whatever load
> was ours to take back, we would only kill the port engine ahead
> of the cargo door leaving the starboard engine running. There
> was a ridge about five miles or so north of the landing strip
> that was watched quite closely. Japanese gun emplacements
> were sited on the strip. When clouds covered their location,

they would begin firing. We would only have to start one engine and be on our way.[53]

By Christmas, the defensive perimeter was four miles deep
by five miles wide and subjected to limited ground attack.[54]
Seabees built a 6,000-foot long by 150-foot wide bomber airfield
called Piva Uncle at the small inland village of Piva four miles
inland from Cape Torokina.[55] The Marston mat-covered field, which
was to become the home of the SCAT contingent on Bougainville,
was in partial operation by Christmas, and had aircraft revetments
in place by January 5. A nearby fighter strip called Piva Yoke was
completed by January 22.[56] These fields provided aircraft bases
220 miles from Rabaul, half the distance than from the airfield at
Munda, New Georgia.

In the early occupation, Japanese troops occasionally shelled
the perimeter area with 75 millimeter guns and 90 millimeter mortars. By Nixon's count, 35 shells landed near his air-raid bunker

Nixon and fellow SCAT officer on Bougainville early 1944

one night.[57] Japanese soldiers moved artillery pieces onto the leeward mountain slopes outside the defensive perimeter. Enlarging the perimeter pushed the artillery far enough away from the airstrips to temporarily remove this threat. Subsequently, the Americans reinforced the perimeter with foxholes, trenches, pillboxes, and gun emplacements—all manned 24 hours a day to keep the Japanese troops at bay.

Malaria had been such a problem for the marines on Guadalcanal that the Bougainville invasion force included malarial control units. More than a square mile of swamps were drained within the defensive perimeter to rid the area of primary mosquito reproduction sites. Troops carried protective clothing, bug spray, netting, and medicine and were trained to eliminate stagnant water. Once again, the best protection from the mosquitos was sleeping in mosquito netting, when the mosquitos were active at night.

Navy, marine, army, and New Zealand aircraft began a massive attack on Rabaul when the Bougainville airfields became operational. Fighters from Munda airstrip staged through Torokina

SCAT aircraft at Piva Uncle airstrip on Bougainville 1944

Courtesy of DC-3 Memorial Web Site and Mag/SCAT Association

to mount their attacks. Bombers flew out of Piva Uncle at least once a day from early January until the Japanese abandoned Rabaul in mid-February.

Medal of Honor winner Gregory "Pappy" Boyington, of Black Sheep Squadron fame, flew F4U Corsair fighters from Bougainville. Boyington was shot down over the sea and presumed missing during a raid on Rabaul. He was, in fact, taken prisoner aboard a Japanese submarine and spent the rest of the war in Japanese prisoner of war camps. Boyington was being held at the infamous Omori camp at the end of the war.[58]

Nixon's Fitness Reports place him on Bougainville from January 1 until March 1, 1944.[59] Koonce described Nixon as an excellent officer, hard working, and trustworthy. Colonel Carl J. Fleps, the Route Two Superintendent, recommended Nixon for a citation.[60]

Nixon subsequently moved up to the Green Islands. Located 135 miles northwest of Empress Augusta Bay, Green Islands airbases again cut the distance to Rabaul in half. PT boats took a small scouting party into the Green Islands on January 10 and on January 30 came back with a reinforced reconnaissance party. The latter group scouted landing zones on the beaches and investigated airfield sites. A force of six thousand largely New Zealand troops invaded the islands on February 15. The invasion fleet passed into the lagoon and put the main force ashore on Nissan Island. Avenger torpedo bombers and Dauntless fighter aircraft provided cover, but the Japanese resistance was so light that the aircraft returned to base without dropping a bomb.[61] Navy Seabees began constructing an airstrip and a PT boat base before Nissan was completely cleared.

Fleps ordered Nixon to take a crew of seven enlisted men to the Green Islands on March 1, 1944.[62] Crewman Joseph Ray Tolman recalls:

> I took a SCAT flight up to Bougainville from Guadalcanal
> to stage out to the Green Islands. Lieutenant Nixon, our

commanding officer, and Lieutenant James Stewart, our executive officer, along with our seven enlisted men, flew out of Piva Uncle in an R4D. The crew consisted of two pharmacy mates, two aircraft mechanics, two cargo handlers, and one personnel handler.

We were supposed to be the first flight into the new fighter air strip on the Green Islands, but we were waved off because of a soft spot in the runway. When we flew in the next day, an aircraft returning from a raid on Rabaul had made an emergency landing there. So we were the second plane to land.

Our SCAT unit set up operations and living area at the landing end of the fighter airstrip. At first we had just a Quonset hut and three tents. The tents had floors and screened sides, so were reasonably comfortable. Nixon and Stewart had their own tents. Although we were not under aerial attack, the Japanese Marines left on the island would snipe at the Seabees from time to time.[63]

Nixon reports that he landed at the Green Islands in PBY.[64] Probably he visited the Green Island airstrip construction site and then returned to his duties at Bougainville.

The airstrip was scheduled to be finished by March 5, but the soft spot in the runway had to be repaired before the strip was ready for action. By March 6, the Seabees completed the fighter airstrip along with roads and supporting facilities. This was the day that the SCAT crew arrived. Not wasting any time, the Seabees set to work building a bomber airfield alongside the fighter strip.

The Green Island fighter strip was completed just in time. On March 8, aircraft stationed at Bougainville relocated to the strip to escape a Japanese attack.[65] Japanese ground troops assaulted the Empress Augusta Bay perimeter, bringing Piva Uncle and Piva Yoke under artillery fire. It took the Japanese army four months to mount a sustained attack on the perimeter. Despite initial successes, American troops pushed the Japanese back— inflicting 2,400 dead and 3,000 wounded.[66] An ingenious method used to help defeat the Japanese attackers was to bounce search-light beams off the low-lying clouds. When the Japanese attacked the perimeter's defenses at night, they were illuminated and repulsed.[67]

Japanese troops on Bougainville were hardly in any shape to mount an effective assault on the American position. When the Allies interdicted Japanese supply convoys, their daily food ration dipped below the equivalent of one pound of rice. By growing their own rice and sweet potatoes, their equivalent food intake quadrupled. Even shelter was a problem; Japanese troops resorted to living and storing provisions in caves.

The first SCAT cargo aircraft landed at the Green Islands on March 11 carrying three thousand pounds of mail.[68] Two weeks later, Admiral Halsey visited the Green Islands on a farewell tour prior to taking command of the Third Fleet. He lavished praise on the Seabees for their airstrip construction heroics.[69]

The Green Islands airstrip was a red-alert area requiring cargo to be unloaded, and the aircraft to be reloaded, as fast as possible. Tolman explains how this was done under Nixon's direction:

> With big groups of aircraft carrying 5,500 pounds of cargo each way, it was necessary to move the static weight as quickly as possible. Passengers could walk, and litters usually had extra handlers. We devised a program where we arranged for the units receiving a full load of cargo to send trucks and men to pick up their cargo directly from the aircraft. Those with heavy loads going out did the same in reverse order. If an aircraft had a number of different consignments, we would off load the cargo onto our trucks and have the consignees pick up their material from them. Out going cargo on our loading dock was transferred to our trucks for loading an empty aircraft. With this help from the organizations that received the bulk of the static weight, we were able to unload and load the aircraft with an average on the ground time of eight

minutes per aircraft per flight. Our SCAT detachment eventually received a Unit Citation for expediting cargo this way.[70]

After Nixon rotated out, the practice of loading cargo directly onto the consignee's trucks was discontinued, and the SCAT crew was enlarged.

Nixon's off hours were filled with writing letters, reading, and playing poker. Nixon's poker prowess became legendary—but greatly exaggerated. Lester Wroble recalls:

> I ran into Nixon again when my Patrol Service Unit was transferred to the Green Islands. He was running the hamburger stand over by the air strip and playing a lot of poker. Nixon was a careful player. He never lost big. There were some very large pots sometimes, but Nixon was not in them.[71]

Nixon passed up an opportunity to have dinner with celebrated aviator Charles Augustus Lindbergh because he had agreed to host a poker game.[72] In his memoirs, Nixon was incredulous that he missed this chance, but he recalled that the etiquette surrounding poker games was taken very seriously.[73] Nixon corrected this oversight when he invited Lindbergh to dinner at the White House.

First recipient of the Distinguished Flying Cross and a national hero, Lindbergh secured an appointment as a United Aircraft civilian representative studying the F4U Corsair fighter aircraft's performance in combat. He flew his first mission out of the Green Islands on May 22, 1944, accompanying three Corsairs over Rabaul. On Emirau Island, he attended a reception for Halsey, conferred with Medal of Honor winner Major Joseph Jacob Foss, and flew several bombing and strafing missions over Kavieng. Lindbergh moved on to Nadzab, New Guinea, where he flew P-38 Lightning fighters. Later he joined the 475th Fighter Group in Hollandia and strafed barges along the sea coast. While flying with the 475th, Lindbergh developed and demonstrated fuel management techniques that greatly increased the P-38's range.[74] This was a major contribution to MacArthur's campaign, as fewer

SCAT nurse Dorothy Sawyer was forced to overnight on the Green Islands due to rapidly deteriorating weather.

Courtesy of Richard Nixon Library and
Birthplace and the Richard Nixon Estate

island bases were required for airstrips. While on patrol off Ceram Island on July 28, 1944, Lindbergh shot down a Japanese Sonia fighter aircraft. During his four months in the Pacific, the 42-year-old Lindbergh flew 50 combat missions and logged 178 combat hours.[75]

Dorothy Sawyer was a surprise overnight visitor to the male-garrisoned Green Islands. Sawyer, a young SCAT nurse, and the flight crew were grounded because of deteriorating weather. Nielson, copilot of the SCAT flight that brought Sawyer, relates:

The weather was turning for the worse so our pilot, Gary Monroe, chose to stay overnight, rather than risk an uncertain flight. Dick Nixon, the local SCAT Officer in Charge, took us to dinner in the mess tent. The food was very good, as the navy and marine cooks seemed to have a way of disguising the rations. After dinner Dick took us to a makeshift club, which was little more than a bamboo lean-to on the back of one of the Quonset huts. It had a improvised counter and served beer, as I remember.

Dorothy was put up for the night in Dick's Quonset hut office, and two guards were assigned. The hut was about 20 feet long and 10 feet high and had a lock on the door. Gary and I slept in Dick's tent, which was one of those pyramidal designs with a floor and a frame around the sides. I wound up sleeping on a stretcher and awoke stiff and sore the next day. That was the only time I met Dick personally during the war.[76]

On May 3, the SCAT Route Two Superintendent ordered Nixon from Bougainville to Espiritu Santo and New Caledonia for temporary aviation duty and to return there.[77] In any light, he was back on the Green Islands by June 5.[78] On June 14, Nixon received orders to terminate his duties on the Green Islands and report to the SCAT commander on Espiritu Santo.[79] Tolman remembers that SCAT officials recalled Nixon to help set up a new air transport unit that was headed to the Marianas.[80]

Nixon's last overseas Fitness Report places him at the Green Islands from April 1 through July 2, 1944, although again he appears to have moved on prior to that date.[81] Koonce rated Nixon's performance as officer in charge of the Green Islands SCAT unit as Exceptional.

Within three weeks of receiving the Espiritu Santo assignment, Nixon was ordered back to the States.[82] He took a flight to Hawaii on July 9 and arrived on July 10.[83] Nixon boarded the 14,000-ton transport ship USS *George F. Elliott* (AP105). *Elliott* docked in San Diego on July 17, 1944, and Nixon reported to the Naval Air Station San Diego for reassignment.[84]

After a three-week leave, Nixon joined the Fleet Air Wing 8 in Alameda, California. He was a building and grounds officer, with responsibility for three hangars and their adjacent areas.[85] His supervisor, Peter Boyle, remarked on Nixon's Fitness Report that he performed his duties in an excellent manner. In late November, Nixon was ordered to the Bureau of Aeronautics in Washington, D.C., for instruction in military contract termination.[86] He boarded a train in Los Angeles on December 19. From December 30, 1944, to January 29, 1945, Nixon attended an Army Industrial College Contracts Termination course at the Pentagon.[87]

Upon graduation, Nixon worked for several weeks in the New York City Navy Contracts Office, and then moved on to a number of assignments involving the winding up of production contracts with aircraft supply firms. Nixon worked for two months at the Barr Budd Company in Philadelphia.[88] He spent two months at various local sites, three months as assistant to the commanding officer for termination in New York City, and four months as officer in charge of negotiations with the Glen L. Martin Company in Baltimore.[89] Frequently, his assignments were so short that his supervisors did not complete his Fitness Report ratings. They did include such comments as: excellent, entirely satisfactory, military and personal character excellent, outstanding ability, and unusual tact and judgement.

Nixon was promoted to lieutenant commander in October 1945. Following a successful interview to become the Republican candidate for California's Twelfth Congressional District seat, Nixon requested a release from service. He was honorably discharged from active duty on December 31, 1945.

Nixon returned to Whittier, California, in January 1946 and successfully campaigned against Democratic incumbent Representative Horace Jeremiah "Jerry" Voorhis. He won the election by 65,586 votes to 49,994. Thirty-four-year-old Nixon was sworn in as a member of the Eightieth Congress in January 1947. He was assigned to the Education and Labor Committee, which produced the Taft-Hartley Act; the Herter Committee, which investigated the need for the Marshall Plan; and the House Committee on Un-American Activities, which investigated subversive organizations. The latter assignment catapulted Nixon to national fame as he doggedly pursued the Alger Hiss case. He won reelection to the House in 1948.

In 1950, Nixon defeated Democratic Congresswoman Helen Gahagan Douglas for a Senate seat from California. Republican presidential candidate Dwight David Eisenhower selected Nixon as his running mate in 1952. The ticket won a landslide victory over Illinois governor Adlai Stevenson and Senator John Jackson Sparkman. Nixon was 40 years old when he became vice president in January 1953. In June, he was promoted to commander in the Naval Reserve.

Nixon traveled abroad extensively, representing the United States and the Eisenhower administration. Eisenhower's heart attack in 1955 and subsequent illnesses elevated the office of vice president to national attention. Eisenhower and Nixon won the 1956 presidential election, as they easily defeated Stevenson and Tennessee Senator Estes Kefauver.

Nixon became the Republican candidate for president in 1960 and campaigned from a position of strength. He and his vice-presidential running mate Henry Cabot Lodge Jr. lost to the Democratic ticket of Kennedy and Johnson by less than 0.4 percent of the popular vote. Nixon returned to California and joined the Los Angeles law firm of Adams, Duque, and Hazeltine. He sought the governorship of California in 1962, but was handily defeated by incumbent Edmund Gerald "Pat" Brown.

Nixon moved to New York City in 1963 and joined the law firm of Mudge, Stern, Baldwin, and Todd. The firm changed its name to Nixon, Mudge, Rose, Guthrie, and Alexander.[90] In 1967, Nixon's law firm merged with the law firm of Caldwell, Trimble, and Mitchell to form Nixon, Mudge, Rose, Guthrie, Alexander, and Mitchell.[91] Nixon traveled the country supporting various Republican candidates and earning their backing for another run at the presidency. He retired from the Naval Reserve in June 1966.

After rolling up 1968 Republican primary victories, Nixon won the party nomination on the first ballot. He chose Maryland Governor Spiro Theodore Agnew as his vice-presidential running mate.

Nixon and Agnew defeated the democratic candidate Hubert Horatio Humphrey and his running mate Edmond Sixtus Muskie. The popular vote was 31,710,470 to 30,898,055, and the Electoral College vote was 301 to 191. Alabama Governor George Corley Wallace's third-party candidacy threatened to throw the election into the House of Representatives but did not carry enough electoral votes to do so.

During Nixon's first term in office as the 37th president, he welcomed home the Apollo 11 astronauts, signed the Strategic Arms Limitation Treaty with the Soviet Union, created a Federal revenue-sharing program with the States, initiated a broad environmental protection effort, and opened trade and cultural relationships with mainland China. He nominated Warren Earl Burger, Harry Andrew Blackmun, Lewis Franklin Powell, and William Hubbs Rehnquist for seats on the Supreme Court. Nixon visited Peking to begin the diplomatic normalization process, and he traveled to Moscow to finalize agreements on issues ranging from arms control to a joint trade commission. Domestic unrest over the American involvement in the Vietnam War and the related invasion of Cambodia continued.

Nixon and Agnew were renominated by the 1972 Republican National Convention and faced the Democratic ticket of Senator George Stanley McGovern and Robert Sargent Shriver Jr. McGovern was a decorated world War II B-24 pilot.[92] Nixon and Agnew won the election handily. The popular vote was 46,740,323 to 28,901,598, and the Electoral College vote was 520 to 17. Nine months after inauguration, Agnew resigned from office, pleading No Contest to an income tax evasion charge. Nixon chose House Minority Leader Gerald Rudolph Ford to replace Agnew. Ford was the first vice president to be appointed to the office under the rules of the 25th Amendment.

In his second term of office, Nixon began withdrawing American forces from Vietnam, directed Secretary of State Henry Alfred Kissinger to negotiate a cease-fire in the Middle East, and battled inflation arising largely out of the oil price hike leveed by the OPEC nations. The burglary at the Democratic National Headquarters in the Watergate Office Building, its subsequent cover-up, and campaign finance irregularities led to a Senate investigation and several trials. Nineteen government or campaign finance officials, including three cabinet officers, were convicted. Nixon resigned from office on August 8, 1974, while impeachment proceedings were under way in the House of Representatives.

The Nixons moved to their residence near San Clemente, California, and he took up writing his memoirs. One month after leaving office, President Gerald Ford pardoned him. The Nixons moved to New York City in 1980, and relocated to Park Ridge, New Jersey, in 1981. Nixon wrote six more books. He died on April 22, 1994, at the age of 81, and is buried at the Richard Nixon Library and Birthplace in Yorba Linda, California.

Nixon held elective office for 19 years. He served in the navy for three and a half years of which one year was in the Pacific Theater. Nixon remained in the Naval Reserve for 20 years after his discharge. For his service in the Pacific Theater, he was awarded the Asiatic-Pacific Campaign Medal with two engagement stars, the American Campaign Medal, and the World War II Victory Medal.

Nixon received a citation for his work on Bougainville and the Green Islands from the South Pacific Area commander, Admiral John H. Newton:

> For meritorious and efficient performance of duty as Officer-in-Charge of the South Pacific Combat Air Transport Command at Bougainville and later at Green Islands from January 1 to July 16, 1944. During this period Lt. Nixon displayed sound judgement and initiative in organizing South Pacific Combat Air Transport Command activities at both Bougainville and Green Islands. He established the efficient liaison which made possible the immediate supply by air of vital material and key personnel and the prompt evacuation of battle casualties from these stations to rear areas. His

able leadership, tireless efforts and devotion to duty were in keeping with the highest traditions of the United States Naval Service.[93]

He also received a commendation for his work on ending military production contracts from Rear Admiral H. B. Sallada, chief of the Bureau of Aeronautics:

> As Bureau of Aeronautics Contracting Officer for Termination for the period 19 August 1945 to 30 November 1945, you performed duties of great responsibility with outstanding initiative, skill and fairness. Your devotion to duty was an inspiration to all who served with you. These outstanding services were in accordance with the highest traditions of the Naval Service.[94]

Chapter 4
Gerald R. Ford
Officer of the Deck

Gerald Rudolph Ford Jr. was a partner in the Grand Rapids, Michigan, law firm of Ford and Buchen when he heard the announcement that the Japanese had attacked the American Pacific Fleet at Pearl Harbor. He applied for a navy commission and asked for an assignment in Naval Intelligence. Joining the navy was a natural choice for Ford because Grand Rapids had a well-established Navy Reserve program, and he had been an active member of the Sea Scouts.[1] When he discovered how long it might take to join the intelligence branch, Ford applied for the navy's V-5 flight-training program. He maintained an active interest in working in Naval Intelligence and later considered transferring assignments.[2] Had he persevered, he would have been stationed in Washington, D.C., not long after John Kennedy transferred to South Carolina.

Ford contacted Lieutenant Commander Thomas J. Hamilton who was in charge of V-5 physical fitness instructor training. Hamilton, an All Star Naval Academy quarterback, was recruiting young football coaches as instructors and knew Ford from his Yale coaching days.[3] After passing a physical examination, Ford was commissioned an ensign on April 13, 1942. He reported to the Naval Academy at Annapolis, Maryland, for training in the navy's aviation cadet V-5 Instructors' School. Upon graduation, Hamilton sent Ford to the V-5 Pre-Flight School at Chapel Hill,

North Carolina. College campuses were frequently used for such schools because service in the military had stripped the schools of a large fraction of their student bodies, thereby leaving buildings and administrations largely idle.

The navy encouraged competitive sports, which were expected to make pilots physically and mentally sharp to help prepare them for combat. Ford coached football, soccer, and boxing. Beginning as a platoon leader, he moved up to battalion commander for the 7th and 13th Battalions. Later he transferred to headquarters as officer in charge of incoming battalions, quartering of cadets, and preparation of cadet records.[4] Ford was promoted to lieutenant (jg) in June 1942 and to lieutenant in March 1943 while at Chapel Hill.

During the little spare time that he had, Ford took private pilot's lessons hoping to become an aviator. Advancing age—29 was considered too old—and poor eyesight were too great a hurdle to overcome, so Ford applied for combat service. After 12 months at Chapel Hill, Ford was ordered to the New York Shipbuilding Corporation in Camden, New Jersey, for duty in fitting out the new light aircraft carrier USS *Monterey* (CVL 26).[5]

The *Independence* class *Monterey* was a converted light cruiser (the USS *Dayton*) of the *Cleveland* class. *Dayton*'s keel was laid down in December 1941, and *Monterey* was launched in February 1943. The Pacific war was rapidly becoming a carrier war, and the fastest way to obtain carriers was to add flight decks to hulls that were already being built. *Independence* class carriers were smaller than the fleet carriers, but could be turned out in large numbers. *Monterey* had a displacement of 11,000 tons, a length of 622 feet, a beam of 109 feet, and a speed of 32 knots. Manned by a crew of 1,569, *Monterey* carried 33 aircraft. By comparison, *Essex* class carriers had a displacement of 33,000 tons, a length of 901 feet, a beam of 130 feet, and a speed of 34 knots. *Essex* class carriers were manned by a crew of 3,373 and carried 86 aircraft.

USS *Monterey* under way

Courtesy of USS *Monterey* CVL-26 Association

Carriers were needed in a hurry. In the early stages of the war, five carriers—*Lexington* (CV 2), *Saratoga* (CV 3), *Yorktown* (CV 5), *Enterprise* (CV 6), and *Hornet* (CV 8)—were based in Hawaii, and two—*Ranger* (CV 4) and *Wasp* (CV 7)—were stationed in the Atlantic.[6] *Lexington* was lost in the Battle of the Coral Sea, and *Yorktown* was lost at Midway. *Wasp* joined the depleted Pacific carrier group, leaving only *Ranger* in the U.S. Atlantic fleet. Within a few months, *Wasp* was lost while escorting a convoy to Guadalcanal, and *Hornet* was lost in the battle of Santa Cruz Islands. When Ford arrived for duty on the *Monterey* in May, *Enterprise*, which was badly in need of an overhaul, left for home, leaving only *Saratoga* and the newly arrived British carrier HMS *Victorious* in the South Pacific.

Ford assumed command of two junior officers and 90 enlisted men.[7] Captain Lestor T. Hundt appointed Ford as Second Division officer as well as the ship's athletic officer.[8] His division handled anchoring, mooring, and fueling lines at sea. During battle, Ford's men operated half of *Monterey*'s 40 millimeter anti-aircraft guns. He left *Monterey* in June for a two-week 40 millimeter gun training course and returned to join *Monterey* for its August shakedown cruise to the Caribbean.[9] Exercises were conducted in the sheltered inland sea. En route *Monterey* stopped in Port of Spain, Trinidad, where Ford was placed in charge of the Shore Patrol detachment.[10]

Carrier accommodations and food service were good. Officers lived in cabins in the forward part of the ship, where—

depending on rank—one to four men occupied a cabin. Ford remembers:

> My first cabin assignment was with a ship's doctor. He was senior to me so had the lower bunk. I don't recall where the cabin was located, but we were junior officers, so probably just below the flight deck on the starboard side. The doctor and I had a wash bowl, two beds—lower and upper bunks—and two small closets. We shared bathroom facilities with others.
>
> My second cabin-mate was Air Group 28 Intelligence Officer Lieutenant Commander Thomas S. Gates. After the war, he became Secretary of the Navy and, subsequently, Secretary of Defense.[11]

Meals were served in the officer's ward room, which could seat one hundred men. A typical meal included meat, vegetable, potatoes, and dessert. When in port, the officers designated a mess officer who collected money and purchased specialty items for their meals.[12]

Food was good for enlisted men as well. William Terheun recalls:

> I was a medical technician on the *Monterey*. The crew were divided into four shifts, which rotated duty around the clock. We ate in three mess halls when we were not at General Quarters. Breakfast was served before the aircraft were launched; that might include pancakes or cornbread and beans. Eggs and milk were made from powder when we were at sea. Lunch might be creamed beef on toast or bean soup. Dinner was often hamburger, meatloaf, or fish. Chicken was often served on Sunday. Coffee was available on station from 4:00 A.M. to 11:00 A.M., and sandwiches were provided when we were at General Quarters.[13]

Monterey left for the Pacific via the Panama Canal in September, stopping in San Diego to replace aircraft. She arrived in

Pearl Harbor in October, where Ford completed a two-day course in fire fighting.

While not in a combat zone, Ford oversaw the conditioning of *Monterey*'s officers and enlisted men. Space and duty schedules made it difficult to conduct calisthenics or large-scale sports, so Ford introduced basketball.[14] He had the ship's forward elevator lowered to provide a court 40 feet by 44 feet and hung backboards from the stanchions on the port and starboard sides of the elevator. Two teams of four or five men played for eight minutes, then rotated off the court and back on again. When in port, both elevators were lowered to accommodate basketball and volleyball.[15]

Admiral Nimitz created two fighting forces using the same ships. When Vice Admiral Raymond Ames Spruance was in command, the carrier task force was designated Task Force 58. When

**Ford tipping the ball during a basketball game
in *Monterey*'s forward aircraft elevator**

United States National Archives

Admiral Halsey was in command, the carrier force was designated Task Force 38. If additional vessels were involved, such as troop ships carrying amphibious forces, the armadas were designated Fifth Fleet and Third Fleet, respectively. Early in the war, Admiral King ordered that the carriers operate independently, so as to minimize the risk of loss of more than one carrier. When the carriers began operating together, they were designated as task groups with a numbering system appropriate to the carrier task force.

As the carrier fleet grew, Nimitz ordered raids on Japanese island outposts. *Yorktown, Essex,* and *Independence* attacked Marcus Island in August 1943. In early September, *Princeton* (CVL 23), and *Belleau Wood* (CVL 24) attacked Baker Island. *Lexington, Princeton,* and *Belleau Wood* attacked Tarawa in the Gilbert Islands several weeks later. In early October six carriers—*Essex, Yorktown, Independence, Belleau Wood, Lexington*, and *Cowpens* (CVL 25)—struck Wake Island.

Monterey experienced its first combat action in November.[16] She joined *Enterprise* and *Belleau Wood* steaming 2,500 miles southwest of Hawaii to attack Makin Atoll (now Butaritari) in the Gilbert Islands. During seven days of patrolling off Makin, enemy aircraft attacked the group four times without serious damage to the ships.

Monterey and *Bunker Hill* (CV 17) patrolled off Makin and Tarawa for five days in late November. In early December *Monterey* and *Bunker Hill* joined Task Group 50.8 under the direction of Rear Admiral Willis Augustus Lee. Moving 500 miles west, the three carriers supported Lee's surface ship bombardment of Nauru Island. Sixteen-inch and five-inch naval shells blasted the island's airbase, while carrier aircraft flew air cover and conducted air strikes.

In mid-December *Monterey* and *Bunker Hill* departed for Espiritu Santo one thousand miles south. On Christmas Day, the two carriers supported Halsey's campaign against the Japanese stronghold of Rabaul by attacking Kavieng, New Ireland. Halsey

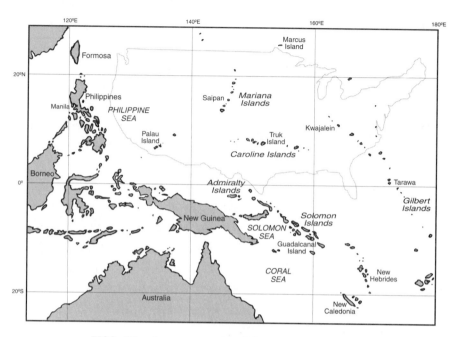

**USS *Monterey* operated in an area larger
than the United States from 1943 to 1944.**

drew the Kavieng fighters off with a raid on the Japanese-occupied island of Buka north of Bougainville, thereby leaving the port and shipping open to attack. Only a few ships were in the harbor at Christmas, so *Monterey* and *Bunker Hill* obliged by attacking again on New Year's Day and then again on January 4, 1944.[17] The battle group came under aircraft attack twice. *Monterey* and *Bunker Hill* returned to Espiritu Santo for rest and reprovisioning.

Monterey moved 1,200 miles northeast and rejoined Lee's Task Group 58.3 at Funafuti Atoll in the Ellice (now Tuvalu) Islands. *Bunker Hill* and *Cowpens,* as well as the battleships *Iowa* (BB 61) and *New Jersey* (BB 62), were included in the group. They steamed 1,400 miles northwest and attacked Kwajalein in the Marshall Islands. Moving northwest an additional 400 miles, the task group conducted air strikes on Eniwetok also in the Marshall Islands before anchoring at Majuro Atoll in the Marshalls on February 4. Occupied by U.S. Naval forces in January, Majuro quickly became a major service and supply center for the Pacific Fleet. Its 56 islets enclose a lagoon 20 miles long by 7 miles wide.

Japanese troops occupied nearby Wotje, Maloelop, Jaluit, and Mille Islands, but those islands were not invaded by U.S. forces. Rather, marine fighter aircraft operating from Majuro's airfields simply neutralized the Japanese forces for the balance of the war.[18] Among the fighter pilots operating out of Majuro was Marine Lieutenant John Herschel Glenn Jr. He flew 59 combat missions in an F4U Corsair over a period of 8 months, earning 2 Distinguished Flying Crosses and 10 Air Medals.[19]

Although Ford saw action directing the aft antiaircraft guns, he wanted a more challenging assignment.[20] After several months of training, Ford qualified as officer of the deck under way in February.[21] Ford relates that his duties were exactly as described in the regulations.[22]

Officially, the officer of the deck is the officer on watch who is in charge of the safety and operation of the ship. He represents the captain and is superior to all officers except the captain and the executive officer. The officer of the deck supervises navigation, ship handling, communications, reports, and the watch team, insuring that the captain's orders are carried out.[23] Each officer of the deck generally stands a four-hour watch while under way. He may stand a two-hour Dog Watch when schedules are shifted for meals.[24] The quartermaster keeps track of noteworthy events in a ship's deck log, and the officer of the deck reviews and signs the log at the end of his shift. The navigator signs the daily deck log and certifies the log at the end of the month; the captain approves the log at the end of the month.[25] A sample *Monterey* log entry illustrates a busy shift:

8 to 12

Steaming as before. 0826 to 0838 Launched aircraft on course 070, speed 10 knots (97 RPM). 0828 to 0844 CONNER (DD-582) alongside starboard quarter receiving...personnel for further transfer to BARNES (CVE-20) to pick up replacement aircraft for this vessel...0915 Maneuvering on various courses at various speeds for approach on tanker. 0920 Alongside tanker PAMANSET (AO-85). 0932 Towline secured to tanker. 0940 Commenced fueling ship....1017 Gasoline hose connected. 1020 Commenced pumping on gasoline hose. 1128 Completed fueling ship having received 309,960 gallons of fuel oil...1144 Cast off from tanker, and proceeding to flying station.

> Signed
> G. R. Ford Jr.
> Lieut. USNR[26]

Signalman 1/c Karl F. Herbst served on the *Monterey* from her commissioning until the end of the war. His assignment was to send and receive Morse code messages between ships using *Monterey*'s 12-inch shielded searchlight. Herbst remembers:

> I was stationed on the bridge when on duty. Gerald Ford was the officer of the deck under way, which meant that he was in command of the ship when the captain was not on the bridge. He was also the athletic officer. I thought Ford was a friendly and intelligent officer and very much a gentleman.[27]

Officer of the deck John F. Latham describes the scene:

> Monterey's bridge was about 12 feet by 20 feet, with port and starboard wings for observation. The bridge contained a helm, radar repeater, compass, TBS radio, and the captain's chair. There was also a small chart room. The bridge was commanded at differing times by the captain, executive officer, or the officer of the deck. Staff consisted of the helmsman, the quartermaster, several signal men, and several lookouts in the wings. At General Quarters, a division officer serving as the officer of the deck returned to his station, and the position was filled by the assistant navigator.[28]

In battle, the executive officer was stationed at the bow or stern of the ship, so that he and the captain would not both be killed by an attack on the bridge.[29]

Monterey, now part of Spruance's Task Force 58, sailed west 1,200 miles in mid-February and attacked Truk Atoll in the Caroline Islands. Truk was well fortified and was the primary anchorage for the Japanese Central Fleet. A majority of the Japanese heavy surface forces withdrew after receiving intelligence reports that a large force was approaching. Japanese battleships and cruisers sailed to the Palau Islands, while the aircraft carriers were split between Singapore and the seas around Japan. After the February attack on Truk, the Japanese never anchored their entire fleet together again.

By noon of the first day, Task Force 58's fighter aircraft controlled the air over Truk. This cleared the way for strafing and bombing of parked aircraft, two light cruisers, two destroyers, and 50 remaining support ships.[30] *Monterey* supported attacks on Truk twice, coming under attack by enemy aircraft. Then *Monterey* steamed 800 miles northwest and attacked Tinian Island in the Marianas before retiring 1,700 miles southwest to Majuro Atoll.

After a brief trip to Pearl Harbor, *Monterey* returned to Majuro. In late March *Monterey*, operating with Task Force 58, sailed west 2,600 miles and attacked Palau Island in the Western Carolines. On its return trip to Majuro, *Monterey* pounded Japanese installations on Woleai Atoll in the Caroline Islands.

Monterey's assistant navigator was forced to leave the ship due to an illness. Ford applied for the position with the encouragement of the ship's navigator, Commander Louis Atwood.[31] Captain Hundt approved his assignment on April 1, knowing Ford had little practical experience.[32] The assistant navigator automatically became the officer of the deck at General Quarters.[33] The latter promotion came as no surprise to fellow officer of the deck Stanley Montunnas:

> There were five or six of us who stood watches as officer of the deck while under way. When the ship went to General Quarters, we returned to our regular assignments and were replaced by the assistant navigator. Jerry Ford was cool, well composed, conscientious, and well liked. Captain Hundt gave Ford the top job.[34]

Ford takes sightings to calculate *Monterey*'s position.

Courtesy of Gerald R. Ford Library

Monterey officer of the deck Horace West agrees:

> We stood watch in four hour shifts. When General Quarters was sounded, the assistant navigator relieved the officer of the deck then turned the watch back to him when it was over.[35]

Captain Stewart H. Ingersoll replaced Captain Hundt on April 10. Before leaving, Hundt prepared Ford's first Fitness Report covering his sea duty. He gave Ford the highest possible mark in Leadership, high marks in all rating categories, and Outstanding with respect to officers of his rank and length of service. Hundt's remarks illustrate his high opinion of Ford's performance to date:

> Lieut. Ford was commissioned as an athletic officer. He
> is a great leader in that specialty. In addition, he has qualified
> and acts as watch officer at sea underway in formation, as a
> division officer and as a 40 millimeter battery officer. He has a
> remarkable personality and an exceptional military character.
> Qualified and heartily recommended for promotion.[36]

Hundt didn't mention Ford's assignment as assistant navigator, presumably because Ford had not been in the position long enough to be evaluated.

Monterey joined *Bunker Hill, Hornet*, and *Cabot* (CVL 28) in Task Group 58.2 as part of Vice Admiral Mark A. Mitscher's Task Force 58. After steaming 2,300 miles southwest, the task force struck installations at Hollandia, New Guinea, in support of General MacArthur's invasion. On its return trip to Majuro in late April, Task Force 58 again struck ships and land installations at Truk. *Monterey* fought off enemy aircraft attacks three times and assisted in sinking a submarine.[37]

Following another Pearl Harbor visit, *Monterey* rendezvoused with Task Force 58 in early June. The task force raided Tinian, Guam, Saipan, and Rota in the Mariana Islands 1,300 miles southeast of Tokyo. *Monterey, Bunker Hill, Wasp*, and *Cabot* patrolled the Marianas for a week, frequently coming under air attack.

In mid-June *Monterey* participated in the Battle of the Philippine Sea. The Fifth Fleet launched an amphibious invasion of Saipan on June 15 with a force of 900 aircraft, 535 ships, and 127,000 invasion troops. Saipan was needed as a base for B-29 bombers to attack the Japanese homeland. The Japanese Mobile Fleet, commanded by Admiral Jisaburo Ozawa, headed for Saipan from Tawi Tawi in the Sulu Sea to engage Spruance's forces and prevent the loss of Saipan. At midnight on June 16, the submarine *Cavalla* (SS 244) spotted a Japanese supply convoy and transmitted that contact the next morning. The next evening *Cavalla* discovered a Japanese task force consisting of

Aircraft launch from _Monterey_ during Marianas Campaign

11 carriers, 5 battleships, 11 heavy cruisers, and an uncounted number of destroyers.[38] On June 19, the submarine _Albacore_ (SS 218) sank Ozawa's flagship carrier, the 31,000-ton _Taiho_, and _Cavalla_ sank the 30,000-ton carrier _Shokaku_.

Spruance, receiving intelligence from the submarines as well as from communication intercepts, prepared to counter Ozawa's thrust, while still protecting the Saipan invasion force. Rather than sending his strike force west to attack Ozawa's Mobile Fleet as his officers wanted, Spruance held his carriers near Saipan to prevent an end run attack on the vulnerable landing forces—a well-known tactic of the Japanese navy.

Ozawa planned to launch his carrier-based aircraft from long range and expected to use the airfields at Guam, Rota, and Yap to refuel and rearm. Spruance dispatched his fighters to destroy Japanese land-based aircraft and used his bombers to neutralize

**Aircraft launching from _Monterey_ to
attack Tinian Island in the Marianas**

Courtesy of United States Navy

the airfields. On June 19, Ozawa launched 326 aircraft from 350 miles west of Saipan to attack the American carriers. What followed was a slaughter. Task Force 58 carrier aircraft downed more than 300 planes, with losses of just 18 fighters and 12 bombers, in what later came to be known as "The Great Marianas Turkey Shoot." One of the secrets of this spectacular success was intercepting the Japanese air controller's radio messages.[39] A second advantage was provided by nature. The atmospheric conditions at flight altitude were such that the aircraft left distinct contrails. American observers could see the Japanese formations coming from tens of miles away and vectored fighters to intercept them.

During the air battle, _Monterey_ came under heavy air attack. _Monterey_'s log records the enemy aircraft engaged:

> 0548 Unidentified aircraft reported to be two Japanese fighters. One plane shot down by MONTEREY'S fighters, bearing 180, 19 miles distant.

1201 Plane shot down bearing 180, distance 2,000 yards. Plane shot down bearing 135, distance 3,000 yards.

1202 Plane shot down bearing 135, distance 4,000 yards.

1308 Four enemy aircraft bearing 070, distance 65 miles. Enemy aircraft were intercepted, bearing 075, distance 60 miles, identified as fifteen torpedo planes.

1418 General quarters, enemy aircraft approaching, six to eight unidentified aircraft bearing 150, distance 20 miles. Firing by ships of the task group commenced. One plane shot down bearing 100, distance 50 miles.

1835 Ships in screen fired at aircraft, no apparent results.

2034 Went to General Quarters, enemy aircraft bearing 230, distance 18 miles.

2134 Firing bearing 325, distance 18 miles.[40]

In addition to General Quarters, Ford had officer of the deck duty from 1600 to 1800 when there was a pause in the air battle.

Late in the afternoon of the second day of battle, Spruance was satisfied that the Saipan invasion fleet was safe. He ordered Mitscher to send 216 Task Force aircraft after Ozawa's Mobile Fleet located 250 miles west of Saipan. The aircraft arrived on the scene at dusk, sank the carrier *Hiyo*, and damaged three carriers. Returning to Task Force 58 in the dark, many planes ditched from a shortage of fuel. Mitscher ordered the carriers to turn on their hooded deck lights and ordered the battleships and destroyers to turn on their searchlights. This action risked exposing the ships to Japanese submarines, but Mitscher had done so successfully at Midway. *Monterey*'s log reads in part:

1613 Commenced flight operations, launched 4 VT, bomb loaded, to participate in strike against enemy surface forces reported bearing 290, distance 215 miles, from this formation.

2114 Commenced flight operations. Recovered 4 torpedo bombers, returned from attack on enemy surface forces, 3 MONTEREY planes and 1 BUNKER HILL plane.

2128 Recovered 1 LEXINGTON fighter plane.

2152 Recovered WASP fighter plane.

2204 Recovered WASP torpedo bomber.

2251 Completed flight operations.[41]

By the end of the following day, rescue operations, including flights over the previous evening's battle scene, picked up 160 pilots and crewmen. The Battle of the Philippine Sea was over as Ozawa retired northwest to Okinawa. He had six carriers and 35 operational aircraft remaining.[42]

Vice Admiral Chichui Nagumo was a bystander to this great air battle. He commanded the Japanese First Air Fleet at Pearl Harbor and in the Indian Ocean, the carrier strike force at Midway, and the Third Fleet in the Solomon Islands with decidedly mixed results. After 16 months in administrative posts in Japan, Nagumo assumed command of the land-based aircraft in the defense of Saipan. Ironically, three of the battleships Nagumo's forces sank at Pearl Harbor participated in the shelling of Saipan. Seeing that the battle was going badly, Nagumo ended his life by the traditional Japanese hara-kiri.[43]

Premier Hideki Tojo was another casualty of the fall of Saipan. Realizing the importance of holding Saipan to avoid Allied bomber strikes on the home islands, Tojo staked his rapidly failing political career on the defense of Saipan. When Saipan fell, Tojo was forced into ignominious retirement.

Four days later *Monterey, Wasp, Bunker Hill,* and *Cabot,* in Task Group 58.2, conducted strikes against Pagan Island north of Saipan, and then steamed 1,200 miles southeast to Eniwetok for three days of rest and provisioning. On July 4, the task group hit Iwo Jima 1,800 miles to the northwest. They returned to Pagan 600 miles south, striking enemy installations and fending off air attacks. In the next two weeks, Task Group 58.2 conducted strikes over Rota and Guam, as well as supporting landing operations on Guam. After temporary duty with several task groups, *Monterey* steamed 1,200 miles east to anchor at Eniwetok for two days before continuing 3,000 miles northeast to Pearl Harbor.

Monterey remained in Pearl Harbor for 24 days, getting under way on August 29.

In early September (about the time George Bush was shot down over Chichi Jima in the Bonin Islands), *Monterey* conducted strikes against Wake 2,400 miles west of Pearl Harbor and continued on to Eniwetok. In mid-September, *Monterey* rendezvoused with Halsey's Third Fleet, which consisted primarily of the Fast Carrier Task Force 38. *Monterey* was assigned to Task Group 38.1, commanded by Vice Admiral John McCain, along with *Wasp, Hornet,* and *Cowpens.* Task Group 38.1 steamed 3,000 miles west to conduct strikes over Manila Bay and Panay Island in the Philippines. Seventeen *Monterey* crew members were wounded when a Japanese fighter strafed her flight deck. Proceeding 2,300 miles southeast, the task group anchored in the Admiralty Islands, north of New Guinea.

In the first week of October, Task Group 38.1 rendezvoused with Task Groups 38.3 and 38.4 and proceeded 2,600 miles northwest to attack Okinawa in the Ryukyu Islands. Carrier aircraft swept over Luzon Island, and bombed and strafed targets in Formosa. The task group was located 50 miles east of Formosa when Japanese aircraft unleashed a vicious counterattack. *Monterey*'s log for October 13 records the incident in part:

> 1830 Enemy planes observed approaching formation from eastward.
>
> 1833 Enemy planes engaged with heavy automatic weapons by formation.
>
> 1836 CANBERRA in station 4180 struck by aerial torpedo.
>
> 1857 CANBERRA reported dead in the water and forced to drop out of formation.
>
> 1859 WICHITA ordered to tow CANBERRA - engagement with enemy planes broken off. Estimated 6 to 8 twin-engine planes shot down by the formation. BELL (DD 587) and BURNS (DD 588) detached to screen WICHITA and CANBERRA.

The action around *Monterey* continued into the next day:

> 1840...Screen opened fire on enemy aircraft bearing 110.
>
> 1849 MONTEREY opened fire. HOUSTON (CL 81) reported to MONTEREY by blinker signal, hit by torpedo, dead in water, 2 DDs, COWELL (DD 547) and McCALLA (DD 488) ordered to stand by.
>
> 1851 MONTEREY opened fire.
>
> 1931...BOSTON (CL 81) and GRAYSON (DD 437) ordered to standby to assist HOUSTON (CL 81), when at 1932 HOUSTON reported abandoning ship.
>
> 2158...On orders ComThirdFlt, BOSTON (CA 69) took HOUSTON (CL 81) in tow.[44]

Monterey's gunners manned their battle stations for 24 consecutive hours.[45] Japanese torpedoes damaged the cruisers *Canberra* (CA 70) and *Houston* (CA 30), which reduced their speed to five knots. Not wanting to risk his entire fleet, but unwilling to abandon the damaged ships, Halsey assigned a van of ships including *Cabot* and *Cowpens* to escort the cripples to Ulithi Atoll for repair.

Monterey's flight deck in action

Courtesy of Gerald R. Ford Library (donated by Dwight A. Smith)

Located 360 miles southwest of Guam in the Caroline Islands, Ulithi was occupied by U.S. Naval forces in late September without significant opposition. The atoll was seized for the specific purpose of creating a fleet anchorage. A reef 20 miles long by 10 miles wide enclosed an 80-foot deep lagoon. Seabees rebuilt a former Japanese airstrip on Falalop Island to accommodate air traffic. Headquarters were established on Asor Island, and a recreation center accommodating nine thousand service men was constructed on Mogmog Island. Sorlen Island was designated as a maintenance depot while fuel, ammunition, and spare parts were stored afloat.[46] By October, six thousand repairmen were working at Ulithi.

General MacArthur's long-planned invasion of the Philippines got under way in mid-October. Task Group 38.1 conducted strikes against targets on Luzon and Mindanao in support of army landings on Leyte before Halsey ordered the ships to Ulithi for rest and repair. These welcome orders caused Ford to miss most of what has been called the greatest sea battle of all time. While *Monterey* was heading for Ulithi, the balance of Task Force 38 steamed in the waters east of the Philippines. Halsey was lending support to the invasion and, by Nimitz's order, was on the lookout for a chance to cripple the Japanese carrier fleet.

Japan was desperately seeking a major naval victory so that an honorable end to the war could be negotiated. The Japanese navy devised a complex plan to oppose MacArthur's impending invasion and gain the victory. The Mobile Fleet was divided into three thrusts: Admiral Shoji Nishimura's Southern Force with support from Vice Admiral Kiohide Shima's detachment, Admiral Takeo Kurita's Central Force, and Ozawa's Northern Force. While the Southern and Central thrusts consisted of surface ships, the Northern Force was composed primarily of carriers—with precious few aircraft. Their assignment was to lure Halsey's task force away from the surface ships, even at the risk of losing the carriers. Sacrificing the carriers was not as desperate as may appear. Few carrier aircraft and fewer qualified pilots remained, and, as the

Allies closed in on the homeland, the remaining battles could be fought with land-based aircraft.

Task Force 38 aircraft attacked the Central Force as Kurita approached the San Bernardino Strait through the Sibuyan Sea. Kurita appeared to be defeated as he retreated west with one battleship lost and two damaged. Halsey, still wary, informed his task group commanders that he planned to send Task Force 34—consisting of four battleships, two heavy cruisers, and two light cruisers under Vice Admiral Lee—to intercept Kurita, should he return to the San Bernardino Strait. Halsey had little concern about the Southern Force, which he assumed could be handled by Admiral Thomas C. Kincaid's Seventh Fleet. Having absorbed elements of the Third Fleet for the Philippines invasion, the Seventh Fleet now consisted of 738 ships and could well operate on its own.

Nishimura's Southern Force, composed of the battleships *Fusi* and *Yamashiro*, the heavy cruiser *Mogami*, and four destroyers, *Asagumo, Mitsushio, Shigure*, and *Yamaguno*, entered the Surigao Strait late in the evening of October 24. At midnight Nishimura was met by 39 PT boats which attacked with torpedoes. Twenty-nine destroyers followed the PT boat attacks. But the real surprise to Nishimura were Admiral Jesse B. Oldendorf's six battleships and assorted cruisers arranged across the exit of the narrow strait. Directed by radar fire control systems, the shelling was devastating and largely unreturned. Of Nishimura's entire force, only *Shigure* survived. *Shigure* was one of three destroyers that transported men and supplies through Blackett Strait on August 1, 1943, when PT 109 was rammed and sunk.

This was to be the last battle fought by large surface ships. Shima, arriving late, entered the Surigao Strait with two heavy cruisers, one light cruiser, and four destroyers and was soon in full retreat. Oldendorf's ships pursued and sank one of the destroyers before retiring. Carrier- and land-based aircraft harassed Shima's retreating ships the next day and sank a light cruiser and a destroyer.

Ozawa's Northern force—consisting of one heavy carrier, three light carriers, two converted battleships, two cruisers, and a phalanx of destroyers—was spotted by Task Force 38 search planes northeast of Cape Engano. Ever eager for a fight, and with Kurita backing off, Halsey raced his carriers 300 miles north to attack the Northern Force. Halsey took Task Force 34 with him, leaving the San Bernardino Strait unprotected. Halsey wanted to use the battleships to finish off the Japanese carrier fleet, and he didn't want to leave the task force unprotected from land-based air attack. Halsey didn't inform Kincaid of his actions, because he did not report through MacArthur's chain of command—an arrangement which would have dire consequences.

Halsey's action left Rear Admiral Thomas L. Sprague to cover the northern approach to the landing beaches with 16 escort carriers, 9 destroyers, and 14 destroyer escorts. Sprague arranged his forces in 3 task units designated "Taffy." Taffy 3, the northern most of these units, was stationed off Samar Island. Commanded by Rear Admiral Clifton A. F. Sprague (no relation), Taffy 3 comprised 6 escort carriers, 3 destroyers, and 4 destroyer escorts. The carriers' aircraft were lightly armed because their primary duty was to support the land forces. Taffy 3 was backed up by Rear Admiral Felix B. Stump's Taffy 2, stationed at the north edge of Leyte Gulf. Taffy 1 was arrayed with Oldendorf's battleships guarding the Surigao Strait.

While Halsey's forces were attacking the Northern Force, Kurita's forces returned, debouched from the San Bernardino Strait, and turned south off Samar Island. Soon Kurita's forces rained 18-inch shells down on Taffy 3. Kincaid pleaded with Halsey for help. Halsey was in no position to respond directly, since he was in a battle with Ozawa's Northern Force. He ordered McCain's Task Force 38.1 (which included *Monterey*) to return at flank speed and to launch long-range air attacks on Kurita's Central Force. Initially some six hundred miles from the Philippines with aircraft patrols in the air, McCain closed on Leyte Gulf at high speed, recovering his aircraft as he went. When Task Force 38.1 reached

350 miles from Leyte, McCain launched long-range fighters fitted out with extra fuel tanks. *Monterey*'s October 25 log records the events in part:

0610 Commenced approach on SAUCATUCK (AO-75).

0635 Tanker alongside to starboard.

0655 Commenced refueling ship.

0825 Completed fueling ship having received 14,300 gallons of aviation gasoline, and 204,170 gallons of fuel oil.

0905 Recovered aircraft on 060º, speed 14 knots.

0915...changed course to 270º.

0940 Formation changed speed to 25 knots and changed course to 225º

0946 Formation changed course to 245º and changed speed to 30 knots.

1237 Formation changed course to 070º, changed speed to 20 knots.

1241 to 1254 Launched aircraft

1322 Formation changed course to 225º and changed speed to 30 knots.[47]

Halsey also ordered the escort carriers guarding his oilers in the Philippine Sea to race westward and join the attack. Nineteen-year-old Glenn Edwin Miller, an aviation radio man assigned to a TBM Avenger on board the 7,800-ton escort carrier *Rudyerd Bay* (CVE 81), recalls:

All blowers and unnecessary equipment were turned off, so that maximum power could be applied to the screws. Shuddering and shaking, *Rudyerd Bay* was plowing through moderately heavy seas at an unheard of 19 knots. When the ship pitched downward after cresting a wave, the screws would come out of the water sending out a high-pitched whine. Halsey might as well have not bothered. Our escort carriers could not get within range in time to affect the battle.[48]

With no other choice, Taffy 3's destroyers and destroyer escorts attacked Kurita with wild abandon, even though they carried

5-inch guns compared to Kurita's 18-inch guns. Taffy 3's aircraft went after the Central Force with one hundred-pound bombs meant for shore attacks. In the meantime, the surface ships laid down smoke to conceal the escort carriers.

From the intensity of the attacks, Kurita believed that he had encountered Halsey's force. After a period of indecision, he turned tail and ran. This was a colossal blunder. Kurita's forces were far superior and could have reached MacArthur's invasion forces. The action was intense and confusing, and Kurita felt it better to withdraw and fight again another day. He may also have been influenced by his intelligence reports that McCain had launched a massive air strike.[49] McCain's long-range air attacks proved ineffectual. His aircraft could not carry heavy bombs or torpedoes due to the need for auxiliary fuel tanks. Reaching Luzon the next day, McCain continued air attacks on Kurita's retiring force. Task Group 38.1 then departed for Ulithi, arriving on October 29.

During the second battle of the Philippine Sea, the Japanese introduced a new terror weapon—kamikazes. Kamikazes, literally meaning Divine Wind, were named after storms that devastated Kublai Kahn's forces during attacks on Japan in the thirteenth century. Poorly trained pilots downed a ceremonial cup of saki, took off, headed in the direction of the American fleet, and hurled their aircraft at the ships. Most of the 2,257 kamikazes launched during the waning months of the war were shot down or missed their targets. Their high-speed dive simply put too much pressure on the plane's control surfaces for the pilot to maneuver effectively.

The Japanese fleet suffered heavily in this disastrous attempt to achieve a great victory at all costs. All three of the Imperial Japanese Navy's forces were routed. The Southern Force lost two battleships, a cruiser, a light cruiser, and three destroyers, with three ships damaged. The Central Force lost one battleship and five cruisers with one battleship, five cruisers, and three destroyers damaged. The Northern Force lost one heavy carrier,

**Japanese kamikaze aircraft hits
USS *Intrepid* in the Philippine Sea**

Courtesy of United States Navy

three light carriers, one light cruiser, and two destroyers with one battleship and one light cruiser damaged. Virtually no carrier aircraft remained.

Monterey left Ulithi on November 2 with McCain replacing Mitscher as commander of Task Force 38. On November 5, the Task Force struck targets on Luzon. Temporarily attached to Task Group 38.4, *Monterey* joined a high-speed dash to the Balabac Strait separating Palawan and Borneo in an unsuccessful attempt to intercept the Japanese Fleet. The Task Group returned to patrol off the Philippines. *Monterey*'s aircraft struck shipping in Manila Bay on November 13 and 14 and struck shore installations on November 19. She came under attack by kamikazes twice, but was not hit. Monterey returned to Ulithi on November 22, striking Yap Island along the way.

USS *Monterey* in Ulithi Harbor

Courtesy of United States Navy

Monterey got under way on December 10. Task force air groups attacked targets on Luzon for three days. *Monterey* fighter aircraft attacked Naga, Bulan, and Legaspi airfields with 5-inch rocket and .50 caliber machine gun fire to support the December 15 landings on Mindoro.[50] On December 17, the task force rendezvoused with the Sea Logistic Support Group three hundred miles east of the Philippines to refuel and take on supplies.[51] Seas were high, and heavier weather threatened. Shortly after noon, McCain ordered that all fueling operations cease.

Ford had deck watch on the *Monterey* from midnight until 4:00 A.M. as the weather worsened on December 18. After his watch, he returned to his cabin to sleep. He was soon awakened by a call to General Quarters. Upon completion of his officer of the deck duties on the bridge, he returned to his bunk. What happened next is best described by Ford himself in *A Time to Heal*:

I hadn't been back in my bunk many minutes before I heard the clang of General Quarters again. Waking, I thought I could smell smoke. I went up the passageway and out to the catwalk on the starboard side which runs around the flight deck, where I started to climb the ladder. As I stepped on the flight deck, the ship suddenly rolled about 25 degrees. I lost my footing, fell to the deck flat on my face and started sliding toward the port side as if I were on a toboggan slide. Around the deck of every carrier is a steel ridge about two inches high. It's designed to keep the flight crews' tools from slipping overboard. Somehow, the ridge was enough to slow me. I rolled and twisted into the catwalk below.[52]

Thirty-one-year-old Ford recovered from his fall and returned to the bridge to resume his duties as officer of the deck. He soon learned that *Monterey* was in a full scale typhoon.

Captain Ingersoll was aware that a storm was approaching and ordered that the ship and aircraft be secured for heavy weather.[53] Precautions such as fences on the flight deck, double security watches, and roving repair crews were put in place.[54]

Ingersoll described the worsening storm and the attendant havoc wreaked on *Monterey* in his action report of December 22.[55] The summary that follows is based upon Ingersoll's report, on *Monterey*'s war diary, and on interviews with *Monterey* officers of the deck Horace West and John Davenport.

Shortly after 8:00 A.M. Task Force 38 changed course to 180 degrees, which put the wind and seas on *Monterey*'s starboard quarter. The wind grew to 65 knots, and *Monterey* rolled up to 34 degrees. As the storm worsened, five F6F fighter aircraft tied down to the aft flight deck broke loose and went over the side. Below deck things got worse in a hurry. At 9:08 A.M. a careening mechanic's tool box snapped the tie downs securing an aircraft on the hangar deck. The aircraft smashed into the other fighters and torpedo bombers, severing their tie downs, and starting severe fires. The aircraft's fuel tanks had been drained, but considerable fuel remained in the aft ends of the belly tanks.

Flaming aviation fuel spread to *Monterey*'s second and third decks. The fire-suppression sprinkler system could not be turned on because of damage to the control station. *Monterey*'s forward elevator was blocked by the damaged aircraft, and pilots tried desperately to secure the loose planes. *Monterey*'s air vents, punctured by the careening aircraft on the hangar deck, were funneling smoke and aviation-fuel fumes into the engine and boiler rooms. The space had to be abandoned, and three of the ship's boilers ceased functioning. These boilers were needed to maintain pressure in the fire-fighting hoses as well as to keep *Monterey* under way.

Commander Atwood advised Ingersoll to head into the prevailing seas and not to try to keep up with the rest of the task force.[56] Ingersoll informed his task group commanding officer, and at 9:12 A.M. *Monterey* changed heading to 240 degrees. This maneuver greatly eased the ship's rolling, in spite of increasing storm intensity. At 9:24 A.M. Ingersoll ordered *Monterey* to go dead in the water to conserve steam for fire fighting and heading control. Crew members donned breathing apparatus to keep the pumps and electrical generators operating. When flames threatened ammunition storage lockers adjacent to the hangar, crew men threw .50 caliber, 40 millimeter and 20 millimeter rounds overboard.

Halsey, recognizing the seriousness of *Monterey*'s problems, authorized abandoning the ship—no easy task in a typhoon. The cruiser *New Orleans* (CA 32) and the destroyers *Twining* (DD 540) and *McCord* (DD 534) stood by to rescue the crew. *Monterey*'s damage control teams got the fires in the hangar deck under control at 10:25 A.M., but the potential for shifting, hot wreckage caused Ingersoll to keep *Monterey* dead in the water. Wind speed increased to 70 knots and gusted to 100 knots. Rescue crews reentered the engine and boiler rooms to restart the boilers. By 11:25 A.M. *Monterey*'s boilers were ready to get under way, but Ingersoll chose to remain hove to and maneuver into the prevailing waves. At 4:25 P.M., the wreckage was secured, the seas subsided, and *Monterey* got under way at 15 knots to rejoin the task force. Ford was on the bridge for the entire time that *Monterey* fought the typhoon and fire—nearly 16 hours.[57]

The typhoon devastated Task Force 38's ships and men. Three destroyers—*Hull* (DD 350), *Monaghan* (DD 354), and *Spence* (DD 512)—capsized and sank, leaving 750 dead. Two other light carriers, *San Jacinto* (CVL 30) and *Cowpens*, were severely damaged, along with two escort carriers, three destroyers, and one cruiser.[58] Nineteen additional ships incurred lesser damage and 146 planes were lost.

Three *Monterey* seamen lost their lives and 33 were injured as a result of the storm and hangar deck fire.[59] Seven aircraft were lost overboard, and 11 were damaged beyond repair. The landing ship officer's platform was swept away, and three 20 millimeter guns were damaged. Approximately two-thirds of the hangar deck was gutted. Electrical circuits were destroyed, the sprinkling system's remote controls were knocked out, and ventilation systems were damaged. Radio transmitters were flooded, beams were buckled by the hangar deck fire, and most of the aircraft spares were destroyed. One hundred thousand rounds of .50 caliber ammunition along with tens of thousands of rounds of 20 and 40 millimeter ammunition were jettisoned.

Halsey ordered *Monterey, Cowpens,* and *San Jacinto* to Ulithi for repairs and reprovisioning. Escorted by *Twining* and *McCord*, they arrived in Ulithi on December 21. Upon inspection, the damage to *Monterey* was found to be so extensive that the ship was sent to Bremerton, Washington, for major repairs.

Ford was detached from duty aboard *Monterey* on December 24 and ordered stateside.[60] Captain Ingersoll prepared Ford's Fitness Report for April 10 to December 24, giving him the highest possible marks in Initiative, Leadership, Moral Courage, Cooperation, Loyalty, Perseverence, Endurance, and Military Bearing. He rated Ford Outstanding with respect to officers of his rank and length of service. His remarks:

**Monterey's hangar deck after December 18, 1943, typhoon.
Photo from USS Monterey Action Report, December 22, 1944.**

Courtesy of United States National Archives

Lieut. Ford is an outstanding officer in all respects. He reported to the ship as Athletic Officer and, though valuable in this assignment, his talents were such that he was most valuable to the ship as Assistant Navigator and Officer of the Deck. He has a thorough knowledge and ready grasp of seamanship and tactics. He is steady, reliable, and resourceful. His judgement and well considered recommendations are reliable. He is an excellent navigator and all around ship's officer. His unfailing good humor, pleasing personality and natural ability as a leader made him well liked and respected by officers and men. He is an excellent organizer and can be relied upon for the successful conclusion of any operation which he may under take. His moral and military character is outstanding. He is well fitted and strongly recommended for promotion when due.[61]

Ford flew to Pearl Harbor, arriving on Christmas Day, and continued home to Michigan for his first leave since he joined *Monterey*. Returning to duty on February 9, Ford reported to the Navy Pre-Flight School at St. Mary's College in Moraga, California. He was assigned as an aviation physical and military officer. The navy's policy was to return V-5 instructors to shore duty after a year at sea; Ford had been aboard *Monterey* for 18 months.

Though St. Mary's was his first choice of shore duty, Ford requested duty aboard the new aircraft carrier *Coral Sea* (CV 43) six weeks after arriving. He went so far as to mention he was considering becoming a career naval officer.[62] His request was not approved. In April 1945, Ford transferred to the Naval Air Reserve Training Command, Glenview, Illinois, where he was an instructor and staff officer.

As part of his duties at Glenview, Ford accompanied base commander Rear Admiral O. B. Hardison on a tour of military bases in the South. As the light plane in which the party was traveling approached Chapel Hill, North Carolina, a heavy rainstorm blanketed the area. In the darkness and confusion, the pilot landed the plane on the wrong runway. Overrunning the airstrip, the plane plunged down an embankment and crashed into some trees. Shortly after all the passengers got out, the plane burst into flames.[63]

Ford was promoted to lieutenant commander in October 1945, while stationed at Glenview. Rear Admiral Ingersoll wrote to a Glenview officer:

> You mention that Jerry Ford is at Glenview as Athletic Officer. I suppose he is going out—all the good ones seem to be—but if he is still around please give him very best regards. He was one of the finest officers I have ever seen, and I would be glad to have him anywhere, in any job, at any time. He was the best Officer of the Deck on my carrier, and I shall never forget him.[64]

Thirty-two-year-old Ford was honorably discharged from active duty on February 23, 1946.

Ford returned to Grand Rapids, Michigan. He joined the law firm of Butterfield, Keeney, and Amberg where his former law firm associate, Philip W. Buchen, was a partner. Ford kept himself busy with legal work, community activities, and, eventually, the company of a young lady named Elizabeth Bloomer "Betty" Warren. In June 1948, he filed for the Republican nomination in Michigan's Fifth District to run against three-term Republican Congressman Bartel John Jonkman. Campaigning largely against Jonkman's isolationist record, Ford won the Republican primary by a margin of two to one.

Ford married Betty Warren in October. He continued campaigning and, on November 2, 1948, won the House seat by a comfortable margin. Ford entered the 1949 House session with former naval officers Lyndon Johnson, John Kennedy, and Richard Nixon. He was assigned to the Committee on Public Works. Ford returned to Congress in 1950, in the first of eleven successive reelections. In his second term, Ford gained a seat on the House Appropriations Committee.

Ford was elected the House Republican Conference Chairman, the number three leadership position in the party, in 1963. In June he was honorably discharged from the Naval Reserve. Later that year, President Johnson called upon Ford to serve on the Warren Commission. His fellow Republican Representatives selected 51-year-old Ford as Minority Leader in 1965. He held that post for eight years.

Spiro Agnew resigned the office of vice president on October 10, 1973. Two days later, Nixon formally offered Ford the vice presidency. Under the 25th Amendment to the Constitution, a new vice president must be approved by a majority of the House and the Senate. Ford's confirmation hearings before the Senate Rules Committee and the House Judiciary Committee went smoothly, and both committees recommended approval. Ford was approved as vice president by a vote of 387 to 35 in the House and by a vote of 92 to 3 in the Senate. He took the oath of office on December 6, 1973, at the age of 60. Eight months later, Richard

Nixon resigned the presidency, and Ford became the nation's 38th president.

One of President Ford's first presidential acts was to name Nelson Aldrich Rockefeller as his vice president. The confirmation hearings were delayed, and it wasn't until December 19, 1974, that Rockefeller's nomination was approved by the House and Senate. In perhaps his most well-known act, Ford pardoned Richard Nixon—one month after taking office. The legal work behind the pardon was prepared by Counselor to the President Philip Buchen—Ford's former law partner.

Ford signed into law bills involving energy decontrol, tax cuts, railroad and securities deregulation, education of handicapped children, housing, and antitrust reform. He nominated John Paul Stevens to serve on the Supreme Court. High rates of inflation and unemployment dogged his administration. On the international front, Ford signed the Helsinki Accords on Human Rights and co-hosted the first International Economic Summit. The Vietnam War ended during his presidency.

Ford was a target of two assassination attempts on visits to California, just two weeks apart. Both female attackers were disarmed before they could harm the president.

Ford withstood a vigorous challenge for the 1976 Republican presidential nomination from California Governor Ronald Wilson Reagan. After winning a close roll call vote, Ford campaigned for the presidency with Robert Joseph Dole as his vice-presidential running mate. Dole was a decorated World War II infantry officer.[65] Ford and Dole lost to a Democratic ticket of James Earl Carter and Walter Frederick Mondale by 39,145,977 votes to 40,827,394 votes. The electoral vote was 240 to 297.

After leaving office in January 1977, President and Mrs. Ford moved to Rancho Mirage, California, where they reside today. He wrote several books, is active in the Republican Party, and serves on numerous charitable and corporate boards.

Ford held elective office for 25 years and appointive office for 3 years. He served in the navy for 4 years of which 13 months were in the Pacific Theater. Ford remained in the Naval Reserve for 18 years after his discharge. For his service in the Pacific Theater, Ford was awarded the American Campaign Medal, the Asiatic-Pacific Campaign Medal with a Silver Star and four Bronze Stars, the World War II Victory Medal, and the Philippine Liberation Ribbon with two Bronze Stars.[66]

Chapter 5

George H. W. Bush
Torpedo Bomber Pilot

George Herbert Walker Bush heard an announcement of the Japanese attack on the American Pacific Fleet at Pearl Harbor when he was 17 years old and a senior at Phillips Academy in Andover, Massachusetts. He decided to become a naval aviator when he graduated. Bush had long been interested in aviation, although he had no flying experience.[1] He enlisted in the navy on his 18th birthday, June 12, 1942, and asked for an assignment as an aviation cadet. One week after the battle of Midway and in dire need of pilots, the navy waived its standard requirement of two years of college. Seaman 2/c Bush was assigned to the V-5 Pre-Flight School at the University of North Carolina at Chapel Hill. Upon arrival in August, he joined the Sixth Battalion, Company K, Second Platoon.

A primary goal of the V-5 program was to get the cadets into top physical condition. Lieutenant Gerald Ford was one of the school's 65 physical fitness instructors when Bush attended, but these two future presidents did not meet.[2] Athletic competition and close order drill accompanied class room instruction. Cadets competed in football, soccer, basketball, boxing, swimming, track, wrestling, gymnastics, and tumbling. Bush earned superior ratings in basketball and soccer, two of his favorite high school sports.[3]

In early November, Bush moved to the Naval Air Station Minneapolis, Minnesota, to begin flight training. Classroom instruction included military history, physics, aeronautics, target recognition, communications, navigation, and elements of torpedo and antisubmarine warfare.[4] Bush took his first flight in an NP-1 Spartan open-cockpit trainer aircraft on November 10, 1942. Among the many maneuvers he accomplished were an inverted spin, an Immelman, and a falling leaf.[5] Eleven days after his first flight, Bush successfully soloed in the NP-1 Spartan. Additional training included night flights and aerial acrobatics. He completed his preliminary flight training in early February 1943, having accumulated more than 80 hours of flight time.

Bush was assigned to the Naval Air Station Corpus Christi, Texas, for further flight training. After flight checkout, he flew an SNV-1 Vultee low-wing training aircraft. Bush learned to fly by instruments in a Link Trainer in March, and in April he flew advanced aerial acrobatics in the North American AT-6 Texan.[6] He attended classes in celestial navigation, strategy, tactics, practical navigation, and airplane identification. Bush was selected as a torpedo bomber trainee and moved to nearby Waldron Field.[7] When asked how he got into torpedo bombers, Bush replied, "We were asked for our preference. I chose torpedo bombers, and they chose me."[8] He completed the flight-training course three days before his 19th birthday and was commissioned an ensign in the Naval Reserve. Reportedly, he was the youngest pilot in the navy at that time.[9]

Bush transferred to the Naval Air Station Fort Lauderdale, Florida, where he flew the Grumman TBF Avenger torpedo bomber. After a month of familiarization flights, Bush practiced carrier landing techniques on a marked-off section of the base runway. In August he moved to the Naval Air Station Glenview, Illinois. Bush performed takeoffs and landings on the 8,000-ton USS *Sable* (IX-81) which cruised on Lake Michigan.[10] *Sable* was a converted paddle wheel excursion ship used for carrier flight training.

**Grumman TBF Avenger aircraft of the
type that George Bush flew**

Courtesy of Northrop Grumman History Center

The TBF Avenger was a huge single-engine aircraft: 16 feet tall and 40 feet long, with a wingspan of more than 54 feet. Powered by a single 1,700 HP Wright engine, the 10,000-pound aircraft had a maximum speed of 270 mph. For all its size, the Avenger was a relatively easy aircraft to fly. Bush told a *Naval Aviation News* reporter that the Avenger was a stable airplane and the easiest to land on an aircraft carrier.[11]

Avengers had a crew of three: pilot, turret gunner, and radioman/tail gunner. The pilot operated two wing-mounted .50 caliber machine guns. The turret gunner was armed with a .50 caliber aft-facing, dorsal gun, and the radioman had a .30 caliber aft-facing belly gun. The radioman's cabin beneath the turret gun was so small that he sat on a pull-down bench during flight and stood in the center cockpit during takeoff and landing. The center cockpit was originally occupied by a bombardier, but that crew position was eliminated.

TBF aircraft were originally designed and built by Grumman Aircraft. Their production rate could not keep up with military needs, in part because Grumman was also manufacturing F6F Hellcat fighters. When automobile manufacturing was canceled by presidential order in late 1941, five General Motors production plants were idled on the East Coast. These plants became the Eastern Aircraft Division of General Motors and produced TBFs—christened TBMs—under subcontract to Grumman. Grumman ceased TBF production in December 1943 and concentrated on the Hellcats. Within 15 months, General Motors produced 400 TBMs a month, and by the end of the war, produced 7,546 such aircraft.[12] Combined with the Grumman-produced TBFs, the total number of aircraft reached 9,839.

Avengers carried either a 21-inch torpedo or 2,000 pounds of bombs. After the success of American dive bombers at Midway, the Avenger was almost exclusively used as a bomber and as an antisubmarine search aircraft. In fact, Bush never flew a torpedo mission.[13] With the introduction of a new torpedo design, Avengers returned to using torpedoes later in the war.

Bush reported to the Naval Air Station Norfolk, Virginia, where VC-51, a composite fighter bomber squadron, was being formed. The squadron was formally commissioned on September 22.[14] At the end of September, VC-51 moved to the Naval Air Station Chincoteague, Virginia. The squadron practiced glide bombing, torpedo attacks, night flying, and simulated carrier landings. On one landing, Bush's aircraft was buffeted by the wakes of two preceding TBFs. He was forced off the runway, and his landing gear collapsed. The aircraft was a total wreck, but Bush and crew escaped unharmed.[15]

Each of the squadron's officers had specific duties. As the squadron's photographic officer, Bush flew photo missions and trained VC-51 crew to take surveillance photos with hand-held cameras. Aerial photography became increasingly important because the navy had little information about the geography and defenses of the Japanese-held Pacific islands. Bush's aircraft was outfitted with three camera mounts in the bomb bay area.[16] Unlike fighter pilots, torpedo bomber pilots did not ordinarily have aircraft assigned to them personally.[17] Bush flew this aircraft, named *Tare Two*, frequently because of the camera mounts.

Aviation Ordnance Man 2/c Leo W. Nadeau and Aviation Radioman 2/c John L. Delaney joined Bush at Chincoteague. Nadeau became Bush's turret gunner, and Delaney became his radioman/tail gunner. Bush flew with these two men for most of his combat service.

Bush's torpedo squadron formally separated from the composite squadron and was commissioned VT-51 on November 8.[18] The squadron received nine General Motors TBM-1C Avengers to replace its original TBFs.[19] On November 18 VT-51 flew to the Naval Air Station Hyannis, Massachusetts, where the squadron practiced gunnery against a towed aerial target and dropped dummy torpedoes in Narragansett Bay. A week later VT-51 hopped over to the Na-

Grumman TBF Avenger aircraft in echelon formation

Courtesy of United States National Archives

val Air Station Charleston, Rhode Island, where the squadron practiced with 24 Grumman F6F Hellcats from fighter squadron VF-51. VT-51 combined with VF-51 to form Air Group 51 and were attached to the new light aircraft carrier USS *San Jacinto* (CVL 30). Whenever the TBMs flew bombing missions, the Hellcats flew cover.

AG-51 pilots witnessed *San Jacinto*'s commissioning in the Philadelphia Naval Yard on December 15. *San Jacinto*, an 11,000-ton aircraft carrier built from the hull of the light cruiser USS *Newark* (CL 100), was to be Bush's home for the next year. *San Jacinto*

Bush with crewmen John Delaney and Leo Nadeau

Courtesy of George Bush Library

was 623 feet long, had a beam of 109 feet, and had a deck 69 feet wide. The last of the *Independence* class of light carriers, *San Jacinto* carried a complement of 25 fighters, 9 torpedo bombers, and 1,600 personnel.

    San Jacinto was named for the April 21, 1836, battle in which a small army of Texans defeated the army of Mexico's General Antonio Lopez de Santa Anna to secure Texas's independence. After the sinking of their namesake cruiser USS *Houston* (CA 30) off Java in 1942, patriotic Texans raised enough money to finance the construction of the light cruiser *Houston* (CL 81), and to finance the conversion of the *Newark* into the light carrier *San Jacinto*. In recognition, *San Jacinto* flew the Texas flag beneath the Stars and Stripes.[20]

    VT-51 transferred to the Naval Air Station Norfolk, Virginia, on January 22, 1944. Two days later, they practiced landings on *San Jacinto*.[21] VT-51 transferred to *San Jacinto* on February 6.[22] Under the command of Captain Harold Montgomery Martin, the carrier left on a two-week shakedown cruise to Trinidad, British

Light aircraft carrier USS *San Jacinto* from which Bush flew Avenger torpedo bombers

Courtesy of United States Navy

San Jacinto officers and VT-51 pilots

Courtesy of United States Navy

West Indies. Pilots practiced carrier takeoffs, carrier landings, and air searches. Landings were accomplished by snagging one of nine arresting cables with the aircraft's tail hook. Unlike Japanese carriers—which stored their aircraft below—U.S. carriers transported their aircraft on the flight deck, and used the minimal space on the hangar deck for maintenance. A safety net protected topside aircraft if an aircraft failed to snag an arresting cable.

Bush shared officer's quarters with pilots Jack O. Guy, Doug W. West, and Francis M. Waters.[23] Accommodations included four bunk beds, lockers, a sink, a medicine chest, a desk, and a porthole. The quarters were located under the catapult, which was on the port side of the forward flight deck. Officers could walk down the hall and out onto a catwalk to catch a breath of fresh air. VT-51 pilots Lou J. Grab and Stanley P. Butchart recall spending many hours on the catwalk with Bush sunning, watching flying fish, and shooting the breeze.[24] Although the officers were housed forward on the ship, the torpedo bomber ready room was aft. To get there, the pilots could walk on the flight deck or on the catwalk along the side of the ship. Enlisted men were housed in the stern, sleeping in bunks four deep, and eating in a large mess hall.[25]

San Jacinto's pilots ate relatively well. VF-51 pilot William Flynn recalls that meals were served by stewards in a ward room which seated one hundred men.[26] Plates and silverware were used, and tables had white table cloths. A typical meal included meat, vegetable, potatoes, and dessert. Milk and potatoes were made from powdered mixtures. And there was always coffee, plenty of coffee.

San Jacinto left for the Pacific on March 28, transited the Panama Canal, and arrived in Pearl Harbor on April 20. VT-51 transferred to Naval Air Station Kaneohe, Territory of Hawaii, and practiced gunnery and glide bombing for 12 days. *San Jacinto* and *Essex* aircrews then practiced group tactics for two days.[27] VT-51 reboarded *San Jacinto* on May 2 as she set sail to Majuro

Atoll in the Marshall Islands. *San Jacinto* arrived on May 8 and joined Vice Admiral Mark Mitscher's Fast Carrier Task Force 58.[28]

In mid-May, *San Jacinto*, *Essex*, and *Wasp* raided Marcus and Wake Islands. The carriers sailed within 600 miles of Japan, but encountered no sea-going opposition. Bush's first combat flight was a May 23 glide bombing attack on a Japanese command post at Heel Point, Wake Island.[29] Squadron commander Donald J. Melvin led four aircraft, with each TBM releasing four 500-pound bombs on the targets. The attacking aircraft encountered antiaircraft fire but were not hit. In a letter to his parents, 19-year-old Bush confessed to a certain amount of nervousness, but not of fear.[30] The raiding party returned to Majuro on May 31 for rest and reprovisioning.

Task Force 58 joined Admiral Spruance's Fifth Fleet on June 6 and headed 700 miles northwest to the Mariana Islands.[31] Fifth Fleet, consisting of 600 ships and 300,000 servicemen, was set to invade Saipan, Guam, and Tinian Islands. More than 200 aircraft from 15 aircraft carriers launched attacks on the Saipan airfields. *San Jacinto* and her sister light carrier *Monterey* participated in the

Lieutenant (jg) George Bush preparing for a flight
Courtesy of George Bush Library

action. Bush flew missions against land targets, on antisubmarine patrols, and on reconnaissance flights.

Bush bombed Aslito Airfield on Saipan on June 12, his 20th birthday. He dropped four 500-pound bombs, and then flew a photo reconnaissance mission to assess the mission's bomb damage. On a June 13 flight, equipment failure forced Bush to return to *San Jacinto*. Switching to another Avenger, he dropped depth charges on a fleet of armed trawlers. Two days later, Bush made glide bombing attacks against Japanese installations on the island of Rota.[32]

During the June 15 invasion of Saipan, Task Force 58 came under heavy attack by Japanese aircraft in what became known as the Battle of the Philippine Sea. Fifth Fleet's Combat Air Patrol aircraft shot down seven enemy aircraft, and its antiaircraft batteries added one more.[33] Bush watched the scene from *San Jacinto*'s deck, six months to the day after *San Jacinto*'s commissioning. The next day, Bush flew combat strikes against ground targets on Guam to deny the use of the air fields by Japanese carrier aircraft. On June 18, Bush patrolled west of Saipan helping search for the Japanese fleet.

When hundreds of fighters from Admiral Ozawa's Mobile Fleet attacked on June 19, VT-51's pilots flew their torpedo bombers off *San Jacinto* to clear the decks for fighter aircraft emergency landings. Bush's Avenger, loaded with four 500-pound depth charges for antisubmarine patrol, was on the catapult when enemy aircraft attacked at noon. Because *San Jacinto* was not turned into the wind, Bush had to wait for the attacking aircraft to pass.[34]

**Task Force 58 carriers turning into
the wind to launch aircraft over Saipan**

Courtesy of United States National Archives

Shortly after launching, his aircraft experienced a sudden loss of oil pressure during climb-out, possibly due to ingesting *San Jacinto*'s defensive flak. Under the circumstances, the flight director would not take Bush back on board, so he had no choice but to ditch. Bush set the ailing Avenger down in the water, and he, Nadeau, and Delaney scrambled into a life raft in the two minutes before the Avenger sank. Rowing away from the sinking aircraft, the three men were shaken by the depth charge explosions as the aircraft sank to the mines' discharge depth. They were picked up within half an hour by the destroyer USS *CK Bronson* (DD 668).[35]

Throughout the day, American fighter aircraft engaged enemy aircraft, and American bombers kept the airfields on Saipan and Guam inoperable. The result was a spectacular loss for the Japanese. More than three hundred attacking aircraft were shot down in what came to be known as "The Great Marianas Turkey Shoot." Nadeau watched the action from the deck of the *Bronson* as the air battle raged overhead.[36] Bush went below to sleep.[37]

Finally freed of his concern for the safety of the Saipan invasion forces, Spruance ordered Mitscher to seek out and destroy the Japanese Mobile Fleet. On June 20, scout planes located the Japanese fleet 250 miles west of Task Force 58. Mitscher ordered an all-out attack, even though it was late in the day. Jack Guy recalls:

> I got a call to go to the torpedo ready room in the afternoon. Only two TBMs were available, and they had been assigned to Melvin and Hole. I suggested that we not send both of our squadron leaders and volunteered to go instead. Melvin agreed with this. We were given a distance and bearing, and we set out using our onboard navigation boards. When we arrived over the Japanese fleet, it was just turning dusk. I attacked an aircraft carrier with four 500 pound bombs. My tail gunner confirmed the hits. When I was returning, I joined up with another TBM, which turned out to be Melvin's aircraft.

He was the best navigator in the fleet and got us back to the carrier.[38]

Guy damaged a Japanese *Hiyataka* class aircraft carrier, and Melvin sank a destroyer. Both were awarded the Navy Cross for their actions.[39]

When the aircraft returned to the fleet after dark, Mitscher ordered Task Force 58 battleships and destroyers to turn on their search lights and the carriers to illuminate their hooded deck lights. The daring approach worked with most of the pilots being recovered—either on deck or in the water. Guy picks up the story:

> Melvin had brought us back right over San Jacinto. I got into the landing pattern, but was waved off twice. The third time I came around, the landing signal officer gave me the cut sign, and I was down. It was the only night landing I ever did in the war.

Melvin ditched his TBM near a destroyer, and the crew were rescued.[40]

A bizarre incident occurred on *San Jacinto* that evening. Landing signal officer Ralph M. Bagwell explains:

> When our planes returned from attacking the Japanese carrier force, it was dark and many were running out of gas. Admiral Mitscher ordered the carriers' deck lights turned on, and planes began landing anywhere they could. We took 11 planes aboard the *San Jacinto* that were not ours, and most had never made a night landing. About 30 minutes after the last one landed, I noticed another plane about six miles out. He was coming in on a straight line and slowly decreasing his altitude. I thought it was a straggler. I began giving him landing signals, and he appeared to be following them. As he got closer, I noticed his landing light was not on, which was a signal that his tail hook was not down. Therefore, I waved him off, expecting him to go around. I asked my assistant to shine a hand-held light on him to check his tail hook. Much to our surprise, the light revealed that it was a Japanese plane. We called the bridge, and they saw it too. The plane then went

around, but we turned our deck lights off so he did not attempt to land a second time.[41]

Butchart and Grab were on the flight deck that night and witnessed the entire episode.[42]

When the battle was over, 20-year-old Bush and his crew transferred from *CK Bronson* to the carrier *Lexington* by breeches buoy—a scary experience for even the most seasoned veteran. Four days later, the destroyer USS *Terry* (DD 513) picked up the three men and transferred them to the *San Jacinto*.[43] Bush resumed flying strikes against land targets, patrolling for submarines, and flying photo reconnaissance missions. Task Force 58 steamed eastward, reaching Eniwetok Island on July 6.

The Task Force resumed battle on July 18 with four days of strikes on Guam and Rota, and then turned its attention to Palau, Yap, and Ulithi. During a reconnaissance flight over Palau, Delaney snapped a spectacular picture of an exploding Japanese mine layer.[44] Several Hellcats from Bush's flight cover strafed the ship and set off its cargo of mines. Continuing on the mission, Bush scored a direct hit on an armed trawler and sank the craft. In late July, Task Force 58 steamed back to Saipan to rest and replenish supplies.[45]

Task Force 58 got under way for the Bonin Islands (now Ogasawara) on August 1. Japanese military leaders recognized the value of the Bonin Islands as early as 1875, fortified them in 1914, and added radio and weather stations. In 1944, Japan installed a naval base, added antiaircraft guns, and increased troop strength to the level of a reinforced brigade. Carrier aircraft attacked Japanese communications and shipping at Iwo Jima and Chichi Jima on August 4 and 5. Shortly after the attacks, Task Force 58 encountered a typhoon, which did minor damage to *San Jacinto*. The Task Force retired 750 miles southwest to Eniwetok to resupply and repair damage. Bush was promoted to lieutenant (jg) effective August 1.[46]

Spruance relinquished command to Admiral Halsey, and the Fleet reorganized as the Third Fleet. On August 28, the carriers

San Jacinto, USS *Franklin* (CV 13), and *Enterprise* headed back to the Bonin Islands as part of Task Group 38.4. Halsey wanted to neutralize the radio transmitting stations on Chichi Jima before Third Fleet invaded the Palau Islands. Only six hundred miles from Japan, the transmitters were a vital link in the Japanese communications network.

VT-51 Avengers attacked Radio Station Number Six on Yoake Peak during September 1. Antiaircraft fire was so intense that no one got a good hit. Although support buildings were left in flames, the key communications tower was still standing. Eliminating the tower was key to the mission's success, so Melvin planned another strike for the next day. In the meantime, the balance of the Third Fleet steamed south toward the Palaus.

After the September 2 morning's briefing, Bush's friend Lt. (jg) William G. White, VT-51's gunnery officer, asked if he could accompany the flight to observe the weapons under combat conditions. White was responsible for maintenance of the TBM turret guns, training of gunners, and supervision of all ordnance material.[47] Bush gave White Nadeau's turret gun seat for this mission, since the covering Hellcats would protect against Japanese aircraft. In fact, Nadeau related that, in the 57 missions he flew with Bush, he never used his turret gun to defend against attacking aircraft.[48]

Shortly after 7:15 A.M., four VT-51 Avengers left *San Jacinto* for a second attack on the communications center. Melvin led the flight composed of Ensign Milton G. Moore, West, and Bush. Twelve Hellcat fighters and eight SB2C dive bombers from the carrier *Enterprise* accompanied the flight.[49]

The Avengers climbed to eight thousand feet and proceeded to Chichi Jima 70 miles away. Arriving over the target, Melvin and West attacked from South to North. They each dropped four 500-pound bombs on the radio station tower and headed out to sea. Bush pushed over in a glide-bombing attack on four communications buildings 2,000 feet from the tower. Moore was on his right

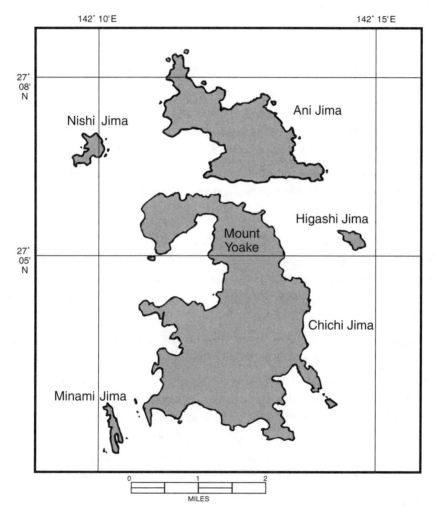

142° 10'E 142° 15'E

27° 08' N

Nishi Jima

Ani Jima

Higashi Jima

27° 05' N

Mount Yoake

Chichi Jima

Minami Jima

0 1 2
MILES

**Bush's aircraft crashed about three
miles northeast of Higashi Jima.**

wing.[50] Flying through intense antiaircraft fire, Bush experienced a flash of light followed by an explosion. Continuing his dive, Bush released his bombs at 4,000 feet and headed out to sea. The time was 8:30 A.M.[51]

Joe L. Foshee, West's turret gunner, describes what happened next:

> We were flying on Melvin's wing and going after the radio tower. Bush was going after a different target about 2,000 feet away. There was heavy anti-aircraft fire, and I saw Bush's aircraft smoking as we pulled out over the ocean. Bush was about 1,000 feet below us as he maneuvered to get out to sea. He dived his aircraft to pick up speed and leveled off several times to extend his range. I'd say Bush got down to 1,500 to 2,000 feet.[52]

Bush's cockpit filled with smoke as he tried to get as far away from shore as possible.[53] He radioed Melvin and his crew that they had to bail out. As Bush climbed out of the cockpit, he was forced backward by the airstream and struck his head on the tail surface. Bush's parachute deployed early and snagged on the tail section—ripping several of the panels. After a faster than normal descent, Bush plunged into the ocean, surfaced, unbuckled his parachute, and inflated his Mae West life preserver. Melvin, flying cover with West and Moore, made a pass over Bush's life raft so Bush could find it. Bush inflated the life raft, climbed aboard, and started paddling away from the island.

Moore and West strafed several Japanese boats that put out to pick up the downed airmen and forced them back to shore. Charles Yancy Bynum, Moore's turret gunner, remembers:

> We were flying on Bush's right when we attacked. Bush went first and was hit before we released our bombs. I saw Bush pull up, and I saw smoke coming from his plane. He flew the plane out to sea and leveled off so the crew could bail out. Two parachutes came out, but one of them streamed. I started to follow the one parachute down, but Moore turned

so I lost track before it hit the water. Of course, I didn't know who it was at the time.

Moore saw two Japanese gunboats come out to pick up the downed airman, and he drove them back by strafing. When he pulled up, I fired my .50 caliber turret gun at the boats. We stayed overhead as long as we could, but we were running low on fuel. We knew that the fighters were still overhead and that a rescue submarine was nearby.[54]

Rumors abounded regarding Japanese mistreatment of prisoners of war, especially of pilots whom the government had declared to be criminals. Chichi Jima's army commandant Major General Yoshio Tachibana had more than mistreatment in mind. He delighted in eating the livers of captured pilots and would sometimes substitute their flesh for his officers' meals. During the Tokyo War Crimes Trial, Major Sueo Matoba testified to the execution of American airmen and the subsequent eating of their flesh.[55] A military tribunal convicted Tachibana and 21 of his officers of cannibalism. Six of them, including Matoba, were hanged.

Melvin radioed Bush's position four miles northeast of Chichi Jima to the nearby submarine USS *Finback* (SS 230).[56] The 1,500-ton submarine, captained by Annapolis graduate Lieutenant Commander Robert R. Williams, was on her 10th war patrol.[57] *Finback* was on station near the Bonin Islands as part of the Lifeguard League, whose submarines were assigned to rescue downed pilots and crew. Nimitz established the League in late 1943, when the number of aircraft carriers began to increase dramatically. The Lifeguard League illustrated the high value the navy placed on returning its downed airmen. The practice was a large morale booster, but it was also good business. A great deal of time and money had been invested in training the aircraft crews. By the end of the war, Lifeguard League submarines had retrieved more than 500 grateful airmen.[58]

On September 1, *Finback* rescued Avenger pilot Ensign Thomas R. Keene and his crew Aviation Ordnance Man 3/c James T.

AIRCRAFT ACTION REPORT

DECLASSIFIED SECRET RESTRICTED

VI. LOSS OR DAMAGE, COMBAT OR OPERATIONAL, OF OWN AIRCRAFT (of those listed in II only).

	(a) TYPE OWN A/C	(b) SQUADRON	(c) CAUSE: TYPE ENEMY A/C, TYPE GUN, OR OPERATIONAL CAUSE	(d) WHERE HIT, ANGLE	(e) EXTENT OF LOSS OR DAMAGE, REMARKS
1	TBM-1C	VT-51	Heavy and Med. A/A	Engine	Crashed in Ocean--Lost
2					
3					
4					
5					
6					
7					
8					
9					
10					
11					
12					
13					
14					

VII. PERSONNEL CASUALTIES (in aircraft listed in II only; identify with planes listed in VI by Nos. at left).

(a) NO.	(b) SQUADRON	(c) NAME, RANK OR RATING	(d) CAUSE	(e) CONDITION OR STATUS
1.	VT-51	Lt.(jg) W. G. White, USNR	Occupant of TBM-1C lost	Missing in action
2.	VT-51	J. L. Delaney, ARM 2/c USNR	Occupant of TBM-1C lost	Missing in action
	NOTE:	The pilot (Lt.(jg) G.H.W. Bush) of the TBM-1C which was lost, parachuted to water and was picked up by rescue submarine, which reported him unhurt.		

VIII. RANGE, FUEL, AND AMMUNITION DATA

(a) TYPE A/C	(b) MILES OUT	(c) MILES RETURN	(d) AV. HOURS IN AIR	(e) AV. FUEL LOADED	(f) AV. FUEL CONSUMED	(g) TOTAL AMMUNITION EXPENDED, PLANES RETURNING				
						NO. OF PLANES	.30	.50	20MM	MM.
TBM-1C	71	75	2.9	300	190	3	500	960		

IX. COMPARATIVE PERFORMANCE, OWN AND ENEMY AIRCRAFT (use check list at left).

SPEED, CLIMB, at various altitudes

TURNS
DIVES
CEILINGS
RANGE
PROTECTION
ARMAMENT

ALLSET — MFD BY THE ECHY REGISTER CO., PATENTED

VT-51 Aircraft Action Report—Part 1

Courtesy of United States National Archives

AIRCRAFT ACTION REPORT

(OMIT THIS SHEET IF NO ATTACK WAS MADE)

 RESTRICTED SECRET

X. ATTACK ON ENEMY SHIPS OR GROUND OBJECTIVES (By Own Aircraft Listed in II Only).

(a) Location of Target(s) <u>4 Bldgs. (Radio Station) and 1 Tower, at</u> (b) Time Over Target(s) 0825 0830 -9
<u>85.8-50.3 also radio station at 85.6-50.6</u>

(c) Weather and Clouds Over Target _____

(d) Sun or Moon _____ (e) Visibility <u>Good</u>

XI. TARGETS, RESULTS OF ATTACK.

	(a) DESCRIPTION OF TARGET (List All Ships in Group, Whether or Not Individually Attacked)	(b) A/C ATTACKING (c) SQUADRON	(d) BOMBS AND AMMUNITION EXPENDED, EACH TARGET	(e) ALTITUDE OF RELEASE	(f) HITS
1	4 Buildings (Radio) and tower at 85.8-50.3	2 VT-51	8-500# G.P.	4,500	See (G)
2	1 Large, 3 small bldgs. (Radio) at 85.6-50.6	2 VT-51	8-500# G.P.	4,000	See (G)
3					
4					
5					
6					
7					
8					

(g) **RESULTS:** (FOR SHIP TARGETS DRAW DIAGRAM, TOP OR SIDE VIEW OR BOTH, AS APPROPRIATE, SHOWING TYPE AND LOCATION OF HITS. FOR ALL TARGETS GIVE LOCATION AND EFFECT OF HITS, WITH DIAGRAMS OR CHARTS WHERE DESIRABLE. DESCRIBE TARGETS FULLY IN (a), AND IN REPORTING DAMAGE OR DESTRUCTION, IDENTIFY BY NUMBERS AT LEFT. USE ADDITIONAL SHEETS IF NECESSARY).

1. Eight direct hits on target by Lt. Comdr. Melvin, USNR and Lt.(jg) D. W. West, USNR destroyed tower and badly damaged or destroyed buildings.

2. Radio station damaged (See XII for narrative) by bombs dropped by Lt.(jg) G.H.W. Bush, USNR and Ens. M. G. Moore, USNR. Extent of damage unobserved.

(h) Were Photographs Taken? ___No___ Photographs of Damage, When Taken, Should Be Attached.

VT-51 Aircraft Action Report—Part 2

Stovall and Aviation Radioman 3/c John R. Doherty from the *Franklin*. Keene remembers:

> I was flying a TBF on a mission to bomb and strafe Japanese aircraft at an airfield on Iwo Jima. My aircraft lost power, possibly from an anti-aircraft hit. I noticed a black cloud but had no fire or smoke on board. I radioed my crewmen, and both answered that they were okay. Then I made a water landing without injury. We quickly got into the life raft and paddled away from the sinking aircraft. My fellow pilots radioed *Finback* and flew cover until we were rescued.[59]

Finback returned to station off the southwest coast of Chichi Jima. At 6:45 A.M. on September 2, two F6F Hellcat aircraft arrived to fly cover.[60] *Finback* received Melvin's distress call at 9:30 A.M. Williams guided *Finback* around the south end of the island and turned north outside of shore battery range. With the Hellcats providing overhead protection, Williams kept *Finback* on the surface to double his speed. Meanwhile, Bush was kneeling on his life raft and paddling away from shore using the life raft's small paddles.[61] With their fuel running low, Melvin, West, and Moore returned to *San Jacinto* at 10:10 A.M. Fighter aircraft from the *Enterprise* continued providing air cover over Bush.

Lookouts on *Finback*'s conning tower spotted Bush's yellow life raft, and *Finback* pulled alongside at 11:56 A.M. A rescue party went out to the bow, secured the raft, and helped Bush up onto *Finback*'s deck. Despite having been in the life raft for more than three hours, much of it kneeling, Bush was able to walk to the conning tower under his own power. A remarkable 8 millimeter film of the rescue taken by the ship's photographic officer, Ensign William E. Edwards, documented the dramatic rescue.[62] *Finback*'s log book reads:

> Picked up Lt. jg George H. W. Bush, file #173464 USNR, pilot of plane T-3 of VT-51 USS San Jacinto who stated that he failed to see his crew's parachute and believed they had jumped when his plane was still over Chi-Chi Jima or that

they had gone down with the plane. Commenced search of area on chance they had jumped over water.[63]

Bush was *Finback*'s fourth rescued airman in less than 24 hours; he wasn't to be the last. Within an hour of Bush's rescue, Captain Williams learned of another downed airman close to the western shore of nearby HaHa Jima. *Finback* sped to the rescue on the surface, but dove to periscope depth when it was reported that the raft was being shelled by shore guns. Spotting the raft through the periscope, Williams brought the *Finback* alongside without stopping. Lieutenant (jg) James W. Beckman, a Hellcat pilot from the *Enterprise*, didn't grab onto the periscope as Williams hoped. Williams turned *Finback* around and made a second pass. This time Beckman grabbed onto the periscope and was towed five miles offshore, where *Finback* surfaced and took the pilot aboard. *Finback* had its fifth rescued airman in less than a day and a half.[64]

Although carrier aircraft searched the area, Delaney and White were never found. Nadeau explained what must have happened:

> There was not enough room for the turret gunner to wear his parachute, so it was hung on a rack in the cramped radioman's bay. When the order to bail out came, the radioman was to open the fly-away hatch on the starboard side and hand a parachute to the turret gunner as he descended into the bay. While the gunner was snapping the parachute onto

USS *Finback* (SS 230) rescued five downed airmen on September 1–2, 1944.

Bush's rescue by crew of USS *Finback*

U.S.S. FINBACK (SS230)

C-O-N-F-I-D-E-N-T-I-A-L

0645	Two F6F's overhead as escort. Headed east for island. Closed to 9 miles and maintained this position.
0933	Received word of plane down 9 miles NE of MINAMI JIMA. Started around southern end of CHICHI JIMA, maintaining minimum range of 7½ miles to island.
1156	Picked up Lt.(jg) George H.W. BUSH, File No. 173464, USNR, pilot of plane T-3 of VT-51, U.S.S. SAN JACINTO, who stated that he failed to see his crew's parachutes and believed they had jumped when plane was still over CHICHI JIMA, or they had gone down with plane. Commenced search of area on chance they had jumped over water.
1236	Received word of rubber boat seen from air. Position given was in hills of HAHA JIMA but started south anyway, asking for jigs, repetitions, and conformations, until we heard one plane state he was circling over the boat. An unknown plane on the circuit was heard to mention a spot "west of HAHA". This was at least as good as any dope we had, so headed for a position about 9 miles west of HAHA JIMA. This seemed to make our cover feel better, although they tried to con us through the island a few times. Plane reported that the raft, about 1½ miles from beach, was being shelled. Spirits of all hands went to 300 feet.
1505	Dived to 55 feet with planes in sight zooming a spot in water 1 mile WSW of MEGANE IMA.
1530	Sighted rubber boat.
1550	Roared by the rubber boat, backing full and still making 4 knots. We must have misjudged his mast-head height a bit We twisted around and started stalking him.
1620	Pilot hooked on and we headed out away from beach. Tried to make two-thirds speed, but the pilot had one arm around the periscope and the other around the life raft with a bailing bucket bringing up the rear. Stopped to see if he would get in the boat. This took about 10 minutes, during which a discussion developed below concerning the precedence of simultaneous orders to blow, pump, and flood. Finally got way on towing pilot in his boat. Two-thirds speed filled the boat, and there he was in the water again. Finally came up to 38 feet to keep him out of the water until at range of 5 miles from beach, planed up and opened the hatch.

-- 6 --

USS *Finback's* Tenth War Patrol Report for September 2, 1944

his harness, the radioman was to exit the hatch to clear the way.[65]

The VT-51 Action Report records that one of the airmen bailed out, but his parachute did not open.[66] Nadeau believes that airman was radioman Delaney. A Japanese combat report uncovered after the war corroborated the existence of two parachutes, and the subsequent rescue submarine's route.[67]

San Jacinto Officers of the Deck Joseph L. Shapiro and H. L. Blum recorded the events of that morning:

> 0712 Changed course to 060° T, speed to 22 knots, 222 R. P. M., for flight operations.
> 716-0722 Launched 4 VT and 4 VF aircraft....
> 0955-1003 Recovered 8 F6F's and 3 TBM's—one TBM Bu No. 46214, having crashed at sea 9 miles NE of the southern tip of Chichi Jima due to enemy anti-aircraft fire. Pilot, Lieut. (jg), G. H. W. Bush, USNR, was rescued by submarine, but crew composed of Lt. (jg), W. G. White, USNR and Delaney, J. L., ARM 2c, USN, are believed to be missing in action.[68]

The eight F6Fs recovered were from *San Jacinto*, not the F6Fs flying cover over Bush's flight. By 5:45 P.M., *San Jacinto* recovered all of its aircraft and headed toward the Mariana Islands.

Meeting Bush in *Finback's* ward room, Keene explained that they would have to remain on board until the submarine completed its combat patrol.[69] Bush was pressed into duty as junior officer of the deck—standing watch on the conning tower between 6 to 8 P.M. and 4 to 6 A.M.[70] *Finback* sank two freighters and was depth charged twice while the airmen were aboard.[71]

The pilots hot bunked in officers' quarters, since sleeping accommodations were crowded with three extra officers on board. When not on watch or sleeping, the officers ate, read, sipped coffee, watched movies, played cards, or wrote letters in the ward room.[72] Showers were limited to one per week, and typical attire was pants and sandals, with undershirts donned for meals.[73]

Thirty days after the rescue, *Finback* reached Midway, and the three pilots were flown to Pearl Harbor. After R&R at the navy-leased Royal Hawaiian Hotel on Waikiki Beach, Bush was back in the air flying TBMs out of the Naval Air Station Barbers Point.[74]

Bush chose to return to *San Jacinto* even though he had the right to rotate home. Eight weeks after being shot down, he and Keene flew to Guam in a Navy C-47 passenger aircraft.[75] They were in Guam several days before rejoining their carriers in Ulithi.[76]

During Bush's absence, *San Jacinto* launched air attacks on the Palau Islands, Formosa, Okinawa, and the Philippines, and then joined in the Battle of Leyte Gulf. Operating in Halsey's Task Force 38, aircraft from *San Jacinto* pursued Admiral Ozawa's Northern Force and sank the Japanese carrier *Zuiho*.[77] This time the Avengers carried torpedoes. On October 30, Japanese kamikaze aircraft struck Task Force 38 off Samar Island, seriously damaging the aircraft carriers *Franklin* and *Belleau Wood*. Two kamikaze aircraft were shot down near *San Jacinto* but caused little damage. *San Jacinto* returned to Ulithi on November 2. In Bush's absence, Nadeau filled in as a spare turret gunner in VT-51 aircraft.[78]

On November 5 Task Force 38 headed to the Philippines. Rejoined by Nadeau and adding Aviation Radio Man 1/c Joseph H. Reichert, Bush flew missions over the island of Luzon. On a November 13 mission to Manila Bay, he dropped four 500-pound armor-piercing bombs, which struck two light cruisers docked side by side.[79] *San Jacinto* headed back to Ulithi, arriving on November 22.

San Jacinto left Ulithi for Guam on November 29. Bush flew an antisubmarine patrol along the way, his 58th and last flight in the Pacific theater.[80] Upon *San Jacinto*'s arrival, Air Group 45 replaced Air Group 51. Eight of VT-51's original 13 pilots remained.

VT-51 pilots and crew returned to the United States on board the escort carrier USS *Bougainville* (CVE 100). Commissioned in June 1944, *Bougainville*'s primary mission was to ferry aircraft and personnel to and from the battle zone. Bush remembers his

Bush with replacement tail gunner
Joe Reichert, *left,* and radioman Leo Nadeau, *right*

accommodations consisted of a crowded stateroom in the officer's quarters.[81] In fact, there were 15 officers in each stateroom.[82] *Bougainville* left Guam in early December, stopped off at Pearl Harbor, and arrived in San Diego on December 22.[83]

Bush caught a flight to Pittsburgh on December 23 and boarded an overnight train. He reached his fiancée Barbara Pierce's hometown of Rye, New York, on Christmas Eve, and they continued on to his parents' home in Greenwich, Connecticut.[84] Bush and Pierce were married on January 6, 1945. After his leave was up, Bush reported to the Naval Air Station Norfolk, Virginia, for additional training.

Bush, Guy, West, and Moore carried out a series of assignments in Florida, Michigan, and Maine, and then returned to Norfolk. In March, Bush joined Squadron VT-153 at the Naval Air Station Lewiston, Maine, in preparation for returning to the Pacific. VT-153 was being trained to fly off an *Essex* class carrier.[85] In May, VT-153 transferred to the Oceana Naval Air Station, Virginia Beach, Virginia, and continued training for the invasion of Japan. Bush was there on September 2, 1945, when the Japanese government signed the peace treaty ending the war—exactly one year after he was shot down over Chichi Jima. Within two weeks, Lieutenant (jg) George Bush was honorably discharged from active duty.

George and Barbara Bush moved to New Haven, Connecticut, where Bush entered Yale University with a major in economics. He was a member of Phi Beta Kappa and a captain of Yale's baseball team in his senior year. After he was graduated in 1948, Bush headed west to Odessa, Texas, to work for Dresser Industries as an oil field equipment clerk. In November, he was promoted to lieutenant in the Naval Reserve.

Dresser sent Bush on a series of assignments that covered oil fields from Bakersfield to Compton, California. In 1950, he returned to Odessa, the heart of Texas oil country.

Not content to remain in a mundane job, 26-year-old Bush and his neighbor John Overby formed the Bush-Overby Oil

Development Company. Bush attracted capital through his Eastern connections, and Overby identified encouraging oil drilling sites. Bush-Overby was moderately successful, but a more promising venture arose. In 1953 the two men joined forces with J. Hugh Liedtke and William C. Liedtke, prominent local attorneys. Together they formed Zapata Petroleum Company, with Hugh Liedtke as president and Bush as vice president. Zapata became a public company, and its shares were listed on the American Stock Exchange. Their first project was an immediate success: 130 oil wells drilled in the Jameson Field produced oil.[86]

Thirty-one-year-old Bush ventured into offshore oil drilling in 1955. He and the Liedtkes formed the Zapata Off Shore Company to perform contract drilling. Through a series of stock exchanges, Hugh Liedtke took control of Zapata Petroleum, while Bush controlled Zapata Off Shore Company. Liedtke merged Zapata Petroleum with Penn Oil Company to create Pennzoil. Subsequently, Pennzoil took over United Gas Pipeline Company, a much larger company. Pennzoil won a $10 billion lawsuit against Texaco when Texaco interfered with Pennzoil's takeover of Getty Oil. Busy running his company, Bush resigned from the Naval Reserve in October 1955.

Bush moved the headquarters of Zapata Offshore to Houston in 1959. The son of a Connecticut senator, Bush campaigned for the chairmanship of the county Republican party. He won by acclamation when his opponent dropped out. Bush worked diligently to build the party organization and succeeded in increasing its membership and contributions. In 1964, 40-year-old Bush ran against incumbent Democratic Texas Senator Ralph Webster Yarborough in his first try for elected office. He reached too far. Yarborough won the election by 300,000 votes in a heavily Democratic state.

The Voting Rights Act of 1965 created the Seventh District in northwest Houston. Seeing an opportunity to break the Democratic stronghold, Bush entered the 1966 Congressional race. He sold his stock in the Zapata Off Shore Company and resigned his chairmanship and chief executive officer positions. Among the political notables who campaigned for him were former navy officers Richard Nixon and Gerald Ford. This time, Bush was successful. He won the election by a comfortable margin, becoming the first Republican Representative from Texas. The Bushes moved to Washington, D.C., and in January 1967, Bush took his seat in the 90th Congress.

Bush was assigned to the House Ways and Means Committee, a powerful tax law panel headed by chairman Wilbur Daigh Mills. He toured South Vietnam in 1967, meeting with Ambassador Ellsworth Bunker and Pacific Area marine commander Lieutenant General Victor Krulak. Two weeks after he returned, the Viet Cong launched their Tet Offensive, and sent America's involvement in the war on the road to failure. In 1968, Bush won reelection to the House of Representatives.

Believing his experience and conservative credentials would carry the day, Bush entered the 1970 Senate race, expecting to campaign against Yarborough. Plans had to be changed when Lloyd Millard Bentsen Jr., a decorated World War II B-24 bomber pilot, defeated Yarborough in the Democratic primary race.[87] As a conservative Democrat, he presented a different challenge than Yarborough, and Bush lost to Bentsen by 150,000 votes.

President Nixon appointed Bush permanent representative to the United Nations. After the 1972 presidential election, Nixon named Bush the Republican National Committee chairman. He held that position when Nixon resigned from office in 1973.

Gerald Ford appointed Bush head of the U.S. Liaison Office in Beijing, China. Bush was in China for just over a year when Ford nominated him to head the Central Intelligence Agency. After several days of contentious hearings, the Senate confirmed Bush by a vote of 64 to 27. He labored valiantly to restore the Agency's tarnished reputation.

Bush returned to Houston in January 1977. He entered into a number of prosperous business arrangements and spent two years supporting Republican candidates around the country.

In May 1979, Bush entered the race for the presidency. With some bruising primary losses to Ronald Reagan and a mounting campaign debt, Bush effectively withdrew from the race just before the Republican National Convention. Reagan picked Bush to be his vice-presidential running mate. Together, they achieved a landslide victory over the incumbent candidates Jimmy Carter and Walter Mondale, carrying 44 states.

In addition to his duties as president of the Senate, Reagan appointed Bush to chair the president's task force on regulatory reform, the Special Situation Group for crisis management, and the South Florida task force on drug interdiction. He also charged Bush with developing the administration's policy on international terrorism. When Reagan was shot by John Hinckley Jr., Bush returned to Washington, D.C., from a trip to Texas to chair the Special Situation Group.

Reagan and Bush faced the Democratic ticket of Mondale and Geraldine Ann Ferraro in 1984. Reagan and Bush carried 49 states. In July 1985, when Reagan was under anesthesia during surgery for the removal of intestinal polyps, Bush was acting president under the rules of the 25th Amendment. Reagan reclaimed the presidency in seven hours, when the effects of the anesthesia subsided.

Bush announced his candidacy for the presidency in 1987. Early primary challenges by Robert Dole put the Republican nomination in some doubt, but Bush triumphed in New Hampshire. He continued collecting delegates until he had enough to clinch the nomination. At the 1988 Republican Convention, Bush selected James Danforth Quayle, senator from Indiana, as his vice-presidential running mate. They were pitted against the Democratic ticket of Michael Stanley Dukakis, governor of Massachusetts, and Lloyd Bentsen, Bush's political nemesis from Texas. Bush and Quayle emerged victorious, making Bush the 41st president of the United States. The popular vote was 48,881,278 to 41,805,374, and the Electoral College vote was 426 to 111. Bush became the first vice president elected directly to the presidency since Martin Van Buren in 1836.

The late eighties and early nineties were a period of international upheaval. Early in Bush's presidency, the Chinese army brutally crushed a student protest against the government in Tiananmen Square. The Union of Soviet Socialist Republics broke up, the Berlin Wall fell, Germany reunified, and the Warsaw Pact disbanded. The United States negotiated Strategic Arms Reductions with the Soviet Union and with Russia. When dictator Manuel Noriega threatened American interests in Panama, Bush sent in military forces. Noriega was captured and returned to the United States for trial. In perhaps his greatest triumph, Bush rallied Allied forces against the Iraqi invasion of Kuwait. Following five weeks of air attacks, Allied land forces ejected Iraqi troops occupying Kuwait, within one hundred hours of the start of the battle. Near the end of his presidency, Bush sent American forces into Somalia to restore order and help distribute emergency supplies of food and medicine.

Bush signed into law the Americans with Disabilities Act and a revision of the Clean Air Act. He extended the General Agreement on Tariffs and Trade and signed the North American Free Trade Agreement. Rising fuel prices, coupled with savings and loan failures, led to an economic recession. Bush nominated David Hackett Souter and Clarence Thomas to serve on the Supreme Court.

Republican Convention delegates nominated Bush and Quayle for a second term of office. After a strenuous campaign, largely reflecting economic issues, they were unseated by Arkansas Governor William Jefferson Clinton and his running mate, Tennessee Senator Albert Arnold Gore Jr. The popular vote was 39,104,545 to 44,909,889, and the Electoral College vote was 168 to 357.

President and Mrs. Bush reside in Houston, Texas, and Kennebunkport, Maine. Bush wrote four books. The Bushs' son George Walker Bush became the 43rd president. Only once in the history of the United States, 170 years earlier, have a father and son been elected to the presidency.

Bush held elected office for 16 years and appointed office for 7 years. He served 3 years in the navy of which 8 months were in the Pacific Theater. Bush remained in the Naval Reserve for 10 years. For his service in the Pacific Theater, Bush was awarded the Distinguished Flying Cross, an Air Medal with two gold stars, the Asiatic-Pacific Campaign medal with three battle stars, the World War II Victory Medal, and the American Campaign Medal. Bush's DFC citation reads:

> The President of the United States
> takes pleasure in presenting the
> DISTINGUISHED FLYING CROSS
> to Lieutenant George Herbert Walker Bush
> United States Naval Reserve

for service set forth in the following:

> For heroism and extraordinary achievement in aerial flight as Pilot of a Torpedo Plane in Torpedo Squadron Fifty One, attached to the U. S. S. San Jacinto, in action against enemy Japanese forces in the vicinity of the Bonin Islands, on September 2, 1944. Leading one section of a four plane division in a strike against a radio station, Lieutenant, Junior Grade, Bush pressed home an attack in the face of intense antiaircraft fire. Although his plane was hit and set afire at the beginning of the dive, he continued his plunge toward the target and succeeded in scoring damaging bomb hits before bailing out of the craft. His courage and devotion to duty were in keeping with the highest traditions of the United States Naval Reserve.

> For the President
> The Secretary of the Navy[88]

Epilogue

At the close of 1944, all five future presidents were back in the United States. Johnson was in Washington, D.C., as a Texas representative. Kennedy was in Boston, after appearing before a Naval Retirement Board. Nixon was in Washington, D.C., attending a navy contracts termination course. Ford was in Grand Rapids, Michigan, on leave. Bush was in Greenwich, Connecticut, also on leave.

Japan was on the ropes. In March, Iwo Jima fell, and American B-29 bombers from Saipan ravaged Tokyo with two days of firebombing. Okinawa was captured in June. Task Force 38 maneuvered at will off Japan in July and August, sending aircraft against airbases, ammunition dumps, factories, ships, and trains. On August 6 an American B-29 bomber, flying from the island of Tinian in the Marianas, dropped an atomic bomb on Hiroshima, which obliterated the city. Tokyo did not respond. A similar weapon was dropped on August 9, devastating Nagasaki. And still the Japanese rulers would not capitulate.

Finally, at an August 10 Imperial Conference, Hirohito intervened and announced his decision to accept the Allies' unconditional surrender demands. Four days later, Army Minister Korechika Anami, Army Chief of Staff Yoshijiro Umezu, and Navy Chief of Staff Soemu Toyoda continued to argue for defense of the mainland. Hirohito—receiving assurances that he would continue

195

to reign subject to the authority of the Allied Supreme Commander—directed his ministers of state to draw up an Imperial Rescript to be broadcast directly to the Japanese people. One last military uprising, formulated to seize the emperor and continue the war, was put down that evening. Hirohito broadcast the Rescript on August 15 directing his people to lay down their arms. The war in the Pacific was over at last.

Two of the future presidents left the navy during the war. Thirty-three-year-old Lieutenant Commander Johnson returned to Congress in July 1942. Twenty-seven-year-old Lieutenant Kennedy was discharged in March 1945 due to incapacitation from colitis.

Three future presidents left the navy after the war ended. Twenty-one-year-old Lieutenant (jg) Bush was released in September 1945. Thirty-two-year-old Lieutenant Commander Nixon left in December. Finally, thirty-two-year-old Lieutenant Commander Ford returned to civilian life in February 1946.

All five future presidents were honorably discharged, and three were decorated. Johnson was awarded a Silver Star for his flight over New Guinea. Kennedy received the Navy and Marine Corps Medal for his role in saving the lives of the crew of PT 109. Bush earned the Distinguished Flying Cross for his actions in attacking Japanese communications facilities on Chichi Jima.

Johnson remained in Congress after the war. Within 16 months, he was joined by Kennedy and Nixon, both of whom served on the Education and Labor Committee. Ford entered Congress two years later, after a brief law career. Bush entered Congress 22 years after the war's end, following a career in the oil industry.

The war in the Pacific was primarily a naval war. At the outbreak of hostilities, Japan was on a near parity with the United States in terms of the numbers and displacement of ships, as well as the numbers of aircraft that could reasonably be committed to the Pacific. Her intention was to strike quickly, secure necessary resources, and establish a defensive perimeter from which she could protect her positions. There was no plan to defeat the United States and her Allies. At best, Japanese leaders hoped to negotiate an agreement by which Japan would retain control of most of her possessions, much as she had done at the termination of the Russo-Japanese war.

Japan made two fundamental errors. First, the rough equivalence in naval power at the beginning of the war was dwarfed by United States naval power produced during the war. Second, Americans were outraged at the Japanese atrocities in China, as well as their attack on the Pacific Fleet at Pearl Harbor, and were not about to slink quietly away. Americans demanded action and were quick to volunteer for the war effort.

The industrial capability of the United States, when focused on war material, was overwhelming. Paul Kennedy, in *The Rise of the Great Powers*, estimated that the United States had more than 10 times the economic ability to wage war than did Japan. Furthermore, America's factories and material sources did not come under attack as did Japan's. In aircraft carriers alone, the United States outproduced Japan 141 to 17. In merchant ships the United States outproduced Japan 34 million tons to 4 million tons, when Japan desperately needed merchant ships to import critical materials to its island nation. Finally, the United States outproduced Japan by 325,000 to 75,000 aircraft. Even if one halved the above numbers because the United States was fighting a two-ocean war, the disparity remains staggering.

At the war's end, Japan's vaunted navy was in shambles, having been reduced largely by submarine and carrier aircraft attack. Japan lost 21 aircraft carriers, 10 battleships, 40 cruisers, 124 destroyers, 132 submarines, and 8,000,000 tons of Merchant Marine ships.

Given that the war in the Pacific was a naval war, it is not at all surprising that the five future presidents fought in that theater. The rapidly expanding navy had an active program to recruit college graduates and rapidly commission them as Naval Reserve officers. Living conditions were more comfortable than slogging through African desert sands or European mud and snow. Finally, the navy held a certain amount of glamour for impressionable young men.

Each of the future presidents had his own personal reasons as well. Johnson, a House Naval Affairs Committee member and a lieutenant commander in the Navy Reserve, could hardly change services when the war broke out. Kennedy was a man of the sea from his early childhood, and he was able to secure a direct commission. Nixon, as a lawyer, could be commissioned as an officer in 60 days. Ford had a background in sea scouts, and there was an active Navy Reserve program in his hometown. Bush wanted to be a navy fighter pilot and entered the navy right out of high school.

The five future presidents volunteered rather than wait to be drafted. These were not nascent paladins hungering to lead troops to glorious victory. None were Naval Academy graduates, and none seriously entertained the notion of a military career. They, like most young American men at the time, simply felt a duty to serve their country. The navy provided an attractive means to fulfill that duty.

Notes

Chapter 1
Lyndon B. Johnson: President's Representative

1. Booth Mooney, *The Lyndon Johnson Story* (New York: Farrar, Straus and Company, 1964), 28.
2. Doris Kearns, *Lyndon Johnson and the American Dream* (New York: Harper and Row, 1976), 90.
3. Ronnie Dugger, *The Politician: The Life and Times of Lyndon Johnson, The Drive for Power from the Frontier to Master of the Senate* (New York: W. W. Norton and Company, 1982), 238.
4. Mooney, *The Lyndon Johnson Story*, 31.
5. Robert Caro, *Means of Ascent: The Years of Lyndon Johnson* (New York, Vintage Books, 1990), 20.
6. Shelby Scates, *Warren G. Magnuson and the Shaping of Twentieth-Century America* (Seattle: University of Washington Press, 1997), 101.
7. John Connally became secretary of the navy in the Kennedy administration, governor of Texas, and secretary of the treasury in the Nixon administration.
8. "Naval Travel Orders" (Austin, Tex.: Lyndon Baines Johnson Library and Museum, n.d.), LBJA Subject File, (Naval Orders); see also James Reston, *The Lone Star: The Life of John Connally* (New York: Harper and Row, 1989), 77.
9. Lyndon Johnson, "Roosevelt Meeting Notes" (Austin, Tex.: Lyndon Baines Johnson Library and Museum, Subject File, Container 73—Naval Career, 1942).
10. Lyndon Johnson, "Complete Itinerary" (Austin, Tex.: Lyndon Baines Johnson Library and Museum, 1942).
11. Chief of the Bureau of Navigation to Lieutenant Commander Lyndon Johnson, "Orders of April 29, 1942, Modified" (Austin, Tex.: Lyndon Baines Johnson Library and Museum, 1942), LBJA Subject File, Container 73, Naval Career.
12. Admiral McCain is the grandfather of Arizona Senator John McCain, a former navy captain.
13. Johnson, "Complete Itinerary."
14. Lyndon Johnson, "Notes of meeting with General MacArthur" (Austin Tex.: Lyndon Baines Johnson Library and Museum, 1942), LBJA Subject File, Container 73, Naval Career.

15. William Breuer, *Sea Wolf: A Biography of John D. Bulkeley, USN* (San Francisco: Presidio Press, 1989), 295.

16. Lyndon Johnson, "Diary" (Austin, Tex.: Lyndon Baines Johnson Library and Museum, 1942), AC66-1, no container.

17. Eric Bergerud, *Fire in the Sky: The Air War in the South Pacific* (Boulder, Colo.: Westview Press, 2000), 53.

18. Rodney Cardell, *Wings around Us: Wartime Memories of Aviation in Northern Australia* (Brisbane, Australia: Amphion Press, 1991), 14.

19. Martin Caidin and Edward Hymoff, *The Mission* (Philadelphia: J. B. Lippincott Co., 1964), 71.

20. Henry Sakaida, *Winged Samurai: Saburo Sakai and the Zero Fighter Pilots* (Mesa, Ariz.: Champlin Fighter Museum Press, 1985), 51.

21. Glenn Shaffer, telephone conversation with author, May 2001.

22. Wesley Craven and James Cate, Eds., *The Army Air Forces in World War II, Vol. 1, Plans and Early Operations January 1939 to August 1942* (Chicago: The University of Chicago Press, 1950), 416.

23. Richard Suehr, telephone conversation with author, April 2001.

24. Craven and Cate, *The Army Air Forces in World War II, Vol. 1*, 476.

25. William Hess, *Pacific Sweep: The 5th and 13th Fighter Squadrons in World War II* (Garden City, New York: Doubleday & Company, Inc., 1974), 43.

26. Eric Hammel, *Aces against Japan: The American Aces Speak, Vol. 1* (Novato, Calif.: Presidio Press, 1992), 40.

27. Craven and Cate, *The Army Air Forces in World War II, Vol. 1*, 477.

28. Carlos Dannacher, communication with author, May 2001.

29. Sakai, who shot down 64 Allied aircraft, died in September 2000.

30. Roger Freeman, *B-26 Marauder at War* (New York: Charles Scribner & Sons, 1977), 21.

31. Radiogram US TWN NR 18, GR92 to 19 Bomb Group, Received 2200 June 7, 1942 (Maxwell Air Force Base, Ala.: Air Force Historical Research Agency).

32. Radiogram US TWN NR 17, GR64 to 3 Bomb Group, Received 2200 June 7, 1942 (Maxwell Air Force Base, Ala.: Air Force Historical Research Agency).

33. Radiogram US TWN NR 28, GR50 to ACH Townsville, Received 0330 June 9, 1942 (Maxwell Air Force Base, Ala.: Air Force Historical Research Agency).

34. Radiogram US TWN NR 16, GR63 to 22 Bomb Group, Received 2200 June 7, 1942, see also Radiogram US TWN NR 33 GR53 to ACH Townsville, Received 0730 June 9, 1942 (Maxwell Air Force Base, Ala.: Air Force Historical Research Agency).

35. Radiogram US TWN NR 8, GR22 to Horn Island, Received 1300 June 8, 1942 (Maxwell Air Force Base, Ala.: Air Force Historical Research Agency).

36. Radiogram US TWN GR 28, GR50 to ACH Townsville, Received 1330 June 8, 1942 (Maxwell Air Force Base, Ala.: Air Force Historical Research Agency).

37. "22nd Bomb Group June-July 1942 Mission Report June 8 & 9, 1942" (College Park, Md.: United States National Archives), Box 139, WWII Combat Operations Reports, Records of the Army Air Forces, Record Group 18.

38. Caidin and Hymoff, *The Mission*, 106.

39. Robert Marshall, telephone conversation with author, July 1999.

40. "22nd Bomb Group June-July 1942 Mission Report June 8 & 9, 1942."

41. Walter Krell to Henry Sakaida, November 1984.

42. Fred Eaton and Jack Carlson, "Narrative Report of Mission of June 8, 1942" (Townsville, Australia: 435th Bombardment Squadron, Office of the Intelligence Officer, June 10, 1942, Maxwell Air Force Base, Ala.: Air Force Historical Research Agency).

43. "22nd Bomb Group June-July 1942 Mission Report June 8 & 9, 1942."

44. Albert Tyree, telephone conversation with author, June 2000.

45. Robert Marshall, telephone conversation with author, July 1999.

46. Wallace Fields, communication with author, March 2001; see also Wallace Fields, *Kangaroo Squadron: Memories of a Pacific Bomber Pilot* (Shamrock Tex.: by the author, 1982), 71.

47. Fields, *Kangaroo Squadron*, 72.

48. "Radiogram US TWN NR 20, GR107 to ACH Townsville, June 9, 1942" (Maxwell Air Force Base, Ala.: Air Force Historical Research Agency).

49. Paul Gambonini, communication with author, May 2001.

50. Albert Stanwood, communications with author, July 1999 and November 2000.

51. "History of the 22nd Bombardment Group, 1 Feb 1940–31 Jan 1944" (Maxwell Air Force Base, Ala.: Air Force Historical Research Agency), 23.

52. Curran Jones, communications with author, April 2001.

53. David Ghen, communications with author, December 2000.

54. "19th Bombardment Squadron, Mission Report, June 9, 1942" (Maxwell Air Force Base, Ala.: Air Force Historical Research Agency).

55. "2nd Squadron, 22nd Bomb Group Report of June 8–9, 1942" (Tucson, Ariz.: International Archive of the B-26 Marauder, Pima Air and Space Museum).

56. Byron Darnton, "Rep. Johnson Sees Airmen in Action" (New York: *The New York Times*, June 12, 1942), 7.

57. Johnson, "Diary."

58. W. L. White, *Queens Die Proudly* (New York: Harcourt, Brace and Company, 1943), 248; see also Craven and Cate, *The Army Air Forces in World War II, Vol. 1*, 477.

59. Walter Edmonds, *They Fought With What They Had* (Boston: Little, Brown and Co., 1951), 70; see also Hammel, *Aces against Japan*, 46.

60. Frank J. Olynyk, *USAAF (Pacific Theater) of Enemy Aircraft in Air-to-Air Combat World War 2* (Aurora, Ohio: self-published, 1985), 8.

61. Donald Green, Curran Jones and Richard Suehr, communications with the author, May 2001.

62. Michael Claringbould, communication with the author, May 2001.

63. "39th Fighter Squadron Diary," June 9 excerpt provided by Squadron member and 39th Association Treasurer, Roy Seher; and "22nd Bomb Group June-July 1942 Mission Report June 8 & 9, 1942."

64. "435th Squadron History, 19th Bombardment Group." (Maxwell Air Force Base: Air Force Historical Research Association, n.d.).

65. Sakaida interview with Walter Krell, May 2, 1985.

66. "435th Squadron History."

67. Johnson, "Complete Itinerary."

68. Herbert Brownstein, *The Swoose: Odyssey of a B-17* (Washington, D.C.: Smithsonian Institution Press,1993), 92.

69. Brownstein, *The Swoose*, 97; White, *Queens Die Proudly*, 266; Johnson, "Complete Itinerary."

70. Johnson, "Diary."

71. Brownstein, *The Swoose*, 97.

72. Noel Tunny, *Fight Back from the North* (Brisbane, Australia, by the author, 1992), 8.

73. Johnson, "Diary."

74. White, *Queens Die Proudly*, 263.

75. Johnson, "Diary."

76. Ibid.

77. Johnson, "Complete Itinerary."

78. "Commander Lyndon B. Johnson's Army Silver Star Medal Citation" (Washington, D.C.: Department of the Navy, Naval Historical Center, September 1997).

Chapter 2

John F. Kennedy: PT Boat Skipper

1. Rose Kennedy, *Times to Remember* (New York: Doubleday, 1974), 243; see also James Burns, *John Kennedy: A Political Profile* (New York: Harcourt, Brace & Company, 1960), 47.

2. "Appointment in Naval Reserve" (Boston: John Fitzgerald Kennedy Library, October 1941), Box 11 A, John F. Kennedy Personal Papers; see also Joan Blair and Clay Blair, Jr., *The Search for JFK* (New York: Berkley Publishing Corporation and G. P. Putnam's Sons, 1976),128.

3. Charles Wellborn, "Memorandum to the Chief of the Bureau of Navigation, Subject: Ensign John Fitzgerald Kennedy, - active duty, request for" (Boston: John Fitzgerald Kennedy Library, October 1941), Box 11 A, John F. Kennedy Personal Papers.

4. "Report on the Fitness of Officers, 10-27-41 to 1-19-42" (Boston: John Fitzgerald Kennedy Library, n.d.), Box 11 A, John F. Kennedy Personal Papers.

5. "Memorandum from the Chief of the Bureau of Navigation to Ensign John F. Kennedy I-V(S), USNR, Subject: Change of Duty" (Boston: John Fitzgerald Kennedy Library, January 1942), Box 11 A, John F. Kennedy Personal Papers.

6. "Airmailgram" (Boston: John F. Kennedy Library, July 20, 1942), Box 11 A, John F. Kennedy Personal Papers.

7. Nigel Hamilton, *J.F.K. Reckless Youth* (New York: Random House,1992), 496.

8. Robert Bulkley, *At Close Quarters: PT Boats in the United States Navy* (Washington, D.C., U.S. Government Printing Office,1962), 60. Captain Robert Bulkley is not related to Vice Admiral John Bulkeley.

9. Ibid.

10. "Orders to proceed to the Motor Torpedo Boat Squadrons Training Center" (Boston: John Fitzgerald Kennedy Library, September 26, 1942), Box 11 A, John F. Kennedy Personal Papers.

11. Blair and Blair, *The Search for JFK*, 166.

12. "Orders to proceed to Jacksonville, Florida" (Boston: John Fitzgerald Kennedy Library, January 8, 1943), Box 11 A, John F. Kennedy Personal Papers.

13. Blair and Blair, *The Search for JFK*, 169.

14. Admiral John Harlee in *PT TV Sea Stories #1*, prod. by Ned Jay (Atlanta:, self-published, 1992), videocassette.

15. "Transfer Orders" (Boston: John Fitzgerald Kennedy Library, February 16, 1943), Box 11 A, John F. Kennedy Personal Papers.

16. Hamilton, *J. F. K: Reckless Youth*, 522.

17. James Mooney, Ed., *Dictionary of American Naval Fighting Ships, Vol. 6* (Washington, D.C.: United States Government Printing Office), 135.

18. Robert Donovan, *PT 109: John F. Kennedy in World War II, Fortieth Anniversary Edition* (New York: McGraw-Hill Book Company, Inc., 2001), 5.

19. A Harvard Law School graduate, Reed served as special assistant to the attorney general and later as assistant secretary of the treasury in Kennedy's administration.

20. "Deck Log Book, Administrative Remarks, U.S.S. *Rochambeau*, Month of March, 1943" (College Park, Md.: United States National Archives, 1943).

21. James Reed, telephone conversation with author, February 7, 2000.

22. Donovan, *PT 109*, 29; see also "Deck Log of U.S.S. L.S.T. 449," April 1943 (College Park, Md.: United States National Archives, 1943).

23. Jack E. Britain, telephone conversation with the author, July 2000.

24. Richard Frank, *Guadalcanal: The Definitive Account of the Landmark Battle* (New York: Random House, 1990), 71.

25. John Searles, *Tales of Tulagi: Memoirs of World War II* (New York: Vantage Press, 1992), 15.

26. John Searles, telephone conversation with the author, March 2000.

27. Dr. Emilio D. Lastreto, telephone conversation with the author, March 2000.

28. Hugh Cave, *Long Were the Nights: The Saga of a PT Boat Squadron in World War II* (Washington, D.C.: Zenger Publishing Co., 1943), 34.

29. Searles, *Tales of Tulagi*, 20.

30. Lester Gamble, telephone conversation with the author, March 2000.

31. Clark Faulkner, telephone conversation with the author, April 2000.

32. Cave, *Long Were the Nights*, 67.

33. M. G. Harris, Hormel Company, telephone conversation with the author, July 2000.

34. Clark Faulkner, telephone conversation with the author, April 2000.

35. Cave, *Long Were the Nights*, 183.

36. Searles, *Tales of Tulagi*, 39.

37. Coletta, *United States Navy and Marine Corps Bases*, 330.

38. William Hess, *Pacific Sweep: The 5th and 13th Fighter Commands in World War II* (Garden City, New York: Doubleday & Company, 1974), 65; see also Eric Hammel, *Aces against Japan: The American Aces Speak, Vol. 1* (Novato, Calif.: Presidio Press, 1992), 94.

39. Samuel Morison, *History of the United States Naval Operations in World War II, Vol. 6: Breaking the Bismarcks Barrier* (Boston: Little, Brown and Company, 1968), 123.

40. "Deck Log of U.S.S. L.S.T. 449."

41. Hugh Robinson, telephone conversation with the author, March 2000.

42. John Iles, telephone conversation with the author, March 2000.

43. Henry Doscher, telephone conversation with the author, January 2000.

44. "Log Book of PT 109 for April 1,1943 to June 30, 1943" (College Park, Md.: United States National Archives, 1943).

45. Kenneth Prescott, telephone conversation with the author, March 2000; see also, Searles, *Tales of Tulagi*, 45.

46. Bryant Larson, telephone conversation with the author, August 2000.

47. Allan Webb, telephone conversation with the author, May 2000.

48. "Report on Fitness of Officers 4/11/43 to 5/29/43" (Boston: John Fitzgerald Kennedy Library, June 9, 1943), Box 11 A, John F. Kennedy Personal Papers.

49. John Kennedy to Dad and Mother (Boston: John Fitzgerald Kennedy Library, May 1943), Box 5, John F. Kennedy Personal Papers.

50. Hugh Robinson, telephone conversation with the author, March 2000.

51. Pat Munroe, telephone conversation with the author, June 2000.

52. Coletta, *United States Navy and Marine Corps Bases*, 282.

53. John Searles, telephone conversation with the author, March 2000.

54. Searles, *Tales of Tulagi*, 46.

55. Kenneth Prescott, telephone conversation with the author, March 2000.

56. Searles, telephone conversation with the author, March 2000.

57.　Clark Faulkner, telephone conversation with the author, April 2000.

58.　John Kearney, telephone conversation with the author, March 2000.

59.　Kenneth Prescott, telephone conversation with the author, March 2000.

60.　Searles, *Tales of Tulagi*, 45.

61.　Ibid., 48.

62.　John Searles, telephone conversation with the author, May 2000.

63.　Dr. Robert Gran, telephone conversation with the author, January 2000.

64.　"Air Command Solomon Islands, Intelligence Summary: Summary and Review for Week Ending June 25, Solomons Area" (Maxwell Air Force Base, Ala., Air Force Historical Research Agency, n.d.), microfilm A7633.

65.　Kenneth Prescott, telephone conversation with the author, March 2000.

66.　Bulkley, *At Close Quarters*, 118.

67.　John Iles, telephone conversation with the author, March 2000.

68.　Dick Keresey, *PT 105* (Annapolis, Md.: Naval Institute Press, 1996), 62.

69.　Donovan, *PT 109*, 69.

70.　Gerard Zinser, telephone conversation with the author, November 1998.

71.　*Los Angeles Times*, August 30, 2001. Zinser died on August 21, 2001.

72.　Blair and Blair, *The Search for JFK*, 206.

73.　Thomas Warfield, "ComMTB Action Report of 1-2 August 1943" (Boston: John Fitzgerald Kennedy Library, August 1943), Box 11 A, John F. Kennedy Personal Papers.

74.　Blair and Blair, *The Search for JFK*, 211.

75.　Henry Brantingham, *Fire and Ice* (San Diego, ProMotion Publishers, 1995), 45.

76.　"ComMTB Action Report of 1-2 August 1943."

77.　Brantingham, *Fire and Ice*, 45.

78.　William Liebenow, telephone conversation with the author, June 2000.

79.　Donovan, *PT 109*, 157.

80.　Keresey, *PT 105*, 81.

81.　Arthur Berndtson, telephone conversation with the author, April 2000.

82.　Raymond Macht, telephone conversation with the author, June 2000.

83.　Tameichi Hara, *Japanese Destroyer Captain* (New York, Ballantine Books, 1961), 181.

84.　Keresey, *PT 105*, 89.

85.　Surely *Amagiri*'s speed was less than 40 knots as the maximum design speed for her class of ships was 38 knots.

86.　William Liebenow, telephone conversation with the author, June 2000.

87.　John Maguire in *PT Sea Stories #1*, prod. by Ned Jay, Atlanta, Ga., 1992, videocassette.

88.　Dick Keresey, telephone conversation with the author, April 2000.

89.　"Memorandum to Commander Motor Torpedo Boat Flotilla One, Subject: Sinking of PT 109 and subsequent rescue of survivors" (Boston: John Fitzgerald Kennedy Library, August 22, 1943), Box 11 A, John F. Kennedy Personal Papers.

90.　Bulkley, *At Close Quarters*, 123.

91.　Robert Donovan, *Boxing the Kangaroo: A Reporter's Memoir* (Columbia, Missouri: University of Missouri Press, 2000), 9.

92.　Katsumori Yamashiro to Senator John Kennedy, trans. by classmate (Boston: John Fitzgerald Kennedy Library, November 15, 1958), Box 132, P.T. 109 Correspondence: Japanese.

93.　Kohei Hanami, statement forwarded to Senator John Kennedy by Gunji Hosono (Boston: John Fitzgerald Kennedy Library, January 28, 1960), Box 132, P.T. 109 Correspondence: Japanese.

94.　*The Evening Post* (Wellington, New Zealand), August 1, 1963.

95. John Searles, telephone conversation with the author, March 2000.

96. Paul Fay, telephone conversation with the author, August 2000.

97. William Liebenow, telephone conversation with the author, June 2000.

98. William Battle, telephone conversation with the author, September 2000.

99. "Memorandum to Commander Motor Torpedo Boat Flotilla One, Subject: Sinking of PT 109 and subsequent rescue of survivors" (Boston: John Fitzgerald Kennedy Library, 22 August 1943), Box 11 A John F. Kennedy Personal Papers; see also John Hersey, "Survival" *The New Yorker*, June 17, 1944, 31-43.

100. Kennedy appointed White deputy attorney general in 1961 and Supreme Court justice in 1962. He retired from the Supreme Court in 1993 after serving 31 years.

101. Dennis Hutchinson, *The Man Who Once Was Wizzer White: A Portrait of Justice Byron R. White* (New York: The Free Press, 1998), 135–38.

102. Gerard Zinser, telephone conversation with the author, November 1998.

103. Walter Lord, *Lonely Vigil: Coastwatchers of the Solomons* (New York: The Viking Press, 1977), 218.

104. Donovan, *PT 109*, 121.

105. Alvin Cluster, telephone conversation with the author, April 2000; see also Stanmore Marshall, telephone conversation with the author, July 2001.

106. Danny and Karin Kennedy, communications with author, Gizo, Solomon Islands, August 2000.

107. John Maguire, *Sea Stories #1*, prod. by Ned Jay, Atlanta, 1992, videocassette.

108. Admiralty Chart 1735, South Pacific Ocean, Solomon Islands, Plans in the New Georgia Group, printed in the United Kingdom, June 1998, nautical chart.

109. John Hersey, "Survival," *The New Yorker*, June 17, 1944, 37.

110. Biuku Gasa, videotaped interview, trans. by Alfred Bisili, *PT Sea Stories #2*, prod. by Ned Jay, Atlanta, 1992, videocassette.

111. Aaron Kumana Interview, Solomon Islands Oral History (Boston: John Fitzgerald Kennedy Library, March 1986), MS-84-57.

112. Biuku Gasa, videotaped interview.

113. Biuku Gasa Interview, Solomon Islands Oral History (Boston: John Fitzgerald Kennedy Library, March 1986), MS-84-57.

114. Aaron Kumana Interview.

115. Biuku Gasa Interview.

116. The coconut shell segment is on display at the John Fitzgerald Kennedy Presidential Library in Boston, Mass. It is not a complete coconut shell as is often envisioned.

117. The Burns Philp Company operated a store on Gizo when it was the area's administrative center.

118. Lord, *Coastwatchers*, 266.

119. Ibid.

120. Ibid., 272.

121. Donovan, *PT 109*, 157.

122. Hersey, "Survivor."

123. John Maguire in *PT Sea Stories #2*, prod. by Ned Jay, Atlanta, 1992, videocassette.

124. Colonel George M. Hill to Senator John F. Kennedy (Boston: John Fitzgerald Kennedy Library, October 1957), John F. Kennedy Pre-Presidential Papers Senate Files: General Files, 1953-1960; 1958-1960, President's Files, P. T. Boat Letter.

125. Biuku Gasa Interview.

126. Donovan, *PT 109*, 161.

127. "Logbook of USS PT 157, 28 June 1943 to 31 October 1943" (College Park, Md.: United States National Archives, 1943).

128. Alvin Cluster, telephone conversation with the author, April 2000.

129. Arthur Berndtson, telephone conversation with the author, July 2000.

130. William Battle, telephone conversation with the author, September 2000.

131. William Liebenow, telephone conversation with the author, July 2000.

132. Raymond Laflin, telephone conversation with the author, June 2000.

133. James Smith, telephone conversation with the author, June 2000.

134. William Liebenow, telephone conversations with the author, June and July 2000.

135. Theodore Aust to the author, June 2000.

136. Arthur Berndtson, telephone conversation with the author, April 2000.

137. Welford West, telephone conversation with the author, June 2000.

138. Alvin Cluster, telephone conversation with the author, April 2000.

139. Welford West, telephone conversations with the author, June and July 2000.

140. Raymond Macht, telephone conversations with the author, June and August 2000.

141. Raymond Laflin, telephone conversation with the author, June 2000.

142. William Liebenow, telephone conversation with the author, June 2000.

143. Gerard Zinser, telephone conversation with the author, November 1998.

144. Theodore Aust to the author, June 2000.

145. Danny Kennedy, communication with the author, July 2000.

146. William Liebenow, telephone conversation with the author, August 2000.

147. "Logbook of USS PT 157, 28 June 1943 to 31 October 1943" (College Park, Md.: United States National Archives, 1943).

148. "Terrain Study No. 40, Area Study, New Georgia Group, Allied Geographical Section, Southwest Pacific Area," December 17, 1942.

149. Stanley Kendall to the author, June 2000.

150. Stanwood Marshall, telephone conversation with the author, July 2001.

151. Gerard Zinser, Sea Stories #1, prod. by Ned Jay, Atlanta, 1992, videocassette; see also Gerard Zinser to Walter Fallon, January 18, 1993, copy courtesy Joseph Gunterman.

152. Biuku Gasa Interview.

153. Gene Schade, "Diary of Squadron 9" (Germantown, Tenn.: PT Boats, Inc.), 13.

154. Paul Fay, telephone conversation with the author, August 2000. Fay served as undersecretary of the navy in the Kennedy administration and was, for a short period, acting secretary of the navy.

155. Dr. Joseph Wharton, interview by Clay Blair Jr. (Laramie, Wyo., American Heritage Center, University of Wyoming, n.d.), audiotape.

156. James Reed, telephone conversation with the author, February 2000.

157. Kenneth Prescott, telephone conversation with the author, March 2000.

158. Paul Fay, *The Pleasure of His Company* (New York: Harper & Row, 1966), 130.

159. David Levy, telephone conversation with the author, June 2000.

160. Alvin Cluster, telephone conversation with the author, June 2000.

161. James Reed, telephone conversation with the author, February 2000.

162. Donovan, *Boxing the Kangaroo*, 102.

163. John Kennedy to Mother & Dad (Boston: John Fitzgerald Kennedy Library, September 12, 1943), Box 11 A, John F. Kennedy Personal Papers.

164. "PT 59 Log Book for October 1, 1943 to December 31, 1943" (College Park, Md.: United States National Archives, November 1943); see also Keresey, *PT 105*, 154.

165. Isaac John Mitchell is not related to John Newton Mitchell, future attorney general of the United States. Attorney General Mitchell served in PT boats in the Pacific after Kennedy returned to the States.

166. Kenneth Prescott, telephone conversation with the author, April 2000.

167. Three PT Boats in Formation (Boston, John Fitzgerald Kennedy Library, 1943), black and white photograph.

168. Le Roy Taylor to the author, November 2000.

169. Bulkley, *At Close Quarters*, 135.

170. Le Roy Taylor to the author, December 2000.

171. W. Glen Christianson, telephone conversation with the author, June 2000.

172. Tameichi Hara, *Japanese Destroyer Captain* (New York: Ballantine Books, 1961), 192.

173. "Agreement to promotion to Lieutenant" (Boston: John Fitzgerald Kennedy Library, October 22, 1943), Box 11 A, John F. Kennedy Personal Papers.

174. "PT 59 Log Book for October 1, 1943 to December 31, 1943" (College Park, Md.: United States National Archives, 1943).

175. Victor Krulak, interview with the author, June 2000.

176. "Second Parachute Battalion (Reinforced) War Diary from October 27 to November 4, 1943, Operations on Choiseul, British Solomon Islands" (College Park, Md.: United States National Archives, 1943), 1.

177. "PT 59 Log Book for October 1, 1943 to December 31, 1943" (College Park, Md.: United States National Archives, 1943).

178. "Second Parachute Battalion (Reinforced) War Diary," 9.

179. Ibid., 6.

180. Warner Bigger, telephone conversations with the author, February and March 2001.

181. Thomas Siefke, telephone conversation with the author, March 2001.

182. Michael Vinich, telephone conversation with the author, March 2001.

183. "Second Parachute Battalion (Reinforced) War Diary," 7.

184. Warner Bigger, telephone conversations with the author, February and March, 2000.

185. John Rentz, "Bougainville and the Northern Solomons" (Washington, D.C.: Historical Section, Headquarters United States Marine Corps, 1948), 112.

186. "Second Parachute Battalion (Reinforced) Unit Journal from October 27 to November 4, 1943, Operations on Choiseul, British Solomon Islands" (College Park, Md.: United States National Archives, 1943), 4.

187. Charles Ridewood, telephone conversation with the author, August 2000.

188. "PT 59 Log Book for October 1943 to December 31, 1943" (College Park, Md.: United States National Archives, November 2, 1943); see also "Motor Torpedo Boat Squadron Nineteen Administrative Log" (College Park, Md., United States National Archives, November 1943), 32.

189. Harry Towne, telephone conversation with the author, February 2001.

190. "Second Parachute Battalion (Reinforced) Unit Journal," 5.

191. Dick Keresey, telephone conversations with the author, April and September 2000; see also Keresey, *PT 105*, 153.

192. Glen Christiansen, telephone conversation with the author, April 2000.

193. Leo Campbell, telephone conversation with the author, August 2000.

194. Warner Bigger, telephone conversation with the author, March 2000.

195. Edward Thomas, telephone conversation with the author, March 2001.

196. Harry Towne, telephone conversation with the author, February 2001.

197. Rea Duncan to Roy Homerding, January 21, 1986.

198. Vivian Scribner to the author, November 2000 and March 2001.

199. Dick Keresey, telephone conversation with the author, May 2000.

200. Ibid.

201. "PT 59 Log Book for October 1943 to December 31, 1943" (College Park, Md.: United States National Archives, November 3, 1943); see also "Motor Torpedo Boat Squadron Nineteen Administrative Log" (College Park, Md., United States National Archives, November 1943), 32.

202. "PT 59 Log Book for October 1943 to December 31, 1943" (College Park, Md.: United States National Archives, November 1943).

203. Ibid.

204. Dr. E. R. Bahnson, communications with the author, August 2000.

205. "PT 59 Log Book for October 1943 to December 31, 1943."

206. S. McGinn, R. Drew, and C. Derrick, "Report of Medical Survey" (Boston: John F. Kennedy Library and Museum, December 6, 1944), Box 11 A. John F. Kennedy Personal Papers.

207. "Orders to proceed to the Motor Torpedo Boat Squadrons Training Center" (Boston: John Fitzgerald Kennedy Library, December 21, 1943), Box 11 A, John F. Kennedy Personal Papers.

208. Blair and Blair, *The Search for JFK*, 345.

209. Kenneth Prescott, telephone conversation with the author, March 2000.

210. "Report on the Fitness of Officers, 4-13-43 to 12-21-43" (Boston: John Fitzgerald Kennedy Library, n.d.), Box 11 A, John F. Kennedy Personal Papers.

211. "Ship's Log of USS Breton" (College Park, Md.: United States National Archives, December 23, 1943).

212. James Shaffer, *Geographic Locations of U.S. APOs 1941–1984*, Fifth Edition (War Cover Club, 1985), 57.

213. Lester Sperberg, telephone conversation with the author, August 2000.

214. Sidney Sherwin Jr., telephone conversation with the author, August 2000.

215. William Y'Blood, *The Little Giants: U.S. Escort Carriers against Japan* (Annapolis, Md.: Naval Institute Press, 1987), 417.

216. "Ship's Log of USS. Breton," December 26, 1943.

217. Ibid., January 7, 1944.

218. Note from John F. Kennedy to Edward Prescott, return address Palm Beach, Florida, n.d., made available by Kenneth Prescott.

219. Herbert Parmet, *Jack: The Struggles of John F. Kennedy* (New York: The Dial Press, 1980), 117.

220. Searles, *Tales of Tulagi*, 58.

221. Clark Faulkner, telephone conversation with the author, April 2000.

222. "Report on the Fitness of Officers June 11 to December 26, 1943" (Boston: John Fitzgerald Kennedy Library, January 8, 1945), Box 11 A, John F. Kennedy Personal Papers.

223. "Report of Medical Survey" (Boston: John Fitzgerald Kennedy Library, December 6, 1944), Box 11 A, John F. Kennedy Personal Papers.

224. "Report of Naval Retiring Board" (Boston: John Fitzgerald Kennedy Library, December 27, 1944), Box 11 A, John F. Kennedy Personal Papers.

225. "Memo from Secretary of the Navy to John F. Kennedy approving the recommendation of the Naval Retiring Board" (Boston: John Fitzgerald Kennedy Library, March 16, 1945), Box 11 A, John F. Kennedy Personal Papers.

226. "Lt. John F. Kennedy's NMCM citation" (Washington, D.C.: Naval Historical Center, May 1944).

Chapter 3
Richard M. Nixon: Ground Aviation Officer

1. Richard Nixon, "Senator Richard Nixon Chronology of Government and Navy Service" (Yorba Linda, Calif.: The Richard Nixon Library and Birthplace, n.d.), RMN Navy Jacket, PPS 264.2.

2. Edwin J. Felher to Richard Nixon (Yorba Linda, Calif.: The Richard Nixon Library and Birthplace, January 6, 1942), telegram.

3. Roger Morris, *Richard Milhous Nixon: The Rise of an American Politician* (New York: Henry Holt and Company, 1990), 240.

4. "Tour of Duty/Reports Commendation" (Yorba Linda, Calif.: The Richard Nixon Library and Birthplace, n.d.), RMN Navy Jacket, PPS 264.407.

5. Jacob Beuscher to Navy Cadet Selection Board (Yorba Linda, Calif.: The Richard Nixon Library and Birthplace, May 4, 1943), RMN Navy Jacket, PPS 264.407.

6. William Rogers became secretary of state in Nixon's first administration. G. Mennen Williams became governor of Michigan.

7. "Tour of Duty/Reports Commendation."

8. "Memorandum from The Chief of Naval Personnel to Lieutenant (jg) Richard M. Nixon, Subject: Change of Duty" (Yorba Linda, Calif.: The Richard Nixon Library and Birthplace, October 10, 1942), RMN Navy Jacket. PPS 264.407.

9. "Bulletin from The Chief of Naval Personnel to All Shore Stations in Continental United States" (Yorba Linda, Calif., Richard Nixon Library and Birthplace, March 3, 1943), SCAT folder, PPS 264.137.

10. "Fitness Report of Richard M. Nixon March 19 to May 7 1943" (Yorba Linda, Calif.: Richard Nixon Library and Birthplace, n.d.), RMN Navy Jacket, PPS 264.407.

11. "Statement of Travel" (Yorba Linda, Calif.: Richard Nixon Library and Birthplace, n.d.), SCAT folder, PS264.152.

12. "Memo from Chief of Naval Personnel to Richard M. Nixon, Subject: Change of Duty, Second Endorsement" (Yorba Linda, Calif.: Richard Nixon Library and Birthplace, May 27, 1943), PS264.151.

13. "Memo from Chief of Naval Personnel to Richard M. Nixon, Subject: Change of Duty, Third Endorsement" (Yorba Linda, Calif.: Richard Nixon Library and Birthplace, May 27, 1943), PS264.158.

14. Lester Wroble, telephone conversation with the author, June 2000.

15. John Niven, *The American President Lines and its Forebears 1848-1984* (Newark, N.J.: University of Delaware Press, 1984), 143; see also James Mooney, Ed., *Dictionary of American Naval Fighting Ships, Volume 5* (Washington, D.C.: United States Government Printing Office, 1970), 374.

16. "Memo from Chief of Naval Personnel to Richard M. Nixon, Subject: Change of Duty, Fourth and Fifth Endorsements" (Yorba Linda, Calif.: Richard Nixon Library and Birthplace, June 17, 1943), SCAT folder, PS264.158 and 159.

17. "Memo from Chief of Naval Personnel to Richard M. Nixon, Subject: Change of Duty, Eighth and Ninth Endorsements" (Yorba Linda, Calif.: Richard Nixon Library and Birthplace, June 27 and 28, 1943), SCAT folder, PS 264.160.

18. "Memo from the Commander Fleet Air South Pacific to Lieutenant (junior grade) Richard M. Nixon, Subject: Change of Duty" (Yorba Linda, Calif.: Richard Nixon Library and Birthplace, June 30, 1943), SCAT folder, PS 264.161.

19. "Memo from the Commander Fleet Air South Pacific to Lieutenant (junior grade) Richard M. Nixon, Subject: Change of Duty - First Endorsement" (Yorba Linda, Calif.: Richard Nixon Library and Birthplace, July 2, 1943), SCAT folder, PS 264.161.

20. "Duty Assignment" (Yorba Linda, Calif.: Richard Nixon Library and Birthplace, September 19, 1943), RMN Navy Jacket, PPS 264.407.

21. Norman Anderson and William Snyder, "SCAT," *Marine Corps Gazette*, September 1992.

22. William Snyder, presentation of certification at the opening of the Marine Aviation History Museum, Marine Corps Air Station Miramar, May 2000.

23. Robert Allen and Otis Carney, "The Story of SCAT, Parts I and II," Air Transport, December 1944 and January 1945.

24. "SCAT," *Flying*, October 1944, 119.

25. "Fitness Report, 1 July to 30 September, 1943" (Yorba Linda, Calif.: Richard Nixon Library and Birthplace, n.d.), RMN Navy Jacket, PPS 264.407.

26. Richard Nixon to Patricia Nixon (Yorba Linda, Calif.: Richard Nixon Library and Birthplace, August 24, 1943), letter on display.

27. William Sears, telephone conversation with the author, November 1999.

28. Richard Nixon, *In the Arena: A Memoir of Victory, Defeat and Renewal* (New York: Simon and Schuster, 1990), 230.

29. William Harris, telephone conversation with the author, November 1999.

30. Joseph Lash, *Eleanor and Franklin: The Story of Their Relationship, Based on Eleanor Roosevelt's Papers* (New York: W. W. Norton & Company, 1971), 689.

31. Doris Goodwin, *No Ordinary Time: Franklin & Eleanor Roosevelt: The Home Front in World War II* (New York: Touchstone & Simon & Schuster,1994), 465.

32. Lash, *Eleanor and Franklin*, 686.

33. "Memo from the Commanding Officer to Lieutenant (jg) Richard Nixon, Subject: Promotion" (Yorba Linda, Calif.: Richard Nixon Library and Birthplace, October 1, 1943), SCAT folder, PPS 264.163.

34. Terry Nobles, telephone conversation with the author, October 1999.

35. A. H. Peterson to the Honorable Richard Nixon, November 6, 1952.

36. Paul Coletta, *United States Navy and Marine Corps Bases, Overseas* (Westwood, Conn.: Greenwood Press, 1985), 106.

37. William Starke, *Vampire Squadron: The Saga of the 44th Fighter Squadron in the South and Southwest Pacific* (Anaheim, Calif.: Robinson Typographics, 1985), 9; see also Eric Bergerud, *Fire in the Sky: The Air War in the South Pacific* (Boulder, Colo.: Westview Press, 2000), 71.

38. "Fitness Report, 10 October to 15 December 1943" (Yorba Linda, Calif.: Richard Nixon Library and Birthplace, n.d.), RMN Navy Jacket, PPS 264.407.

39. "Memo from The SCAT Personnel Officer to Lieutenant Nixon" (Yorba Linda, Calif.: Richard Nixon Library and Birthplace, November 16, 1943), SCAT folder, PPS 264.168.

40. William Snyder, communications with the author, June and August 2000.

41. H. Jesse Walker, communications with the author, October 1999.

42. Otis Carney, telephone conversation with the author, October 1999.

43. "Commander Richard M. Nixon, U.S. Naval Reserve, Retired" (Washington, D.C., Naval Office of Information, 1969).

44. Terry Nobles, telephone conversation with the author, November 1999.

45. John Hayes, *James A. Michener: A Biography* (Indianapolis: The Bobbs-Merrill Company, 1984), 61.

46. James Michener, *The World is My Home: A Memoir* (New York: Random House, 1992), 91.

47. "Memo from The SCAT Personnel Officer to Lieutenant Nixon" (Yorba Linda, Calif.: Richard Nixon Library and Birthplace, December 10, 1943), SCAT folder, PPS 264.170.

48. Clovis Davis, telephone conversations with the author, October 1999.

49. "Fitness Report, 16 December to 31 December 1943" (Yorba Linda, Calif.: Richard Nixon Library and Birthplace, n.d.), RMN Navy Jacket, PPS 264.407.

50. Oliver Gillespie, *The Pacific: Official History of New Zealand in the Second World War 1939-1945* (Wellington, New Zealand, War History Branch, Department of Internal Affairs, 1952), 130.

51. "COMSCAT Personnel Officer to Richard Nixon" (Yorba Linda, Calif.: Richard Nixon Library and Birthplace, n.d.), SCAT folder, PPS 264.172.

52. John Rentz, "Bougainville and the Northern Solomons" (Washington, D.C.: Headquarters, U.S. Marines, 1948), 90.

53. Howard Nielson, telephone conversation with the author, February 2000.

54. Robert Sherrod, *History of Marine Corps Aviation in World War II* (Washington, D.C., Combat Forces Press, 1952), 207; see also "Air Command Solomon Islands—Intelligence Section Weekly Summary and Review, December 25 to December 31,1943" (Maxwell Air Force Base, Ala.: Air Force Historical Research Agency, 1944).

55. Starke, *Vampire Squadron*, 70.

56. Samuel Morison, Breaking the Bismarcks Barrier 22 July 1942–1 May 1944 (Boston: Little, Brown and Company, 1968), 395.

57. Richard Nixon, *RN: The Memoirs of Richard Nixon* (New York: Gosset & Dunlap, 1978), 28.

58. Robert Martindale, *The Thirteenth Mission: Prisoner of the Omori Prison in Tokyo* (Austin, Tex.: Eakin Press, 1998), photo insert.

59. "Fitness Report, 1 October 1943 to 1 March, 1944" (Yorba Linda, Calif.: Richard Nixon Library and Birthplace, n.d.), RMN Navy Jacket, PPS 264.407.

60. Carl J. Fleps, "Memo from The Superintendent Route Two to The Commander SCAT, Subject: Citation, recommendation for" (Yorba Linda, Calif.: Richard Nixon Library and Birthplace, March 18, 1944), RMN Navy Jacket, PPS 264.407.

61. "Air Solomons Command Weekly Intelligence Summary and Review, Week of February 12-18, 1944" (Maxwell Air Force Base, Alabama, Air Force Historical Research Agency, 1944), microfilm roll A7633.

62. "Memo from The Superintendent Route Two to R. M. Nixon, Lieut., USNR" (Yorba Linda, Calif.: The Richard M. Nixon Library and Birthplace, February 27, 1944), SCAT folder, PPS 264.176.

63. Joseph Tolman, communications with the author, August 2000.

64. Nixon, *RN: The Memoirs of Richard Nixon*, 28.

65. Gillespie, *The Pacific*, 190.

66. Tanikawa Kazou, *Japanese Monograph No. 44: History of the Eighth Area Army November 1942 to August 1945* (Tokyo: Military History Section, Headquarters Army Forces Far East, October 1942), 70.

67. "Air Solomons Command Weekly Intelligence Summary and Review, Week of March 11–17, 1944" (Maxwell Air Force Base, Ala.: Air Force Historical Research Agency, 1944), microfilm roll A7633.

68. "Historical Records of the 13th Troop Carrier Squadron, April 1944" (Maxwell Air Force Base, Ala.: Air Force Historical Research Agency, n.d.), Microfiche A0969.

69. "Nixon Speech Notes" Trans. by Susan Naulty (Yorba Linda, Calif.: The Richard Nixon Library and Birthplace, 1946).

70. Joseph Tolman to the author, August 2001.

71. Lester Wroble, telephone conversation with the author, June 2000.

72. Stephen Ambrose, *Nixon: The Education of a Politician 1913–1962* (New York: Simon and Schuster, 1987), 111.

73. Nixon, *RN: The Memoirs of Richard Nixon*, 29.

74. George Kenney, *General Kenney Reports: A Personal History of the Pacific War* (New York Dual, Sloan and Pearce, 1949), 412.

75. Charles Lindbergh, *The Wartime Journals of Charles A. Lindbergh* (New York: Harcourt, Brace Jovanovich, Inc.,1970), 888.

76. Howard Nielson to the author, February 2000.

77. "Memo from The Superintendent, Route Two to R. M. Nixon" (Yorba Linda: The Richard Nixon Library and Birthplace, May 3,1944), SCAT folder, PPS 264.186.

78. Major Dyer to R. M. Nixon (Yorba Linda: The Richard Nixon Library and Birthplace, June 5,1944), PPS 264.189a, telegram.

79. "Memo from The Superintendent, Route 2, to R. M. Nixon" (Yorba Linda, Calif.: Richard Nixon Library and Birthplace, June 14, 1944), SCAT folder, PPS 264.190A.1.

80. Joseph Tolman, communications with the author, August 2000.

81. "Fitness Report, 1 April to 2 July 1944" (Yorba Linda, Calif.: Richard Nixon Library and Birthplace, n.d.), RMN Navy Jacket, PPS 264.407.

82. "The Commander, Aircraft South Pacific Force to Lieutenant Richard M. Nixon, Subject: Change of Duty" (Yorba Linda, Calif.: Richard Nixon Library and Birthplace, n.d.), SCAT Folder, PPS 264.192.1.

83. "The Commander, Aircraft South Pacific Force to Lieutenant Richard M. Nixon, Subject: Change of Duty, First and Second Endorsement" (Yorba Linda, Calif.: Richard Nixon Library and Birthplace, n.d.), SCAT Folder, PPS 264.192.2.

84. "Travel orders and endorsements" (Yorba Linda, Calif.: Richard Nixon Library and Birthplace, 1944), SCAT Folder, PPS 264.194.

85. "Fitness Report for 9 August to 20 December, 1944" (Yorba Linda, Calif.: Richard Nixon Library and Birthplace, n.d.), RMN Navy Jacket, PPS 264.407.

86. "The Chief of Naval Personnel to Lieut. Richard M. Nixon, Subject: Change of Duty" (Yorba Linda, Calif.: Richard Nixon Library and Birthplace, November 1944), SCAT Folder, PPS 264.227.

87. "Fitness Report for 30 December 1944 to 29 January 1945" (Yorba Linda, Calif.: Richard Nixon Library and Birthplace, n.d.), RMN Navy Jacket, PPS 264.407.

88. "Fitness Report for 3 February to 29 March, 1945" (Yorba Linda, Calif.: Richard Nixon Library and Birthplace, n.d.), RMN Navy Jacket, PPS 264.407.

89. "Fitness Report for 29 March to 28 May, 1945," "Fitness Report for 1 June to 31 August, 1945," and "Fitness Report for 1 September to 30 December, 1945 (Yorba Linda, Calif.: Richard Nixon Library and Birthplace, n.d.), RMN Navy Jacket, PPS 264.407.

90. Nixon, *RN: The Memoirs of Richard Nixon*, 248.

91. Ibid., 279.

92. William Van Osdol, *Famous Americans in World War II: A Pictorial History* (St. Paul, Minn.: Phalanx Publishing Company, 1994), 86.

93. Citation for meritorious service from the commander of the South Pacific forces, dated September 25, 1944, on display at the Richard Nixon Library and Birthplace, Yorba Linda, California.

94. "Memo from the Chief of the Bureau of Aeronautics to Lieutenant Commander R. M. Nixon, Subject: Commendation" (Yorba Linda, Calif.: Richard Nixon Library and Birthplace, December 10, 1945), SCAT folder, PPS 264.253.

Chapter 4

Gerald R. Ford: Officer of the Deck

1. Gerald Ford to the author, August 1998.

2. Gerald Ford to Lt. Commander Horace Dawson (Ann Arbor, Mich.: Gerald R. Ford Presidential Library, May 22, 1942), Box 1, Application for a Navy Commission Folder.

3. James Cannon, *Time and Chance: Gerald Ford's Appointment with History* (New York: HarperCollins, 1994), 33.

4. Gerald Ford to Lt. Commander Frank Wickhorst (Ann Arbor, Mich.: Gerald R. Ford Library, n.d.), Box 1, Naval Orders and Correspondence Folder.

5. "Memo from The Chief of Naval Personnel to Lt. Gerald Ford, Jr., Subject: Change of Duty" (Ann Arbor, Mich.: Gerald R. Ford Library, May 14,1943), Box 1, Officer's Order Jacket.

6. Clark Reynolds, *The Fast Carriers* (Annapolis, Md.: Naval Institute Press, 1968), 22.

7. Michael Unsworth, "Best Officer of the Deck" *Michigan History Magazine*, 10, January 1944.

8. Dave LeRoy, *Gerald Ford—Untold Story* (Arlington, Va.: R. W. Beatty, LTD., 1974), 53; see also Gerald Ford to Lieutenant Commander Frank Wickhorst (Ann Arbor, Mich.: Gerald Ford Library, 1944), Box 1, Naval Orders and Correspondence.

9. "Memo from The Commandant, Fourth Naval District to Lt. Gerald Ford, Jr. Subject: Temporary Additional Duty" (Ann Arbor, Mich.: Gerald R. Ford Library, June 10, 1943), Box 1, Officer's Order Jacket; see also Bruce Young, "History of the U.S.S. *Monterey*: Part I Chronology" (Ann Arbor, Mich.: Gerald R. Ford Library, n.d.), Box 2, U.S.S. *Monterey* History Folder.

10. "Memo from The Commanding Officer USS *Monterey*, Subject Shore Patrol Duty" (Ann Arbor, Mich.: Gerald R. Ford Library, August 9, 1943), Box 1, Navy Orders and Correspondence Folder.

11. Gerald Ford to the author, July 2000.

12. Thomas Whisler, telephone conversation with the author, July 2000.

13. William Terheune, telephone conversation with the author, July 2001.

14. Gerald Ford to the author, August 1998.

15. Gerald Ford to Lt. Commander Frank Wickhorst.

16. *Monterey*'s participation in the Pacific battles are taken largely from her log books, her War Diary, and from History of the U.S.S. *Monterey*, Part 1 Chronology (Ann Arbor, Mich.: Gerald R. Ford Library, n.d.), Box 2, USS *Monterey* Folder.

17. Samuel Morison, *History of the United States Naval Operations in World War II, Volume 6: Breaking the Bismarcks Barrier* (Boston: Little, Brown and Company,1968), 411.

18. Paolo Coletta, *United States Navy and Marine Corps Bases, Overseas* (Westport, Conn.: Greenwood Press, 1985), 198.

19. John Glenn and Nick Taylor, *John Glenn: A Memoir* (New York: Bantam Books, 1999), 103.

20. Gerald Ford, *A Time to Heal: The Autobiography of Gerald R. Ford* (New York: Harper & Row Publishers and The Reader's Digest Association, 1979), 58.

21. W. J. Scott, "Memo From Senior Watch Commander to Commanding Officer U.S.S. *Monterey*, Subject: Lt. G. R. Ford—Qualification for watch stand of" (Ann Arbor, Mich.: Gerald R. Ford Library, February 20, 1944), Box 1, Navy Orders and Correspondence Folder. The memo is countersigned by Captain Hundt.

22. Gerald Ford to the author, March 2000.

23. Bill Bearden and Bill Wedertz, *The Bluejackets' Manual* (Annapolis, Md.: United States Naval Institute, 1971), 287.

24. Stanley Montunnas, telephone conversation with the author, August 2001.

25. Bearden and Wedertz, *The Bluejackets' Manual*, 294.

26. "Log Book of the U.S.S. *Monterey* (CVL 26), Month of October 1944" (College Park, Md.: United States National Archives, October 1944), 44.

27. Karl Herbst, telephone conversation with the author, May 2000.

28. John Latham, telephone conversation with the author, August 2001.

29. John Moreno, interview with the author, May 2000. Moreno is a former captain of *Monterey*'s sister ship USS *San Jacinto* (CVL 30).

30. Clark Reynolds, *The Fast Carriers*, 138.

31. John Latham, telephone conversation with the author, August 2001.

32. Gerald Ford to Lt. Commander Frank Wickhorst, n.d.

33. Gerald Ford to the author, August 1998 and August 2001.

34. Stanley Montunnas, telephone conversation with the author, August 2001.

35. Horace West, telephone conversation with the author, July 2000.

36. Lester Hundt, "Report on Fitness of Officers: Gerald Ford 6/28/43 to 4/10/44" (Ann Arbor, Mich.: Gerald R. Ford Library, n.d.), Bureau of Naval Personnel File—Officer's Fitness Report Jacket, 1942–1951.

37. Theodore Taylor, *The Magnificent Mitscher* (New York: W. W. Norton and Company, 1954), 206.

38. Clay Blair, *Silent Victory: The U.S. Submarine War against Japan, Volume 2* (Philadelphia, J. B. Lippincott Company, 1975), 622; see also E. Wooldridge, Ed., *Carrier Warfare in the Pacific: An Oral History Collection* (Washington, D.C.: Smithsonian Institute Press, 1993), 160.

39. E. Woolridge, Ed., *Carrier Air Warfare in the Pacific: An Oral History Collection* (Washington, D.C.: Smithsonian Institute Press, 1987), 164.

40. "Log Book of the U.S.S. *Monterey* (CVL-26), June 1, 1944 to June 30, 1944" (College Park, Md.: United States National Archives, 1944), 531.

41. Ibid., 539.

42. Samuel Morison, *History of the United States Naval Operations in World War II: Volume 8, New Guinea and the Marianas* (Boston: Little Brown and Company, 1953), 309.

43. Paul Manning, *Hirohito: The War Years* (New York: Bantam Books, 1986), 99.

44. "U.S.S. *Monterey* (CVL 26), Smooth Deck Log, Month of October 1944," 39.

45. "History of the USS *Monterey* (CVL 26)" (Washington D.C.: Office of Naval Records and History, Ships' History Branch, United States Navy, 1947), 2.

46. Coletta, *United States Navy and Marine Corps Bases, Overseas*, 340.

47. "Log Book of the U.S.S. *Monterey* (CVL-26), Month of October 1944," 74.

48. Glenn Miller, communications with the author, 1982.

49. John McCain and Mark Salter, *Faith of My Fathers: A Family Memoir* (New York: Random House, 1999), 41.

50. U.S.S. *Monterey* (CVL 26) Action Report December 10, 1944 to December 21, 1944 (E. L.) Serial 0036, Annex Easy (College Park, Md.: United States National Archives, December 21, 1944).

51. "U.S.S. *Monterey* (CVL 26) War Diary Month of December 1944" (College Park, Md.: United States National Archives, n.d.), 6.

52. Ford, *A Time to Heal*, 59.

53. Raymond Calhoun, *Typhoon: The Other Enemy, The Third Fleet and the Pacific Storm of December 1944* (Annapolis, Md.: Naval Institute Press,1981), 83.

54. John Davenport, telephone conversation with the author, July 2000.

55. Stewart Ingersol, "Action Report—Operations against Luzon 10 December to 21 December (E.L.) 1944, USS *Monterey* CVL 26 Serial 0036" (College Park, Md.: United States National Archives, December 22, 1944).

56. Horace West, telephone conversation with the author, July 2000.

57. Gerald Ford to the author, August 2001.

58. Calhoun, *Typhoon: The Other Enemy*, 119.

59. Ingersol, "Action Report—Operations Against Luzon" Annex DOG.

60. "Orders from Commanding Officer, U.S.S. *Monterey* to Lt. Gerald R. Ford" (Ann Arbor, Mich.: Gerald R. Ford Library, December 24, 1944), Box 1, Officer's Order Jacket.

61. S. H. Ingersoll, "Report of the Fitness of Officers: Gerald Ford 4/10/44 to 12/24/44" (Ann Arbor, Mich.: Gerald R. Ford Library, n.d.), Navy Orders and Correspondence 1942–46(1).

62. Gerald Ford to Commander W. R. Kane (Ann Arbor, Mich.: Gerald R. Ford Library, March 23, 1945), Naval Orders and Correspondence, 1942–1946(2).

63. Ford, *A Time to Heal*, 60.

64. Rear Admiral S. H. Ingersoll to Lt. Mary Small (WR) (Ann Arbor, Mich.: Gerald R. Ford Library, December 6, 1945), Naval Orders and Correspondence, 1942–1946(2).

65. William Van Osdol, *Famous Americans in World War II: A Pictorial History* (St. Paul, Minn.: Phalanx Publishing Company, 1994), 28.

66. "Transcript of Naval Service" (Washington D.C.: Naval Historical Center, July 12, 2000).

Chapter 5
George H. W. Bush: Torpedo Bomber Pilot

1. Written Interview Responses, *Naval Aviation News* (Washington, D.C.: Naval Historical Center, December 1984).

2. Office of George Bush to the author, February 2000.

3. Joe Hyams, *Flight of the Avenger: George Bush at War* (San Diego: Harcourt Brace Jovanovich, 1991), 37.

4. Ibid., 38.

5. George Bush, *All the Best: My Life in Letters and Other Writings* (New York: Lisa Drew/Scribner, 1999), 29.

6. Ibid., 46.

7. Ibid., 34.

8. Office of George Bush to the author, February 2000.

9. "Lieutenant Junior Grade George Bush, USNR" (Washington D.C.: Naval Historical Center, n.d.).

10. Hyams, *Flight of the Avenger*, 53.

11. Written Interview Responses, *Naval Aviation News*.

12. Charles Scrivner, *TBM/TBF AVENGER in Action* (Carrollton, Tex.: Squadron/Signal Publications, Inc., 1987), 13.

13. Office of George Bush to the author, February 2000.

14. Donald Melvin, "Squadron History, Torpedo Squadron 51" (College Park, Md.: United States National Archives, 1944), 1.

15. Bush, *All the Best*, 36.

16. Robert Stinnett, *George Bush: His World War II Years* (Missoula, Mont.: Pictorial Histories Publishing Company, 1991), 29.

17. Forest Wilson, conversations with the author, February 1999.

18. Melvin, "Squadron History," 1.

19. Ibid., 3.

20. Nicholas King, *George Bush: A Biography* (New York: Dodd, Mead & Company, 1980), 28.

21. Bush, *All the Best*, 40.

22. Melvin, "Squadron History," 1.

23. Jack Guy, telephone conversation with the author, April 2000.

24. Lou Grab and Stanley Butchart, telephone conversations with the author, April 2000. Butchart became a celebrated NASA experimental test pilot.

25. Leo Nadeau, telephone conversation with the author, April 2000.

26. William Flynn, telephone conversation with the author, April 2000.

27. Melvin, "Squadron History," 6.

28. "A Short History of the U.S.S. *San Jacinto*: 3 May, 1944...14 September 1945" (Washington D.C.: Naval Historical Foundation, n.d.), 8.

29. Stinnett, *George Bush*, 43.

30. Bush, *All the Best*, 42.

31. "A Short History of the U.S.S. *San Jacinto*," 9.

32. Stinnett, *George Bush*, 63.

33. "A Short History of the U.S.S. *San Jacinto*," 9.

34. Hyams, *Flight of the Avenger*, 82.

35. Stinnett, *George Bush*, 74.

36. Leo Nadeau, telephone conversation with the author, January 2000.

37. Office of George Bush to the author, February 2000.

38. Jack Guy, telephone conversation with the author, May 2000.

39. "A Short History of the U.S.S. *San Jacinto*," 9.

40. Ibid.

41. Ralph Bagwell, telephone conversation with the author, April 2000.

42. Stanley Butchart and Lou Grab, telephone conversations with the author, April 2000.

43. Stinnett, *George Bush*, 79.

44. *George Bush: His World War II Years*, A&E Biography #AAE-10003, prod. by Arthur Drooker, 50 min., Greystone Communications, Inc., 1992, videocassette.

45. "A Short History of the U.S.S. *San Jacinto*," 10.

46. "Lieutenant Junior Grade George Bush, USNR" (Washington D.C.: Naval Historical Center, April 6, 2001).

47. Melvin, "Squadron History," 7.

48. Lee Nadeau, telephone conversation with the author, January 2000.

49. M. E. Kilpatrick and Donald J. Melvin, "VT-51 Aircraft Action Report, September 2, 1944" (College Park, Md.: United States National Archives, 1944), 30.

50. Charles Bynum, telephone conversation with the author, August 2001.

51. Kilpatrick and Melvin, "VT-51 Aircraft Action Report," 29.

52. Joe Foshee, telephone conversation with the author, May 2000.

53. Bush, *All the Best*, 50.

54. Charles Bynum, telephone conversation with the author, August 2001.

55. Gavan Daws, *Prisoners of the Japanese: POWS of World War II in the Pacific* (New York: Quil/William Morrow, 1994), 321; see also Stinnett, *George Bush*, 151.

56. Kilpatrick and Melvin, "VT-51 Aircraft Action Report," 30.

57. Clay Blair, *Silent Victory: The U.S. Submarine War against Japan, Volume 2* (Philadelphia: J. B. Lippincott Company, 1975), 928; see also *Dictionary of American Naval Fighting Ships, Volume 2* (Washington, D.C.: Naval History Division, 1969), 404 and 405.

58. E. Potter and Chester Nimitz, *Triumph in the Pacific: The Navy's Struggle Against Japan* (Englewood Cliffs, N.J.: Prentice-Hall, Inc., 1963), 147.

59. Thomas Keene, communications with the author, June 2001.

60. Robert Williams, "U.S.S. *Finback* (SS 230)—Report of War Patrol Number 10" (College Park, Md: United States National Archives, October 4, 1944), 6.

61. Office of George Bush to the author, February 2000.

62. *George Bush: His World War II Years*, A&E Biography #AAE-10003.

63. Williams, U.S.S. *Finback* (SS 230), 6.

64. Ibid.

65. Leo Nadeau, telephone conversation with the author, January 2000.

66. Kilpatrick and Melvin, "VT-51 Aircraft Action Report," 30.

67. Hyams, *Flight of the Avenger*, 113.

68. Joseph L. Shapiro and H. L. Blum, "Deck Log of USS *San Jacinto*" (College Park, Md.: United States National Archives, September 2, 1944), 388.

69. Thomas Keene, communications with the author, June 2001.

70. Bush, *All the Best*, 53; see also William E. Edwards to Henry Sakaida, July 19, 1983.

71. *Dictionary of American Naval Fighting Ships, Vol. 2*, 405.

72. Thomas Keene, communications with the author, June 2001.

73. Bush, *All the Best*, 54.

74. Robert Stinnett, *George Bush*, 165.

75. Office of George Bush to the author, February 2000; see also Thomas Keene, communications with the author, June 2001.

76. Thomas Keene, communications with the author, June 2001.

77. "A Short History of the U.S.S. *San Jacinto*," 14.

78. Leo Nadeau, telephone conversation with the author, January 2000.

79. Hyams, *Flight of the Avenger*, 145.

80. Ibid., 156.

81. Office of George Bush to the author, February 2000.

82. Stanley Butchart, telephone conversation with the author, April 2000.

83. *Dictionary of American Fighting Ships, Vol. 1* (Washington, D.C.: Office of the Chief of Naval Operations, Naval History Division,1964).

84. Herbert Parmet, *George Bush: The Life of a Lone Star Yankee* (New York: Lisa Drew/ Scribner, 1997), 60; see also Hyams, *Flight of the Avenger*, 148.

85. Jack Guy, telephone conversation with the author, May 2000.

86. Parmet, *George Bush*, 82.

87. William Van Osdol, *Famous Americans in World War II: A Pictorial History* (St. Paul, Minn.: Phalanx Publishing Company, 1994), 8.

88. Lt. George Bush's DFC Citation (Washington D.C.: Naval Historical Center, n.d.).

Bibliography

PRIMARY SOURCES

Author's Interviews

(in chronological order within organizations, ships, and PT boat numbers)

Lyndon Johnson

James Peterson, 3rd Bomb Group

John Methvin, 3rd Bomb Group

Wallace Fields, 19th Bomb Group

Albert Stanwood, 22nd Bomb Group

Robert Marshall, 22nd Bomb Group

Albert Tyree, 22nd Bomb Group

John Ewbank, 22nd Bomb Group

Gerald Crosson, 22nd Bomb Group

Patrick Norton, 22nd Bomb Group

Paul Bechtel, 12th Fighter Squadron

Richard Suehr, 39th Fighter Squadron

Curran Jones, 39th Fighter Squadron

Frank Royal, 39th Fighter Squadron

Donald Green, 39th Fighter Squadron

Philip Shriver, 40th Fighter Squadron

Carlos Dannacher, 40th Fighter Squadron

Paul Gambonini, 40th Fighter Squadron

Bernard Oliver, 40th Fighter Squadron
Robert Shick, 40th Fighter Squadron
Glenn Shaffer, 40th Fighter Squadron
Kermit Tyler, 44th Fighter Squadron
William Starke, 44th Fighter Squadron
Jack Laurie, 44th Fighter Squadron
William Harris, 70th Fighter Squadron
Louis Kittle, 70th Fighter Squadron
Milton Adams, 70th Fighter Squadron
Doug Canning, 339th Fighter Squadron

John Kennedy

John Kearny, PT 40
Lester Gamble, PT 45
Thomas Kendall, PT 48
David Levy, PT 59
I. John Mitchell, PT 59
W. Glen Christiansen, PT 59
Vivian Scribner, PT 59
John Searles, PT 60
Alan Webb, PT 60
Kenneth Prescott, PT 61
Joe Atkinson, PT 61
Dick Keresey, PT 105
John Iles, PT 105
Bryant Larson, PT 109
Gerard Zinser, PT 109
Jack J. Kempner, PT 109
Edward R. Guenther, PT 109
Pat Munroe, PT 110
Clark Faulkner, PT 124
Stan Marshall, PT 153
William Liebenow, PT 157
Raymond Laflin, PT 157

Welford West, PT 157

James Smith, PT 157

Stanley Kendall, PT 157

Ted Aust, PT 157

Ted Berlin, PT 167

Paul Fay, PT 167

William Battle, PT 171

William Gill, PT 171

John Tiernan, PT 171

Charles Ridewood, PT 236

Leo Campbell, PT 236

William Ping, PT 236

Anthony Prizmonte, PT 236

Murl Wescott, PT 236

Edward Butikofer, PT 236

John Devito, PT 236

Roy Robinson, PT 238

Alvin Cluster, PT Squadron 2

Hugh Robinson, PT Flotilla One

James Reed, Tulagi PT Base

Dr. Emilio Lastreto, Tulagi PT Base

Dr. E. R. Bahnson, Lambu Lambu Cove Base

LeRoy Taylor, PT Squadron 11

Dr. T. Edward Bailey, PT Squadron 11

Bayne A. Sparks, PT Squadron 19

Henry Doscher, SC-761

Jack Britain, LST 449

Orville C. Lewis, SS *Roger Williams*

Victor Krulak, 2nd Marine Parachute Battalion

Warner Bigger, 2nd Marine Parachute Battalion

Roy Homerding, 2nd Marine Parachute Battalion, Company F

Harold Towne, 2nd Marine Parachute Battalion, Company G

Robert Winner, 2nd Marine Parachute Battalion, Company G

Edward Thomas, 2nd Marine Parachute Battalion, Company G

Howard Baxter, 2nd Marine Parachute Battalion, Company G
Anthony Skotnicki, 2nd Marine Parachute Battalion, Company G
George Nicol, 2nd Marine Parachute Battalion, Company G
Michael Vinich, 2nd Marine Parachute Battalion, Company G
Thomas Siefke, 2nd Marine Parachute Battalion, Company G
George Shively, 2nd Marine Parachute Battalion, Headquarters
Lester Sperberg, USS *Breton*
Sidney Sherwin, USS *Indiana*

Richard Nixon

H. Jesse Walker, SCAT
Howard Nielson, SCAT
Robert Bigane, SCAT
William Sears, SCAT
Clovis Davis, SCAT
Terry Nobles, SCAT
Otis Carney, SCAT
Joseph Tolman, SCAT
Lester Wroble, Patrol Service Unit 2

Gerald Ford

Horace West, USS *Monterey*
John Davenport, USS *Monterey*
Thomas Whisler, USS *Monterey*
John Latham, USS *Monterey*
Stanley Montunnas, USS *Monterey*
Karl Herbst, USS *Monterey*
Forest Wilson, USS *Princeton*, USS *Independence*
Glenn Miller, USS *Rudyerd Bay*

George Bush

Thomas Keene, USS *Franklin*, VT-13
John Moreno, USS *San Jacinto*
Leo Nadeau, USS *San Jacinto*, VT-51
Lou Grab, USS *San Jacinto*, VT-51

Stanley Butchart, USS *San Jacinto*, VT-51

Jack Guy, USS *San Jacinto*, VT-51

Joe Foshee, USS *San Jacinto*, VT-51

Harold Nunnally, USS *San Jacinto* VT-51

Charles Bynum, USS *San Jacinto* VT-51

William Flynn, USS *San Jacinto*, VF-51

Ralph Bagwell, USS *San Jacinto*, LSO

PRIMARY SOURCES

Lyndon Johnson

Chief of the Bureau of Navigation. "Naval Travel Orders." Austin, Tex.: Lyndon B. Johnson Library, LBJA Subject File, Container 73—Naval Career, 1942.

———. "Orders of April 29, 1942, Modified." Austin, Tex.: Lyndon B. Johnson Presidential Library, LBJA Subject File, Container 73—Naval Career, 1942.

Eaton, Fred, and Jack Carlson. "Narrative Report of Mission of June 8, 1942." Townsville, Australia: 435th Bombardment Squadron, Office of the Intelligence Officer, Maxwell Air Force Base, Ala.: Air Force Historical Research Agency, June 10, 1942.

Johnson, Lyndon. "Complete Itinerary." Austin, Tex.: Lyndon B. Johnson Library, LBJA Subject File, Container 73—Naval Career, 1942.

———. *Diary.* Austin, Tex.: Lyndon B. Johnson Library, Accession Number AC66-1, 1942.

———. "Notes of meeting with General MacArthur." Austin, Tex.: Lyndon B. Johnson Library, LBJA Subject File, Container 73—Naval Career, 1942.

———. "Roosevelt Meeting Notes." Austin, Tex.: Lyndon Baines Johnson Library and Museum, Subject File, Container 73—Naval Career, 1942.

John Kennedy

Blair, Clay Jr. "Interview of Dr. Joseph Wharton." Laramie, Wyo.: American Heritage Center, University of Wyoming, n.d., audiotape.

Hanami, Kohei, statement forwarded to Senator John Kennedy by Gunji Hosono. Boston: John Fitzgerald Kennedy Library, Box 132, P.T. 109 Correspondence: Japanese. January 28, 1960.

Hill, Colonel George M. to Senator John Fitzgerald Kennedy. Boston: John Fitzgerald Kennedy Presidential Library, Pre-Presidential Papers Senate Files: General Files, 1953–1960, 1958–1960, President's Files P. T. Boat Letter, 21 October 1957.

Note from John Fitzgerald Kennedy to Edward Prescott, made available by Captain Kenneth Prescott. San Antonio, Tex: n.d.

John Fitzgerald Kennedy Personal Papers. Boston: John Fitzgerald Kennedy Presidential Library. Boxes 5 and 11 A. Includes "Appointment in Naval Reserve, October 1941, " "Memorandum to the Chief of the Bureau of Navigation, Subject: Ensign John Fitzgerald Kennedy,—active duty, request for, October 1941," "Report on Fitness of Officers 10-27-41 to 1-19-42," "Memorandum from the Chief of the Bureau of Navigation to Ensign John Fitzgerald Kennedy I-V(S), USNR, Subject: Change of Duty, January 1942," "Airmailgram, July 20, 1942," "Orders to proceed to the Motor Torpedo Boat Squadrons Training Center September 26, 1942," "Orders to proceed to Jacksonville, Florida, January 8, 1943," "Transfer Orders, February 16, 1943," "Report on Fitness of Officers 4/11/43 to 5/29/43," "John Kennedy to Dad and Mother, May 1943," "John Kennedy to Mother and Dad, September 1943," "Agreement to promotion to Lieutenant, October 22, 1943," "Report of Medical Survey, December 6, 1944," "Orders to proceed to the Motor Torpedo Boat Squadrons Training Center December 21, 1943," "Report on Fitness of Officers June 11 to December 26, 1944," "Report of Naval Retiring Board, December 27, 1944," "Memo from Secretary of the Navy to John Fitzgerald Kennedy approving the recommendation of the Naval Retiring Board, March 16, 1945."

Krulak, Victor. "Memorandum from Lieutenant Colonel V. H. Krulak, USMC to The Commandant, U.S. Marine Corps, Subject: Comments on Operations and Material: CHOISEUL Operation, October 27–November 4, 1943." College Park, Md.: United States National Archives, 29 November 1943.

Schade, Gene, "Diary of Squadron 9." Germantown, Tenn.: PT Boats, Inc., 1943.

Warfield, Thomas. "Commander Motor Torpedo Boat Action Report of 1–2 August 1943." Boston: John Fitzgerald Kennedy Presidential Library, Box 11 A, August 5, 1943.

—————. "Memorandum from The Commander Motor Torpedo Boats, Rendova to The Commander in Chief, U.S. Fleet, Subject: PT Operations Night 7–8, 1943." College Park, Md.: United States National Archives, 1943.

White, Byron, and J. McClure. "Memorandum to Commander Motor Torpedo Boat Flotilla One, Subject: Sinking of PT 109 and Subsequent Rescue of Survivors, August 22, 1943." Boston: John Fitzgerald Kennedy Presidential Library, Box 11 A, 1943.

Yamashiro, Katsumori to Senator John Kennedy, trans. by classmate. Boston: John Fitzgerald Kennedy Library, Box 132, P.T. 109 Correspondence: Japanese, November 15, 1958.

Zinser, Gerard to Walter Fallon, January 18, 1993.

Richard Nixon

Major Dyer to R. M. Nixon. Yorba Linda, Calif.: The Richard Nixon Library and Birthplace, PPS 264.189a, Telegram, June 5, 1944.

Lindbergh, Charles. *The Wartime Journals of Charles A. Lindbergh.* New York: Harcourt, Brace and Jovanovich, Inc., 1970.

Nixon, Richard. "Senator Richard Nixon Chronology of Government and Navy Service." Yorba Linda, Calif.: The Richard Nixon Library and Birthplace, n.d., RMN Navy Jacket, PPS 264.2.

—————. "Speech Notes." Trans. by Susan Naulty, Yorba Linda, Calif.: Richard M. Nixon Library and Birthplace, 1946.

"RMN Navy Jacket." Yorba Linda, Calif.: The Richard Nixon Library and Birthplace, PPS 264.407, various dates. Includes: "Tour of Duty/Reports Commendation, n.d." "Memorandum from the chief of Naval Personnel to Richard Nixon, Subject: Change of Duty, October 10, 1942," "Fitness Report of Richard M. Nixon March 19 to May 7, 1943," "Jacob Beuscher to Navy Cadet Selection Board, May 4, 1943," "Duty Assignment, September 19, 1943," "Fitness Report, 1 July to 30 September 1943," "Fitness Report 10 October to 15 December 1943," "Fitness Report 16 December to 31 December 1943," "Fitness Report 1 October 1943 to 1 March 1944," "Memorandum from the Superintendent Route Two to The Commander SCAT, Subject: Citation, n.d.," "Fitness Report 1 April to 2 July 1944," "Fitness Report for 9 August to 20 December 1944," "Fitness Report for 30 December 1944 to 29 January 1945," "Fitness Report for 3 February to 29 March

1945," "Fitness Report for 29 March to 28 May 1945," "Fitness Report for 1 September to 30 December 1945."

Peterson, A. H. to the Honorable Richard Nixon. Yorba Linda, Calif.: Richard Nixon Library and Birthplace, November 6, 1952.

Gerald Ford

Ford, Gerald. Letters to the author, August 28, 1999, March 1, 2000, July 28, 2000 and August 29, 2001.

Gerald Ford Personal Papers. Ann Arbor, Mich.: Gerald R. Ford Presidential Library, Box 1, Accession No. 80-15.

Naval Orders and Correspondence Folder. Ann Arbor, Mich.: Gerald R. Ford Library, Box 1, various dates. Includes: "Memo from The Commanding Officer USS *Monterey*, Subject Shore Patrol Duty, August 9, 1943, " W. J. Scott, "Memo From Senior Watch Commander to Commanding Officer U.S.S. *Monterey*, Subject: Lt. G. R. Ford—Qualification for watch stand of, February 20, 1944," Gerald Ford to Lt. Commander Frank Wickhorst, 1944, Gerald Ford to Commander W. R. Kane, March 23, 1945, Rear Admiral S. H. Ingersoll to Lt. Mary Small (WR), December 6, 1945.

Officer's Fitness Report Jacket, Ann Arbor, Mich.: Gerald R. Ford Library, Lester Hundt. "Report on Fitness of Officers: Gerald Ford 6/28/43 to 4/10/44, " S. H. Ingersoll, "Report of the Fitness of Officers: Gerald Ford 4/10/44 to 12/24/44."

Officer's Order Jacket. Ann Arbor, Mich.: Gerald R. Ford Library, various dates, Box 1, includes: "Memo from The Chief of Naval Personnel to Lt. Gerald Ford Jr., Subject: Change of Duty, May 14, 1943, " "Memo from The Commandant, Fourth Naval District to Lt. Gerald Ford, Jr. Subject: Temporary Additional Duty, June 10, 1943, " "Orders from Commanding Officer, U.S.S. *Monterey* to Lt. Gerald R. Ford, December 24, 1944."

Ford, Gerald to Lt. Commander Horace Dawson. Ann Arbor, Mich.: Gerald R. Ford Presidential Library, Box 1, Application for a Navy Commission Folder, May 22, 1942.

Ingersoll, S. "Action Report—Operations Against Luzon 10 December to 21 December 1944 USS *Monterey* CVL 26, Serial 0036." College Park, Md.: United States National Archives, 22 December 1944.

George Bush

Bush, George. *All the Best: My Life in Letters and Other Writings.* New York: Scribner, 1999.

Bush, Office of George, Letter to the Author, February 2000.

Edwards, William E. to Henry Sakaida, July 19, 1983.

Kilpatrick, M. E., and Donald J. Melvin. "VT-51 Aircraft Action Report, September 2, 1944." College Park, Md.: United States National Archives, 1944.

Williams, Robert. "U.S.S. *Finback* (SS 230)—Report of War Patrol Number 10." College Park, Md.: United States National Archives, October 4, 1944.

PRIMARY SOURCES—NO AUTHOR

Lyndon Johnson

"2nd Squadron, 22nd Bomb Group Report of June 8–9, 1942." Tucson, Ariz.: International Archive of the B-26 Marauder, Pima Air and Space Museum, 1942.

"19th Squadron, 22nd Bomb Group Report of June 8–9, 1942." Tucson, Ariz.: International Archive of the B-26 Marauder, Pima Air and Space Museum, 1942.

"19th Bombardment Squadron, Mission Report, June 9, 1942." Maxwell Air Force Base, Ala.: Air Force Historical Research Agency, 1942.

"22nd Bomb Group June–July 1942 Mission Report June 8 & 9, 1942." College Park, Md.: United States National Archives, Box 139, WWII Combat Operations Reports, Records of the Army Air Forces, Record Group 18, 1942.

"39th Fighter Squadron Diary." Courtesy Roy Seher, 39th Fighter Squadron Association Treasurer.

"Radiograms between Port Moresby, Townsville, Charters Towers, Horn Island, June 7 to 10, 1942." Maxwell Air Force Base, Ala.: Air Force Historical Research Agency, 1942.

John Kennedy

"2nd Marine Parachute Battalion (Reinforced) Unit Journal, From October 27 to November 4, 1943, Operations on Choiseul, British Solomon Islands." College Park, Md.: United States National Archives, 1943.

"2nd Marine Parachute Battalion (Reinforced) War Diary, From October 27 to November 4, 1943, Operations on Choiseul, British Solomon Islands." College Park, Md.: United States National Archives, 1943.

"Aaron Kumana Interview, Solomon Islands Oral History." Boston: John Fitzgerald Kennedy Presidential Library, MS-84-57, March 1986.

"Air Command Solomon Islands, Intelligence Summary: Summary and Review for Week Ending June 25, Solomons Area." Maxwell Air Force Base, Ala., Air Force Historical Agency, microfilm A7633, n.d.

"Biuku Gasa Interview, Solomon Islands Oral History." Boston: John Fitzgerald Kennedy Presidential Library, MS-84-57, March 1986.

"Log Book of PT 59 for October 1, 1943 to December 31, 1943." College Park, Md.: United States National Archives, 1943.

"Log Book of PT 109 for April 1, 1943 to June 30, 1943." College Park, Md.: United States National Archives, 1943.

"Log Book of PT 157 for 1 August to 10 August, 1943." College Park, Md.: United States National Archives, 1943.

"Log book of U.S.S. *Breton* for December 10, 1943 to January 30, 1944." College Park, Md.: United States National Archives, 1944.

"Motor Torpedo Boat Squadron Nineteen Administrative Log." College Park, Md.: United States National Archives, November 1943.

"Terrain Study No. 4, Area Study, New Georgia Group." Allied Geographical Section, Southwest Pacific Area, December 17, 1942.

"Three PT Boats in Formation." Boston: John Fitzgerald Kennedy Library, 1943, black and white photograph.

Richard Nixon

"13th Troop Carrier Squadron Records." Maxwell Air Force Base, Ala.: Air Force Historical Research Agency, Microfiche A0969, n.d.

"Air Solomons Command Weekly Intelligence Summary and Reviews." Maxwell Air Force Base, Ala.: Air Force Historical Research Agency, Microfilm Roll A7633, n.d.

"Bulletin from The Chief of Naval Personnel to All Shore Stations in Continental United States." Yorba Linda, Calif., Richard Nixon Library and Birthplace, SCAT folder, PPS 264.137, March 3, 1943.

"The Chief of Naval Personnel to Lieut. Richard M. Nixon, Subject: Change of Duty." Yorba Linda, Calif.: Richard Nixon Library and Birthplace, SCAT Folder, PPS 264.227, November 1944.

"The Commander, Aircraft South Pacific Force to Lieutenant Richard M. Nixon, Subject: Change of Duty, First and Second Endorsement." Yorba Linda, Calif.: Richard Nixon Library and Birthplace, SCAT Folder, PPS 264.192.2, n.d.

"Commander Richard M. Nixon, U.S. Naval Reserve, Retired." Washington, D.C.: Naval Office of Information, 1969.

"The Commander, Aircraft South Pacific Force to Lieutenant Richard M. Nixon, Subject: Change of Duty." Yorba Linda, Calif.: Richard Nixon Library and Birthplace, SCAT Folder, PPS 264.192.1, n.d.

"COMSCAT Personnel Officer to Richard Nixon." Yorba Linda, Calif.: Richard Nixon Library and Birthplace, SCAT folder, PPS 264.172, n.d.

"Historical Records of the 13th Troop Carrier Squadron, April 1944." Maxwell Air Force Base, Ala.: Air Force Historical Research Agency, n.d., Microfiche A0969.

"Memo from the Chief of the Bureau of Aeronautics to Lieutenant Commander R. M. Nixon, Subject: Commendation." Yorba Linda, Calif.: Richard Nixon Library and Birthplace, SCAT folder, PPS 264.253, December 10, 1945.

"Memo from Chief of Naval Personnel to Richard M. Nixon, Subject: Change of Duty, Second Endorsement." Yorba Linda, Calif., Richard Nixon Library and Birthplace, SCAT folder, PS264.151, May 27, 1943.

"Memo from Chief of Naval Personnel to Richard M. Nixon, Subject: Change of Duty, Third Endorsement." Yorba Linda, Calif., Richard Nixon Library and Birthplace, SCAT folder, PS264.158, May 27, 1943.

"Memo from Chief of Naval Personnel to Richard M. Nixon, Subject: Change of Duty, Fourth and Fifth Endorsements." Yorba Linda, Calif.: Richard Nixon Library and Birthplace, SCAT folder, PS264.158 and 159, June 17, 1943.

"Memo from Chief of Naval Personnel to Richard M. Nixon, Subject: Change of Duty, Eighth and Ninth Endorsements." Yorba Linda, Calif.: Richard Nixon Library and Birthplace, SCAT folder, PS 264.160, June 27 and 28, 1943.

"Memo from the Commander Fleet Air South Pacific to Lieutenant (junior grade) Richard M. Nixon, Subject: Change of Duty," and "First Endorsement." Yorba Linda, Calif.: Richard Nixon Library and Birthplace, SCAT folder, PS 264.161, June 30–July 2, 1943.

"Memo from the Commanding Officer to Lieutenant (jg) Richard Nixon, Subject: Promotion." Yorba Linda, Calif.: Richard Nixon Library and Birthplace, SCAT folder, PPS 264.163, October 1, 1943.

"Memo from The Superintendent Route Two to R. M. Nixon, Lieut., USNR." Yorba Linda, Calif.: The Richard M. Nixon Library and Birthplace, SCAT folder, PPS 264.176, February 27, 1944.

"Memo from The SCAT Personnel Officer to Lieutenant Nixon." Yorba Linda, Calif.: Richard Nixon Library and Birthplace, SCAT folder, PPS 264.168, November 16, 1943.

"Memo from The SCAT Personnel Officer to Lieutenant Nixon." Yorba Linda, Calif.: Richard Nixon Library and Birthplace, SCAT folder, PPS 264.170, December 10, 1943.

"Memo from The Superintendent, Route Two to R. M. Nixon." Yorba Linda, Calif.: The Richard Nixon Library and Birthplace, SCAT folder, PPS 264.186, May 3, 1944.

"Memo from The Superintendent, Route 2, to R. M. Nixon." Yorba Linda, Calif.: Richard Nixon Library and Birthplace, SCAT folder, PPS 264.190A.1, June 14, 1944.

The Real Nixon: Early Life. Prod. by Radford Communications, Inc., New York: Central Park Media Corp., videocassette, 1994.

"Statement of Travel." Yorba Linda, Calif.: Richard Nixon Library and Birthplace, SCAT folder, PS264.152, n.d.

"Telegram from Edwin J. Felher announcing OPA appointment, January 6, 1942, " "Letter to Pat Nixon, August 24, 1943, " and "Citation for Meritorious Service, September 25, 1944." Yorba Linda, Calif.: Richard M. Nixon Library and Birthplace, on display.

"Travel orders and endorsements." Yorba Linda, Calif.: Richard Nixon Library and Birthplace, SCAT Folder, PPS 264.194, 1944.

Gerald Ford

"Log Book of the U.S.S. *Monterey* (CVL-26), June 1, 1944 to June 30, 1944." College Park, Md.: United States National Archives, 1944.

"U.S.S. *Monterey* (CVL-26), Smooth Deck Log, Month of October, 1944." College Park, Md.: United States National Archives, 1944.

"USS *Monterey* (CVL-26) Action Report December 10, 1944, to December 21, 1944, (E.L.) Serial 0036, Annex Easy." College Park, Md.: United States National Archives, December 21, 1944.

"USS Monterey (CVL-26) War Diary Month of December 1944." College Park, Md.: United States National Archives, 1944.

"World War II, A Personal Journey." New York: CEL Communications, videocassette, 1991.

George Bush

George Bush: His World War II Years, A&E Biography #AAE-10003, prod. by Arthur Drooker, 50 min., Greystone Communications, Inc., 1992, videocassette.

"Log Book of USS *San Jacinto*, August 31 to September 5, 1944." College Park, Md.: United States National Archives, 1944.

SECONDARY SOURCES

Agawa, Hiroyuki. *The Reluctant Admiral: Yamamoto and the Imperial Navy.* Translated by John Bester. Tokyo: Kodansha International, LTD., 1979.

Aitken, Jonathon. *Nixon: A Life.* Washington, D.C.: Regency Publishing, Inc., 1993.

Allen, Robert, and Otis Carney. "The Story of SCAT, Parts I and II." *Air Transport*, December 1944 and January 1945.

Ambrose, Stephen. *Nixon: The Education of a Politician 1913–1962.* New York: Simon & Schuster, 1987.

Anderson, Norman, and William Snyder. "SCAT, " *Marine Corps Gazette*, September 1992.

Baren, Harry. "My Combat Mission with Lyndon Johnson," *SAGA*, vol. 29, number 4, 9–15, 73–74, 1964.

Bearden, B., and B. Wedertz. *The Bluejackets' Manual.* Annapolis, Md.: United States Naval Institute, 1971.

Beloit, James, and William Beloit. *Titans of the Seas: The Development and Operations of Japanese and American Carrier Task Forces During World War II.* New York: Harper & Row, 1975.

Bergerud, Eric. *Fire in the Sky: The Air War in the South Pacific*. Boulder, Colo.: Westview Press, 2000.

Blair, Clay. *Silent Victory: The U.S. Submarine War against Japan*. Philadelphia: J. B. Lippincott Company, 1975.

Blair, Joan, and Clay Blair. *The Search for JFK*. New York: Berkley Publishing/G.P. Putnam's Sons, 1976.

Boyington, Gregory. *Baa Baa Black Sheep*. New York: Bantam Books, 1977.

Bradshaw, Thomas, and Marsha Clark. *Carrier Down: The Sinking of the U.S.S. Princeton*. Austin, Tex.: Eakin Press, 1990.

Brantingham, Henry. *Fire and Ice*. San Diego: ProMotion Publishing, 1995.

Breuer, William. *MacArthur's Undercover War*. New York: John Wiley & Sons, 1995.

———. *Devil Boats: The PT War Against Japan*. Novato, Calif.: Presidio Press, 1987.

———. *Sea Wolf: A Biography of John D. Bulkeley, USN*. San Francisco: Presidio Press, 1989.

Brodie, Fawn. *Richard Nixon: The Shaping of His Character*. New York: W. W. Norton & Company, 1981.

Brownstein, Herbert. *The Swoose: Odyssey of a B-17*. Washington, D.C.: Smithsonian Institution Press, 1993.

Buell, Thomas. *The Quiet Warrior*. Boston: Little Brown and Company, 1987.

Bulkley, Robert. *At Close Quarters: PT Boats in the United States Navy*. Washington, D.C.: United States Government Printing Office, 1962.

Caidin, Martin, and Edward Hymoff. *The Mission*. Philadelphia: J. B. Lippincott Company, 1964.

Calhoun, Capt. C. Raymond. *Typhoon: The Other Enemy*. Annapolis, Md.: Naval Institute Press, 1981.

Cannon, James. *Time and Chance: Gerald Ford's Appointment with History*. New York: HarperCollins Publishers, 1994.

Cardell, Rodney. *Wings around Us: Wartime Memories of Aviation in Northern Australia*. Brisbane, Australia: Amphion Press, 1991.

Caro, Robert. *Means of Ascent: The Years of Lyndon Johnson.* New York: Vintage Books, 1990.

————. *The Path to Power: The Years of Lyndon Johnson.* New York: Alfred A. Knopf, 1982.

Casad, D., and F. Driscoll. *Chester W. Nimitz: Admiral of the Hills.* Austin, Tex.: Eakin Press, 1983.

Cave, Hugh. *Long Were the Nights: The Saga of a PT Boat Squadron in World War II.* Washington, D.C.: Zenger Publishing Co., Inc., 1943.

Coletta, Paolo. *United States Navy and Marine Corps Bases, Overseas.* Westport, Conn.: Greenwood Press, 1985.

Costello, William. *The Facts about Nixon.* New York: The Viking Press, 1960.

Craven, Wesley, and James Cate. Eds. *The Army Air Forces in World War 1. Vol. 1, Plans and Early Operations, January 1939 to August 1942.* Chicago: The University of Chicago Press, 1950.

————. *The Army Air Forces in World War II. Vol. 4, The Pacific: Guadalcanal to Saipan, August 1942 to July 1944.* Chicago: The University of Chicago Press, 1950.

Dallek, Robert. *Lone Star Rising: Lyndon Johnson and His Times 1908–1960.* New York: Oxford University Press, 1991.

Darnton, Byron. "Rep. Johnson Sees Airmen in Action." New York: *New York Times,* 1942.

Daws, Gavan. *Prisoners of the Japanese: POWS of World War II in the Pacific.* New York: Quill—William Morrow, 1994.

De Toledano, Ralph. *One Man Alone: Richard Nixon.* New York: Funk & Wagnalls, 1969.

Donovan, Robert. *PT 109: John F. Kennedy in World War II, Fortieth Anniversary Edition.* New York: McGraw Hill Book Company, 2001.

————. *Boxing the Kangaroo: A Reporter's Memoir.* Columbia, Mo.: University of Missouri Press, 2000.

Doscher, J. Henry, Jr. *Little Wolf at Leyte: The Story of the Heroic USS Samuel B. Robert, DE413 in the Battle of Leyte Gulf during World War II.* Austin, Tex.: Eakin Press, 1996.

————. *Subchaser in the South Pacific: A Saga of the USS SC-761 during World War II.* Austin, Tex.: Eakin Press, 1994.

Dugger, Ronnie. *The Politician: The Life and Times of Lyndon Johnson, The Drive for Power from the Frontier to Master of the Senate.* New York: W. W. Norton and Company, 1982.

Edmonds, Walter. *They Fought with What They Had.* Boston: Little, Brown and Co., 1951.

Fields, Wallace. *Kangaroo Squadron: Memories of a Pacific Bomber Pilot.* Shamrock, Tex.: by the author, 1982.

Ford, Gerald. *A Time To Heal: The Autobiography of Gerald R. Ford.* New York: Harper & Row and The Readers Digest Association, Inc., 1979.

Frank, Richard. *Guadalcanal: The Definitive Account of the Landmark Battle.* New York: Random House, 1990.

Freeman, Roger. *B-26 Marauder at War.* New York: Charles Scribner & Sons, 1977.

Glenn, John, and Nick Taylor. *John Glenn: A Memoir.* New York: Bantam Books, 1999.

Goodwin, Doris. *No Ordinary Time, Franklin & Eleanor Roosevelt: The Home Front in World War II.* New York: Touchstone and Simon & Schuster, 1994.

Hamilton, Nigel. *JFK: Reckless Youth.* New York: Random House, 1992.

Hammel, Eric. *Aces against Japan: The American Aces Speak. Vol. 1.* Novato, Calif.: Presidio Press, 1992.

Hara, Tameichi. *Japanese Destroyer Captain.* New York: Ballantine Books, 1961.

Hayashi, S., and A. Coox. *Kogun: The Japanese Army in the Pacific War.* Quantico, Va.: The Marine Corps Association, 1959. First published in Tokyo, 1951, as *Taiheiyo senso rikusen gaishi.*

Hayes, John. *James A. Michener: A Biography.* Indianapolis, Ind.: The Bobbs-Merrill Company, 1984.

Hersey, John. "Survival," *The New Yorker*, June 1944, 31–43.

———. "PT Squadron in the South Pacific," *Look Magazine*, May 10, 1943.

Hess, William. *Pacific Sweep: The 5th and 13th Fighter Commands in World War II.* Garden City, N.Y.: Doubleday & Company, 1974.

Hoffman, Jon. "Silk Chutes and Hard Fighting: U.S. Marine Corps Parachute Units in World War II." Washington, D.C.: U.S. Marine Corps, 1999.

Hoyt, Edwin. *Japan's War: The Great Pacific Conflict.* New York: McGraw-Hill Book Company, 1986.

Hubbard, Douglas. *Diary of a Coastwatcher in the Solomons: Lieutenant Commander F. A. Rhoades, RANVR.* Fredericksburg, Tex.: The Admiral Nimitz Foundation, 1982.

Hutchinson, Dennis. *The Man Who Once Was Whizzer White: A Portrait of Justice Byron R. White.* New York: The Free Press, 1998.

Hyams, Joe. *Flight of the Avenger George Bush at War.* New York: Harcourt, Brace, Jovanovich, 1991.

Ireland, Bernard, and Eric Grove. *Jane's War at Sea: 1807–1997, 100 Years of Jane's Fighting Ships.* New York: HarperCollins Publishers, 1997.

Jay, Ned, Prod. "PT TV Sea Stories #1." Atlanta: self-published, 1992, videocassette.

———. "PT Sea Stories #2." Trans. by Alfred Bisili, Atlanta: self-published, 1992, videocassette.

Johnson, Frank. *United States PT-Boats of World War II.* New York: Blandford Press/Sterling Publishing, 1983.

Kahn, David. *The Codebreakers: The Story of Secret Writing.* New York: Scribner, 1967.

Kazou, Tanikawa. *Japanese Monograph No. 44: History of the Eighth Area Army November 1942 to August 1945.* Tokyo: Headquarters United States Army Japan, 1942.

Kearns, Doris. *Lyndon Johnson and the American Dream.* New York: Harper & Row, 1976.

Kennedy, Paul. *The Rise of the Great Powers.* New York: Random House, 1987.

Kennedy, Rose. *Times to Remember.* New York: Doubleday, 1974.

Kenney, George. *General Kenney Reports: A Personal History of the Pacific War.* New York: Dual, Sloan and Pearce, 1949.

Keresey, Dick. *PT 105.* Annapolis, Md.: Naval Institute Press, 1996.

Kessler, Ronald. *The Sins of the Father: Joseph P. Kennedy and the Dynasty He Founded.* New York: Warner Books, 1996.

Kilduff, Peter. *US Carriers at War*. Annapolis, Md.: Naval Institute Press, 1997.

Kirkland, Richard. *Tales of a War Pilot*. Washington, D.C.: Smithsonian Institution Press, 1999.

King, Nicholas. *George Bush: A Biography*. New York: Dodd, Mead & Company, 1980.

Kornitzer, Bela. *The Real Nixon: An Intimate Biography*. New York: Rand McNally & Company, 1960.

Larrabee, Eric. *Commander in Chief: Franklin Delano Roosevelt, His Lieutenants, and Their War*. New York: Simon & Schuster, 1987.

Lash, Joseph. *Eleanor and Franklin: The Story of Their Relationship, based on Eleanor Roosevelt's Papers*. New York: W. W. Norton & Company, 1971.

Leahy, William. *I Was There: The Personal Story of the Chief of Staff to Presidents Roosevelt and Truman Based on His Notes and Diaries at the Time*. New York: Whittlesey House, 1950.

LeRoy, Dave. *Gerald Ford—Untold Story*. Arlington, Va.: R. W. Beatty, LTD., 1974.

Lindley, John. *Carrier Victory: The Air War in the Pacific*. New York: Elsevier-Dutton, 1978.

Lord, Walter. *Lonely Vigil: Coastwatchers of the Solomons*. New York: The Viking Press, 1977.

MacArthur, Douglas. *Reminiscences*. New York: McGraw-Hill Book Company, 1964.

Manchester, William. *American Caesar: Douglas MacArthur 1880–1964*. Boston: Little Brown and Company, 1978.

Matthews, Christopher. *Kennedy & Nixon: The Rivalry That Shaped Postwar America*. New York: Simon & Schuster, 1996.

Martindale, R. *The Thirteenth Mission: Prisoner of the Omori Prison in Tokyo*. Austin, Tex.: Eakin Press, 1998.

Maxon, Yale. *Control of Japanese Foreign Policy: A Study in Civil-Military Rivalry 1930–1945*. Berkeley, Calif.: University of California Press, 1957.

McCain, John, and Mark Salter. *Faith of My Fathers: A Family Memoir*. New York: Random House, 1999.

Melvin, Donald. "Torpedo Squadron 51 History: 22 September 1943–30 November 1944." College Park, Md.: United States National Archives, 1944.

Michener, James. *The World is My Home: A Memoir.* New York: Random House, 1992.

Miller, John. *Cartwheel: The Reduction of Rabaul.* Washington, D.C.: Historical Division, Department of the Army, 1959.

———. *Guadalcanal: The First Offensive.* Washington, D.C.: Historical Division, Department of the Army, 1949.

Mooney, Booth. *The Lyndon Johnson Story.* New York: Farrar, Straus and Company, 1964.

Mooney, James, Ed. *Dictionary of American Naval Fighting Ships,* Washington, D.C.: Naval History Division, United States Navy, printed by United States Government Printing Office, 1959.

Morison, Samuel. *History of United States Naval Operations in World War II. Vol. 8, New Guinea and the Marianas, March 1944–August 1944.* Boston: Little, Brown and Company, 1953.

———. *History of United States Naval Operations in World War II. Vol. 15, Supplement and General Index.* Boston: Little Brown and Company, 1962.

———. *History of United States Naval Operations in World War II. Vol. 12, Leyte: June 1944–January 1945.* Boston: Little Brown and Company, 1958.

———. *History of United States Naval Operations in World War II. Vol. 6, Breaking the Bismarcks Barrier 22 July 1942–1 May 1944.* Boston: Little Brown and Company, 1968.

———. *History of United States Naval Operations in World War II. Vol. 7, Aleutians, Gilberts, and Marshalls June 1942–April 1944.* Boston: Little Brown and Company, 1951.

———. *History of United States Naval Operations in World War II. Vol. 3, The Rising Sun in the Pacific 1931–April 1942.* Boston: Little Brown and Company, 1965.

———. *The Two Ocean War: A Short History of the United States Navy In the Second World War.* Boston: Little, Brown and Company, 1963.

Morris, Roger. *Richard Milhous Nixon: The Rise of an American Politician.* New York: Henry Holt and Company, 1990.

Morton, Lewis. *United States Army in World War II—The War in the Pacific—Strategy and Command: The First Two Years.* Washington, D.C.: Office of the Chief of Military History, 1971.

Newlon, Clarke. *L. B. J.: The Man from Johnson City.* New York: Dodd, Mead and Company, 1964.

Niven, John. *The American President Lines and its Forebears 1848–1984.* Newark, N.J.: University of Delaware Press, 1984.

Nixon, Richard. *RN: The Memoirs of Richard Nixon.* New York: Grosset & Dunlap, 1979.

———. *In the Arena: A Memoir of Victory, Defeat and Renewal.* New York: Simon & Schuster, 1990.

Olynyk, Frank. *USAAF (Pacific Theater) Credits for the Destruction of Enemy Aircraft in Air-To-Air Combat World War 2.* Aurora, Ohio: by the author, 1985.

Parmet, Herbert. *Jack: The Struggles of John F. Kennedy.* New York: The Dial Press, 1980.

———. *George Bush: The Life of a Lone Star Yankee.* New York: A Lisa Drew Book/Scribner, 1997.

Peattie, Mark. *Pacific Islands Monograph Number Four. Nanyo: The Rise and Fall of the Japanese in Micronesia 1885–1945.* Honolulu: University of Hawaii Press, 1988.

Potter, E. B. *Bull Halsey.* Annapolis, Md.: Naval Institute Press, 1985.

———. *Nimitz.* Annapolis, Md.: Naval Institute Press, 1976.

Potter, E. B., and Nimitz, Chester. *The Great Sea War: The Story of Naval Action in World War II.* New York: Bramhall House, 1960.

Rentz, John. "Bougainville and the Northern Solomons." Washington, D.C.: Headquarters, U.S. Marines, 1948.

Reston, James. *The Lone Star: The Life of John Connally.* New York: Harper and Row, 1989.

Reynolds, Clark. *The Fast Carriers: The Forging of an Air Navy.* Annapolis, Md.: Naval Institute Press, 1968.

Robinson, Pat. *The Fight for New Guinea.* New York: Random House, 1943.

Sakai, Saburo, Martin Caidin, and Fred Saito. *Samurai!* Annapolis, Md.: Naval Institute Press, 1957.

Sakaida, Henry. *Winged Samurai: Saburo Sakai and the Zero Fighter Pilots.* Mesa, Ariz.: Champlin Fighter Museum Press, 1985.

———. *Imperial Japanese Navy Aces 1937–1945.* London: Osprey Aerospace, 1988.

———. *Voices from the Past.* St. Paul, Minn.: Phalanx Publishing Co. Ltd., 1993.

Salecker, Gene. *Fortress against the Sun: The B-17 Flying Fortress in the Pacific.* Conshohocken, Pa.: Combined Publishing, 2001.

Scates, Shelby. *Warren G. Magnuson and the Shaping of Twentieth-Century America.* Seattle: University of Washington Press, 1997.

Scrivner, Charles. *TBM/TBF AVENGER in Action.* Carrollton, Tex.: Squadron/Signal Publications, Inc., 1987.

Searles, John. *Tales of Tulagi: Memoirs of World War II.* New York: Vantage Press, 1992.

Shaffer, James. *Geographic Locations of U.S. APOs 1941–1984, Fifth Edition,* New York: War Cover Club, 1985.

Shaw, Henry, and Douglas Kane. *Isolation of Rabaul: History of U.S. Marine Corps Operations in World War II.* Washington, D.C.: Historical Branch, U.S. Marine Corps, 1963.

Sherrod, Robert. *History of Marine Corps Aviation in World War II.* Mount Pleasant, S.C.: Nautical and Aviation Publishing Company of America, 1987.

Shiroyama, Saburo. *War Criminal: The Life and Death of Hirota Koki.* Tokyo: Kodansha International, Ltd., 1977.

Smith, S., Ed. *The United States Navy in World War II.* New York: William Morrow & Company, Inc., 1966.

Spalding, Henry. *The Nixon Nobody Knows.* Middle Village, N.Y.: Jonathon David Publishers, 1972.

Spector, Ronald. *Eagle against the Sun.* New York: The Free Press, 1985.

Stanaway, John. *Cobra in the Clouds: Combat History of the 339th Fighter Squadron 1940–1980.* Temple City, Calif.: Historical Aviation Album, 1982.

Starke, William. *Vampire Squadron: The Saga of the 44th Fighter Squadron in the South and Southwest Pacific.* Anaheim, Calif.: Robinson Typographics, 1985.

Steinberg, Alfred. *Sam Johnson's Boy: A Close-Up of the President from Texas.* New York: The Macmillan Company, 1968.

Stinnett, R. *George Bush: His World War II Years.* Missoula, Mont.: Pictorial Histories Publishing Company, 1991.

Stone, Peter. *The Lady and the President: The Life and Loss of the S.S. President Coolidge.* Victoria, Australia: Oceans Enterprises, 1999.

terHorst, Jerald. *Gerald Ford and the Future of the Presidency.* New York: The Third Press/Joseph Okpaku Publishing Company, Inc., 1974.

Tillman, Barrett, and Henry Sakaida. "Silver Star Airplane Ride." *Naval History*, U.S. Naval Institute, Vol. 15. No. 2, April 2001, 25 to 29.

Toland, John. *The Rising Sun: The Decline and Fall of the Japanese Empire 1936–1945.* New York: Random House, 1970.

Tregaskis, Richard. *John F. Kennedy and PT-109.* New York: Landmark Books, 1962.

Tunny, Noel. *Fight Back from the North.* Brisbane, Australia: by the author, 1992.

Unsworth, Michael. "Best Officer of the Deck," *Michigan History Magazine,* 10, January 1994.

van der Vat, Dan. *The Pacific Campaign: World War II: The U.S.-Japanese Naval War 1941–1945.* New York: Simon & Schuster, 1991.

Van Osdol, William. *Famous Americans in World War II: A Pictorial History.* St. Paul, Minn.: Phalanx Publishing Company, 1994.

Whipple, Chandler. *Lt. John F. Kennedy: Expendable!* New York: Envoy, 1962.

White, W. L. *They Were Expendable.* New York: Harcourt, Brace and Company, 1942.

———. *Queens Die Proudly.* New York: Harcourt, Brace and Company, 1943.

Wooldridge, E. Ed. *Carrier Warfare in the Pacific: An Oral History Collection,* Washington, D.C.: Smithsonian Institute Press, 1993.

Y'Blood, William. *The Little Giants: U.S. Escort Carriers against Japan.* Annapolis, Md.: Naval Institute Press, 1987.

Young, Bruce. "History of the U.S.S. *Monterey:* Part I Chronology." Ann Arbor, Mich.: Gerald R. Ford Library, Box 2, U.S.S. *Monterey* History Folder, n.d.

Secondary Sources—No Author

"435th Squadron History, 19th Bombardment Group." Maxwell Air Force Base, Ala.: Air Force Historical Research Agency, n.d.

Admiralty Chart 1735, South Pacific Ocean, Solomon Islands, Plans in the New Georgia Group, printed in the United Kingdom, June 1998, nautical chart.

"Commander Lyndon B. Johnson's Army Silver Star Medal Citation." Washington, D.C.: Department of the Navy, Naval Historical Center, September 1997.

"History of the 22nd Bombardment Group, 1 Feb 1940—31 Jan 1944." Maxwell Air Force Base, Ala.: Air Force Historical Research Agency.

"History of the Third Bombardment Group (Light) AAF, Activation March 1944, Fifth Bomber Command." Sobe, Okinawa: United States Army Air Force, October 1945.

"History of the USS *Monterey* (CVL 26)." Washington, D.C.: Office of Naval Records and History, Ships' History Branch, United States Navy, 1947.

"Lieutenant Junior Grade George Bush, USNR." Washington, D.C.:, Naval Historical Center, April 6, 2001.

"Lt. George Bush's DFC Citation." Washington, D.C.: Naval Historical Center, May 12, 1996.

"Lt. John F. Kennedy's NMCM citation" Washington, D.C.: Naval Historical Center, August 16, 1997.

"Lt. Richard M. Nixon's Letter of Commendation Citation." Washington, D.C.: Naval Historical Center, August 16, 1997.

"A Short History of the U.S.S. *San Jacinto*: 3 May, 1944...14 September 1945." Washington, D.C.: Naval Historical Foundation, n.d.

"Transcript of Naval Service, Gerald Ford." Washington, D.C.: Naval Historical Center, July 12, 2000.

Written Interview Responses, *Naval Aviation News*, December 1984.

Index

First and middle names are given when known.